KILLING YOUR NEIGHBORS

KILLING YOUR NEIGHBORS

*Friendship and Violence in Northern Kenya
and Beyond*

Jon D. Holtzman

UNIVERSITY OF CALIFORNIA PRESS

University of California Press, one of the most
distinguished university presses in the United States,
enriches lives around the world by advancing
scholarship in the humanities, social sciences, and
natural sciences. Its activities are supported by the UC
Press Foundation and by philanthropic contributions
from individuals and institutions. For more
information, visit www.ucpress.edu.

University of California Press
Oakland, California

Library of Congress Cataloging-in-Publication Data

Names: Holtzman, Jon, author.
Title: Killing your neighbors : friendship and violence
    in northern Kenya and beyond / Jon D. Holtzman.
Description: Oakland, California : University of
    California Press, [2017] | Includes bibliographical
    references and index.
Identifiers: LCCN 2016015352 (print) | LCCN
    2016016942 (ebook) | ISBN 9780520291911
    (cloth : alk. paper) | ISBN 9780520291928 (pbk. :
    alk. paper) | ISBN 9780520965515 (ebook)
Subjects: LCSH: Samburu (African people)—
    Violence against--Kenya. | Samburu (African
    people)—Kenya--Social conditions. | Ethnic
    conflict—Kenya.
Classification: LCC DT433.545.S26 H645 2017
    (print) | LCC DT433.545.S26 (ebook) |
    DDC 305.896/5—dc23
LC record available at https://lccn.loc.
    gov/2016015352

26   25   24   23   22   21   20   19   18   17
10   9   8   7   6   5   4   3   2   1

For Lengerded

CONTENTS

ACKNOWLEDGMENTS

For anyone who is more or less honest and has chosen the correct profession, anthropology is frequently something of a guilty pleasure. We weren't conscripted into doing this, and I've also heard rumors about several careers that are arguably at least as lucrative, so chances are that we are anthropologists because we enjoy it. I feel extremely fortunate to have had the opportunity to have the experiences I have had through anthropology and to be let into the lives of so many kind and generous people. We should never forget, however—least of all in a book centering on violence—that what we learn in anthropological fieldwork as an intellectual experience and what we get out of it as a personal experience are only possible because of the generosity of people whose circumstances are often less fortunate than our own, and in some cases exceptionally dire. We all hope that we are giving back in some way to the communities we work with, and that, moreover, our work as scholars is meaningful even in a small way by bringing to light knowledge and understanding that is relevant to the most serious issues of our time. But in honesty, even under such circumstances as the saddening events I encountered in the research for this book, the wonderful people whose lives have come together with mine through this and related projects made the fieldwork, for lack of a better word or set of words, really, really fun. Of course, writing the book that is the goal of these experiences can at times prove hard. Consequently, I aim to acknowledge those people who made the enjoyable parts all the more enjoyable and the hard parts at least a bit easier.

Foremost, I acknowledge the many in northern Kenya who not only helped me in overt ways, but whose company has made my research there something that I always wanted to do and always look forward to doing, today as much as any other day. With sadness, gratitude, and the absolutely fondest memories, I start with those who have passed before their time. First among these is Augustine K. Lengerded, one of my first research assistants from near the beginning of my doctoral research, a fantastic friend, a kind soul, one of the most enjoyable people to spend time with one will ever meet, and to whom this book is dedicated. Although he assisted me only with the earliest stages of this project, I have likely learned more about the Samburu from him than from any other individual. That I have also been lucky enough over the years to absorb at least some small measure of his inimitable gift of coaxing out a story and relating it to others has made an important mark on this book. The wit, gentle and ironic wisdom, and the brotherhood of Barnabas Lanyasunya are similarly missed. My gratitude goes, as well, to Musa Letuaa, Otan Lentiyo, Jason Lentiyo, my longtime neighbor Nancy, Damaris and other members of the Lepartinagat family, Lendoogi Lenogseek, Benson, Piringi, and many others I may regrettably overlook in writing these acknowledgments but who have made my years in Kenya more enjoyable and more memorable, and whose absence makes my continuing time there always bittersweet.

Sammy Letoole assisted me in many stages of this project, and his good cheer and eagerness to do whatever needed to be done was indispensable. My great friend, Lemujel Lekutaas, is an irreplaceable model for anyone aspiring to excel at being both a rascal and a sage. I can only hope that if I live as long as him I can become half as good at either. I have continuing gratitude to my longtime host in Loltulelei, Leanoi Lekeren, and the many members of his family who have welcomed me. Among the Pokot, there are no words to sufficiently express my appreciation for the friendship and the contributions of Simba Amarnguli. I am not sure what this book would have been without Simba, but it would have been much less than it is and the time doing the research for this book would have been less ridiculously fun. In Isiolo I thank the several families who hosted me at their camel camps in the countryside, and in town I note the invaluable assistance of "Mr. Mombasa," particularly in introducing me to the surviving family of Sheik Ahmed Yassin, who generously shared their accounts with me. Leshornai was indispensible in introducing me to L and helping me learn his side of the same events. In Nachola, Christopher and his family were kind and giving hosts on many occasions.

A fellowship from the American Council of Learned Societies provided principal funding for the research upon which this book is based. Additional funding came from a FRACAAF grant from Western Michigan University and some support for this project also came by way of a Collaborative Research Grant from the Japanese Society for the Promotion of Science, submitted by Kyoko Nakamura. Indispensable background material was collected over the course of other projects in Samburu funded by two National Science Foundation Grants for Senior Research. In Kenya I am grateful to the Institute of African Studies of the University of Nairobi for affiliation during this project and for the permission of the Republic of Kenya to undertake this research.

To my colleagues, I offer the warmest and sincerest thanks to what has become another home away from home at Kyoto University, where I have been generously hosted numerous times at the Graduate School for African and South Asian Studies, and where much of the manuscript for this book was written as a visiting scholar. I note in particular the generosity and friendship of Professor Itaru Ohta and Kyoko Nakamura. Conversations with these and other colleagues there have been particularly useful in honing several sections of this book. Earlier versions of several chapters were presented at symposia at Kyoto University, as well as at an invited symposium at Hirosaki University hosted by my wonderful friend Toru Soga, and I appreciate the many useful comments in all of these forums. Elsewhere, Dick Werbner, apart from always being the cheerful and funny pal (see Lekutaas above), has offered useful insights in both formal and informal contexts. At Western Michigan University, my former chair, Robert Ulin, was indispensable in facilitating the release from teaching necessary for sustained periods of fieldwork, as well as being extremely supportive in other ways. Also at Western Michigan University, I note several colleagues and former colleagues, particularly Vincent Lyon-Callo, Laura Spielvogel, LouAnn Wurst, and Timothy Green, without whose interesting views on my work this book may have been completed less expeditiously than it has been.

Sundry acknowledgements:

Michael Karanja has been a good friend for many years now. His kindness, his wit, and his valiant attempts to keep my cars moving have all been greatly appreciated .

Sveva and her mother, Kuki Gallman, from time to time offered their assistance and insights, as well as the occasional opportunity to see what hospitality looks like on the other side of the fence.

Homer's distant niece, old and sad before her time I dreamed, wanders silently behind some of these pages.

In the last book I acknowledged Katie Loldia as my most loyal companion from start to finish of that project. Sadly, this dog of dogs has not been seen in our world since early in the main research period for this book, except perhaps fleetingly in the petals of the apricot tree beneath which she now rests, in the few days between their bloom and when they are blown away in the first spring rain. Another dog has sat beside me through much of the writing, a wonderful dog, and fortunately not quite a good enough reader to notice and Envy that she is characterized here as "another dog." I also previously acknowledged my car. There is another car, only slightly reliable but many times heavier when, as with its predecessor, a group of generous and random strangers is the only tonic for extricating it by unconventional means from some situation in which a vehicle was never designed to be: lifting it out of a swamp, guiding it across a precarious river, or pushing it up a slick clay slope on the other side with little traction and a failing engine. I extend particular gratitude and admiration to a group of twenty anonymous Turkana who with generosity and good cheer literally appeared out of an acacia thicket one day to do all these things.

My good friend Matt Paris may not realize it, but beyond the other things he may have inadvertently taught me, watching his knack for figuring out what is important to people and how to have a conversation with just about anyone about just about anything has made me a better anthropologist in general and specifically made this book better. He also very helpfully organized a Kalamazoo shooting session one day, which genuinely enhanced my understanding of how military-style weaponry actually works and was extremely helpful in my discussions of guns in this text.

LG once concluded our discussion with the resolution that the role of BS should generally be acknowledged. And so it should.

My parents, Jordan and Joyce Holtzman, have, as always, remained supportive of me and my work in many diffuse ways. I particularly acknowledge here the role of my father, who—sure the book would be a smash even if he wasn't necessarily totally clear on what it was about— wouldn't stop bugging me until it was done.

I thank again two of my anthropological mentors: my doctoral adviser, Conrad Kottak, and my undergraduate teacher, the late Phil Kilbride. The spirit with which each of these has done anthropology is something I continue to look up to and to aim for.

I cannot say enough about the support I have received from University of California Press. Reed Malcolm has been an incredibly organized, supportive, and attentive editor, and the comments of three reviewers have been extremely helpful in thinking through and honing issues in the book.

Finally I acknowledge Clare Rose Straight Holtzman and William S. Straight Holtzman, funny, bright, wonderful children and the finest of anthropological companions.

INTRODUCTION

"It's the people who were friends before who are enemies now," remarked Simba, my Pokot host in Ol Moran, northern Kenya. Almost bubbly at times, Simba's playful manner made it easy to imagine that—instead of being a respected community leader of about forty—he was an overgrown ten-year-old, a sense only underlined by his tendencies as a ravenous snacker on roasted meat and half-liter bottles of Coca-Cola. Smiles often beamed across his chubby face, in response to our joking with one another, or on occasions when he play-acted hunting down one of his fellow Pokot neighbors, slowly stalking him in a grove, his AK-47 poised in hand. It was a game we found hilarious when he played it for my camera, yet our laughter was also unsettling, knowing that the Kalashnikov was fully loaded and carried by a man who was not just reputed to be an expert in its use, but whose stomach bore the marks of cuts by some accounts made to let blood in ritual purification after killing neighbors—or former neighbors, Samburu herders with whom I have long worked and with whom Simba once lived side by side. Indeed, I had heard about Simba before I met him. Lekeren, my longtime host in Samburu, inquired about my strange doings as I began to extend my research to the other side: the Pokot, with whom the Samburu had been at war since early 2006. He asked me if I had met someone named Simba, who lived near him before the war. "We used to be great friends. He likes to talk and joke a lot," Lekeren explained. "I heard he told people that he wants to kill me."

.   .   .

One of the most disturbing spectacles of recent decades has been brutal acts of violence—indeed, genocide—between groups who long lived together in relative peace: the ethnic cleansing that marked the dissolution of Yugoslavia, the genocide of eight hundred thousand Tutsis in Rwanda in 1994, or Sunni-Shia violence in today's Iraq. The horror of such events goes beyond the dehumanization that we construe as natural among enemies, amplified by war. It is a more incomprehensible dehumanization, which marks a sudden reversal from conditions of everyday intimacy—as in a 2005 massacre of ninety people near Marsabit in northern Kenya, where killing was not directed against strangers or enemies, but rather schoolchildren were called from their dormitories by name and gunned down with automatic weapons.

War no longer occurs predominantly between standing armies of official combatants on well-defined battlefields. This is most often emphasized in the popular imagination in the hyper-reality of nebulous notions such as a "global war on terror," where anywhere may be a site of war and anyone may be a combatant or a victim. If this dizzying trope is the one most familiar to audiences in the Western world—frighteningly disorienting to those living on soil comfortably safe from the violence of "foreign wars"—the reality for many around the world is diametrically opposed to that. War, lethal violence, may not be a product of some faraway and unseen hand, irrespective of the role that global powers and forces play in its inception. Rather, it may be experienced at the hand of your neighbor, someone who before some unforeseen event was perhaps your friend.

This is illustrated perhaps most vividly in the events in Rwanda in 1994. Violence erupted following the death of the president in a likely assassination, and in a period of less than three months, members of the Hutu majority killed over eight hundred thousand members of the Tutsi minority (along with suspected Hutu sympathizers). What is shocking in many of these instances is the brutality inflicted on individuals and groups with whom—prior to some catalyzing moment—the perpetrators of violence had seemingly been on good terms, as neighbors, coworkers, even friends. Thus, it is difficult to comprehend the response of the Hutu church leader Elizaphan Ntakirutimana to the letter of several of his Tutsi pastors, which provides the title of Philip Gourevitch's (1999) chilling book, *We Wish to Inform You That Tomorrow We Will Be Killed along with Our Families*. In response to this call for help before an impending massacre, Ntakirutimana replied to his pastors, "You must be eliminated. God no longer wants you," leaving them, their families, and hundreds of others to be massacred with machetes and farm implements.

Similar examples may be seen in other well-known and lesser-known cases throughout the world. Thus, for instance, the dissolution of Yugoslavia gave rise to violence among Serbs, Bosnian Muslims, Croats, and Kosovars who since the mid-twentieth century had lived as neighbors within a peaceful multiethnic state. Similar events characterize Sunni-Shiite violence in contemporary Iraq, where in the aftermath of the American invasion cities and neighborhoods were cleansed of neighbors of different Muslim religious sects who for generations had lived and interacted peacefully side by side. While every case has unique characteristics and varying accounts, the genocide of half a million communists or suspected communists in Indonesia in the 1960s may be read in similar terms, as may be a range of conflicts in Latin America, recent violence in East Timor, and the long-running civil war in Sri Lanka. While it would be wrong to diminish the central role that external forces (whether at the national or international level) played in fueling these eruptions of violence, in all instances people were killed by those who had been neighbors living in peaceful coexistence prior to these events.

Such a shift from neighbor to killer necessitates a process of dehumanization. One does not normally kill someone defined foremost as your neighbor; that would be murder. To kill such a person requires a cultural shift to put him or her into some other category, a category less human. One way to approach this question is to consider what has sometimes been seen as a cross-cultural aspect of morality, the prohibition on murder. That is, all societies construe murder as bad. Yet societies do not agree on what murder is. Most societies allow, condone, or even encourage killing under some circumstances; hence, murder is killing that occurs in the absence of those validating or even valorizing circumstances. A hypothetical example would be a young man from Texas who enlists in the military and is sent to Afghanistan. There he kills many Taliban fighters, so effectively in fact that he is awarded a medal for valor. Later he leaves the military and goes back to his hometown, where—perhaps suffering from post-traumatic stress disorder—he kills a woman on the street. Where his earlier killing was part of war and culturally validated, this new killing is culturally wrong. He is arrested and condemned to death. His execution is also killing, but it is not murder.

Clearly the circumstances surrounding these various killings are quite different, leading to disparate cultural definitions. There are typically people that society says you may kill and those that society says you may not. What is important in killings between intimates—friends, neighbors, partners in economic activities—is that they involve a shift from defining these people as those you should not kill to those you may kill, or even should kill. Here I examine the process through which peaceful neighbors are transformed into perpetrators and victims of lethal violence— that is, how neighbors and friends become killers of one another.

To examine this process, I take as a case study patterns of violence and peace between Kenyan Samburu herders (Spencer 1965; Straight 2006; Holtzman 2009) and several neighboring groups with whom they oscillate between peaceful cooperation and lethal violence, principally Kikuyu agriculturalists, ethnic Somalis, and pastoralist Turkana and Pokot. This case differs from many of the above-mentioned examples in key ways, but also shares key aspects that help illuminate this broader process. The wars of the Samburu and their neighbors have thankfully never reached the level of genocide or ethnic cleansing that these other examples have. Yet, perhaps even more than these other examples, lethal violence has arisen between Samburu and their intimates—friends, neighbors, and economic partners, who are people you normally should not kill. All the groups with whom the Samburu regularly fight are also groups with whom they are more often than not on friendly terms, herding their livestock together, intermingling, intermarrying, and sometimes forming close personal friendships. Then, at some moment, friction arises— whether because of theft of livestock, competition over grazing, or other problems—and these relationships become transformed into lethal ones.

I argue here that this transformation is a cultural and historical process rather than simply a material or political event. It requires the recategorization of persons, remaking your neighbors as people who can or should be killed. While some amount of friction occurs regularly, even in the best of times—someone's cow gets lost and it is suspected that it was stolen, there is an incident of small-scale theft, or someone murders someone from the other group—it does not always escalate into widespread violence. What I aim to illustrate here is how this recategorization is part of a system of meanings. Specifically, the seeds of violence exist in the understandings or misunderstandings of the opposing group, which are often products of past violence, catalyzed into lethal conflict by some event or series of events. War is given meaning by its participants. There are causes that justify it and explain it. And there are effects that its participants aim for. These are typically not just the obvious material goal of killing enemies. Those engaged in war are communicating things to their own people, such that lethal acts become logical outcomes within the cultural discourse that drives the war. At the same time violence—its patterns, its forms—conveys meanings to one's opponents about the causes of war, its goals, and its rules of conduct. Thus, I suggest, we must look at violence not only in its technical aspects (the brutality of the killing) but also in the way it is driven by and conveys cultural meanings. Wars are the products of stories, and they create stories, stories that may have consequences for generations to come.

ANTHROPOLOGY AND THE CULTURAL MEANINGS OF VIOLENCE

Violence is often construed as the antithesis of the social order (Rapport 2000; Sorel 1999; Daniel 1996; Nordstrom and Robben 1995; Abbink 2000). Recent scholars have, however, suggested that violence should be analyzed as part of a cultural system (George 2004; Steedly 1999), much like anthropologists have long interpreted art, religion, or economics (Geertz 1973). That is, much as Clausewitz saw war as a continuation of politics by other means, violence is in some ways an extreme form of communication, such that it must be understood within the systems of meaning that foment it, shape even its ghastliest forms, and serve as lenses for its interpretation (Whitehead 2004; Taylor 2004; Hinton 2004)—that is, violence is an extension of other aspects of a cultural system.

Since violence is by definition conflictual, the type of cultural system of which it is a part is different from many subjects of anthropological analysis. If in domains such as food or religion one would typically uncover relatively shared meanings, violence inherently involves agents whose interests and subject positions are radically at odds. Consequently, the cultural meanings of violence are always multiple and fragmented (Briggs 1996; Brenneis 1996). Yet, most important to this framework, they are also interlocking (Riches 1986; Stewart and Strathern 2002). On the one hand, varying sets of actors—victims, perpetrators, and observers, often shifting among these subject positions—operate under differing cultural logics that lead to violence and influence the ways victims construe and respond to it, and how varied sets of observers understand, explain, and respond to violence. At the same time, violent acts ultimately emerge as what Gluckman (1940) termed a "social situation," a single event that crystallizes out of the intersection of the divergent visions of varyingly positioned actors, who will understand this shared event very differently and ultimately create disparate interpretations that will influence conditions including, but not limited to, peaceful and violent interactions in the future.

That differently positioned actors or groups explain violence in contrasting ways is not, of course, news. In all likelihood, every society that has ever warred with another has its own account of how and why it all started. As Brenneis (1996) points out in Briggs's important volume on narrative in conflict: "Nowhere is it more likely [than in conflicts] that there will be at least two sides to every story, neither of which can be taken as objective. The indeterminacy inherent in narrative representation may not be immediately evident in every context, but it cannot be avoided in cases of conflict" (p. 42). Every society engaged in war views itself as justified in its actions; its warriors are heroes while its opponents are in one way or another to blame. Even in cases where a society might recognize its own aggression, actions can nonetheless be justified by virtue of past wrongs by their opponents, by the righteousness of their cause, or perhaps by the less than fully human stature attributed to their victims. Although, for instance, it is difficult to concoct a reading of North American history in which Europeans were not aggressors against the native peoples, this conquest was justified by ideology (e.g., Manifest Destiny) that made such a conquest both righteous and teleologically inevitable, while also painting their victims as barbarous savages who perhaps got what they deserved. It is only relatively recently, long after the fact, that popular culture portrayals have painted Native Americans as the victims in "Indian massacres." If there is a war, one of the few things you can rely on is that both sides will believe themselves right and justified, irrespective of an objective reading (when that is possible).

Perhaps the first written account of conflicting versions of the causes of war comes from Herodotus, writing some 2,500 years ago about the differing explanations of the roots of the war between the Persians and the Greeks. He notes that knowledgeable Persians trace the war to the abduction of Io, the daughter of the king, who was kidnapped, raped, and taken away while the Phoenicians were on a trading expedition to Argos. "These standing near to the ship were buying the wares that pleased them most, when suddenly the Phoenicians, passing the word from one to another, made a rush upon them; and the greater part of the women escaped by flight, but Io and certain others were carried off." What ensued was a mutual abduction of women, spurred by this initial abduction of Io. But, as Herodotus goes on to explain:

> The Persians for their part say that things happened thus; and they conclude that the beginning of their quarrel with the Hellenes was on account of the taking of Ilion. As regards Io the Phoenicians do not agree with the Persians in telling the tale thus; for they deny that they carried her off by violent means, and they say on the other hand that when they were in Argos she enjoyed sex with the master of their ship, and perceiving that she was with child, she was ashamed to confess it to her own parents, and therefore sailed away with the Phoenicians of her own will, for fear of being found out. These are the tales told by the Persians and the Phoenicians severally: and concerning these things I am not going to say they happened thus or some other way. (Herodotus 2003: 5)

How would an anthropologist have made sense of these differing accounts? In all likelihood, the answer to this question might depend on whether one was an anthropologist of the Persians or an anthropologist of the Phoenicians. As we strive to view the world through the eyes of inter-locutors who are our informants and often friends, anthropology is in many ways well suited to understanding the cultural logics and meanings of violence. Yet at the same time we are uniquely vulnerable to potential pitfalls. There is a delicate line between the goal of understanding violence and the problematic position of accepting it—even valorizing it—by virtue of our tacit acceptance of our informants' idioms and accounts (e.g., Chagnon 1977). Moreover, we naturally tend toward advocacy for those who share their lives and knowledge with us, fostering portrayals of violence that differ markedly from those on the other side of the encounter (McCabe 2004). Rephrased analytically, traditional ethnographic accounts are inherently partial (in both senses of the word) from the standpoint of understanding violence through a triad of perpetrators, victims, and observers (Riches 1986; Stewart and Strathern 2002), since our methods normally expose us to one segment rather than the full set of actors in a violent encounter. Gaining full(er) insights into all sides of a violent encounter is important not simply to illustrate that various actors have different perspectives but in order to understand how these differing perspectives interact—that is, to understand how the terrain that leads to violence, to peace, or there and back again, is composed of the articulation of varied and conflicting beliefs, practices, attitudes, predispositions, and memories. Any incident of violence is, therefore, a single moment that crystallizes diverse meanings and causal threads while splintering into new ones with consequences into the future.

What, then, can we hope to glean from these (not unexpectedly) contradictory narratives, and what should our purpose be in engaging with them? We have long ago moved past the era when (for instance) the parsimonious account of a seventy-year-old male informant would be taken as the one true account of the social relations (or "culture") of our subjects. Yet I would argue that we have not fully come to terms with how best to capture, analyze, and portray discordant data despite long-standing efforts to do so. Sapir's (1938) classic discussion of contradictory statements from informants—for instance, though one informant claimed Omaha had a particular number of clans, another informant, Two Crows, denied the very existence of some of them—stands as an early anthropological exploration of how nuanced psychological complexities of an informant's subject position influenced data that researchers often mistakenly construed as normatively shared aspects of "Culture." Heider (1988) takes up the question of what factors lead to anthropologists portraying a cultural setting in significantly different terms (e.g., does a group practice or not practice witchcraft? were the Samoans more like Margaret Mead portrayed them or like Derek Freeman did?). Heider employs what he terms the Rashomon effect, drawn from Kurosawa's classic film (and an earlier short story) in which a samurai may or may not have been murdered and his wife may or may not have been raped, portrayed with an only nominally different version of the same story told from the subject positions of several actors. Each character in the film renders his or her account from a perspective that portrays them in the most favorable light, creating radically different portrayals of the events even though the facts are almost indistinguishable. Heider's point is that when ethnographers disagree, it may be important to consider the factors influencing the ethnographer's perspective. Yet, like others employing a similar tack (e.g., Roth and Mehta 2002), his concern largely emphasizes a positivist search for what really happened—the Truth. Certainly there is some value to this. In a case study such as the present one, it is dissatisfying, even ethically problematic, to fall back on some postmodern version of many equally valid and unknowable truths, a luxury afforded to us as scholars but not to the real, feeling people killed by other real, feeling people, with their bones left to be picked at by vultures. We thus stand in a position where we can neither fully discern the truth nor ignore it.

Although we are, in some sense, doomed to never fully accomplish our goal of explaining, or even knowing, what actually happened, the goal of engaging with sometimes irreconcilable visions is nonetheless crucial. Human lives are intrinsically constituted of just such discordant scenes composed of actors with wildly differing visions, yet anthropologists have with a few notable exceptions (e.g., Gluckman 1940) not been particularly adept or even concerned with capturing them. More pertinent to this case study, the reason it is important to engage with these conflicting narratives lies in the extent to which the totality of these narratives may best be understood not as two (or more) sides of a story but as components that constitute a single landscape of social action and meaning. That is, though conflicting parties may not agree with (or even be entirely aware of) the other's account, each version affects the views, attitudes, and behavior of those on the other side of the interaction, leading to actions and attitudes that structured relationships in the past and continue to do so into the present (see also Briggs 1996). If Herodotus asserts an inability to assess the competing accounts of the Persians and Phoenicians, and if anthropologists typically tend toward a position ranging from sympathy to advocacy for those they know well, the real question lies in how these stridently divergent discourses are different parts of a single thing, and the consequences that this holds. Our aim, then, may be to provide not a more "balanced" account, nor a more "true account," once we have sorted the black hats from the white ones, but a more *complete* account that understands the reverberations of one discourse, action, or event on whole sets of actors and groups, while understanding that these reverberations also produce their own reverberations continuing onward.

To construct such an ethnography, I argue, one must strive to be metaphorically the anthropologist of both the Persians and the Phoenicians—or more to the point, of the Samburu with whom I have long worked and the varying groups with whom they oscillate over time between peace and war. This has entailed a methodological, analytical, and theoretical approach that aims to come to terms with how one constructs the ethnography of scenes that are intrinsically multivocal, giving due weight to all sides of these encounters. As background, I have engaged in long-term fieldwork with the Samburu, over the course of which I have become knowledgeable about Samburu accounts of their various interethnic conflicts, how they describe events, explain and justify their positions, and interpret the motivations and actions of their neighbors. While this provided a rich understanding of conflict from a Samburu point of view, it did not encompass the radically different perspectives of their adversaries. Thus, in 2006 I began to engage in multi-sited ethnography, a much touted (e.g., Gupta and Ferguson 1997) but little utilized methodology.[1] That is, I went to collect the points of view of the neighbors on the other side of these violent (and sometimes peaceful) encounters in order to examine the lives of subjects engaged in different sides of a common activity—interethnic violence, but also periods of peaceful coexistence. In the course of this research, I collected accounts of conflicts that form key moments in individual and collective memory, as described from the perspectives of both Samburu and their opponents.

In this endeavor, it is clear that the depth of my ethnographic knowledge of each side is not equal. While the Samburu perspectives are drawn from formal and informal data collected during roughly six years of fieldwork over the course of two decades, the accounts of the other groups in these encounters have been drawn from informal participant observation, informal interviews, and roughly eighty formal interviews. While all ethnographic accounts are inherently incomplete, the Samburu side of this is certainly *more* complete than those of their counterparts. This does not, I would argue, render the ethnography of one side of the encounter good or accurate and the other not. No account I present—whether Samburu, Pokot, Somali, Turkana, or Kikuyu—represents *the* version of what happened and why; rather, each is a legitimate version that may be idiosyncratic in some respects and more representative in others.

Neither, I would hasten to add, does my deeper experience with Samburu create a pro-Samburu bias that is impossible to overcome. Indeed, there is some degree of truth in the assumption held by many of my non-Samburu informants that my years with Samburu would naturally predispose me *against* Samburu, or at least lead me to more closely scrutinize their accounts and motives. As one Pokot man said when I asked about the cause of their conflict with Samburu, "You've stayed with them. You [must] know how they are." Like many others, he assumed not partisanship on my part but rather empathy with him and his non-Samburu peers, based on his assumption that long-term residence among Samburu must necessarily have exposed me to their faults to an infuriating degree. If this somewhat humorously runs counter to commonplace anthropological doxa on empathy with our informants, as anyone who has done extended fieldwork knows, anthropologists' close encounters with the humans who generously share their lives with us can extend from the deeply meaningful to the downright annoying (sometimes on the same day). In some sense, exposure to the views of other groups has not led me to repudiate their perspectives based on my loyalty to Samburu, but rather has served as a mirror to help me understand taken-for-granted Samburu assumptions in a different light (e.g., those who have their cattle stolen by young Samburu men are less likely to dismiss them as typical youthful pranksters than Samburu themselves are).

In analyzing the resulting narratives, this book strives to be an analytical and methodological experiment in multisited and multivocal ethnography, toward the goal of understanding how we as anthropologists might best approach this type of often confounding ethnography. While recognizing that in many contexts all accounts are not equally valid—a position that could potentially do horrific disservice to the victims of violence (Payne 2008)—I suggest that here, as in many contexts, the landscape of narratives is better characterized as being composed of sets of accounts which, if inherently contradictory, suggest *Rashomon*-like subtle permutations of the truth more than mendacity on the part of our interlocutors.

SAMBURU: THEIR WARFARE AND THEIR NEIGHBORS

There are currently about two hundred thousand Samburu inhabiting the semiarid lands of north central Kenya. Most live in Samburu District, though smaller numbers live in neighboring Laikipia District to the south and Marsabit District to the northeast. Culturally they are closely related to the better-known Maasai and speak a mutually intelligible dialect of the same language, Maa. Historically the Samburu were among the world's wealthiest livestock keepers and survived almost exclusively on the products of their animals (Spencer 1965). There are significant ecological differences across the areas where the Samburu live, which affect both the patterns of pastoralism and responses to change, the most significant distinction being between lowlands (*Lpurkel*)—semiarid to arid acacia scrub, lying at around 4,000 feet above sea level—and the highlands (*Ldonyo*) of the Leroghi plateau, which at 5,500–8,000 feet is much cooler and wetter, characterized by open grasslands, with substantial forested areas at the highest altitudes. The population of the highlands has become far more sedentarized, and towns, trading centers, and schools are far more common (Holtzman 2004, 2009).

The aspect of Samburu life that has received the most attention is their age-gender system. The most striking feature of this is the institution of murranhood. Young men are initiated into manhood through circumcision and associated rituals between the ages of fifteen and twenty, and spend the next ten to fifteen years as murran, or bachelor-warriors. Murran are visually distinctive, allowing their hair to grow into long braids (*lmasi*) decorated with red ochre. They are primarily responsible for the most difficult and dangerous jobs in Samburu life, such as long-distance herding and offensive or defensive warfare, but they also are considered the most glamorous sector of Samburu society, cultivating both physical beauty and ability in singing and dancing. Murran are expected to stay at the fringes of domestic life, the most salient aspect of this being the *lminong* (prohibitions) that forbid them to eat food which has been seen by women (Holtzman 2009). Murran move through the life course with

FIGURE I.   A pair of Samburu *murran,* bachelor warriors.

their age set and typically do not marry until initiations have begun for a new age set. Women do not have formal age sets, though their social status is closely tied to the age of their husbands and children, particularly their sons. The murran are particularly significant for our purposes, as they form the main age group involved in interethnic conflict.

Interethnic conflict has been a major feature of Samburu life since long before the colonial period. The Samburu's reputation prior to British colonization was that they were more focused on defensive warfare than offensive, in contrast to larger and more aggressive groups of Maa speakers, such as various Maasai sections. At the time of the first European expeditions into their territories in the late nineteenth century, the Samburu (referred to mainly as Burkineji, "People of the White Goats") were severely weakened by livestock and human disease, and were living in hilly, dryland terrain more suitable for defense (e.g., Von Hohnel 1896). However, oral history suggests that within a few generations prior they were more vigorous militarily, having engaged in major conflicts with groups such as the Turkana, Boran, and Dassanetch, as well as taking part with Maasai and other groups in the war against the Laikipiak, which resulted in the eventual routing of the latter. At the time of British colonization of Samburu District in the 1910s, Samburu were engaged in a major war with the Turkana—one they were apparently losing badly until the British took their side in an alliance against the yet to be pacified Turkana. The British subsequently largely suppressed warfare—with little more than minor conflicts during the colonial period—though the postcolonial government has been less effective or less concerned in maintaining peace. As a consequence, a variety of conflicts with neighboring groups have erupted up to the present, with firearms largely replacing spears since the mid-1990s.

Samburu engage in two main types of aggressive warfare. The first are minor raids (*lwuamban*) that in pregovernment times were focused largely on "spear bloodying"—killing someone from an enemy group as a sign of manhood—and more recently have turned to the theft of livestock. Lwuamban involve small groups, ranging from as few as a half dozen warriors up to about forty people. They can be motivated by a number of reasons, ranging from a simple desire to acquire livestock for feasting, to augmenting one's herd, proving one's manhood, or escaping boredom. These are often carried out in response to the taunting of girlfriends at singing and dancing occasions, and are generally done by murran without the guidance, consent, or knowledge of elders, though *loibonok* (seers/diviners) might be consulted at times to ensure success through supernatural guidance or by providing charms, *ntasim,* to ensure good fortune (see also Straight 2006; Fratkin 2011). Elders' roles in lwuamban may have been greater in the past, prior to government interventions and collective punishment for theft during the colonial period and beyond.

Elders play a much bigger part in *nchore,* large-scale attacks aimed at killing enemies and attaining military victory. Nchore may involve hundreds of combatants, or even more. While most of the combatants in nchore are murran, who also play a central role in their planning, elders' voices and actions are also important since these larger wars are carried out when they are considered to be in the interests of Samburu society as a whole. Thus, while lwuamban are carried out without input from elders (and indeed, may be deliberately hidden from them), elders often aid in planning nchore and provide the resources necessary to carry them out successfully. In the past this may have involved such support as providing oxen for murran to feast on, thus ensuring they had sufficient strength before entering battle, while more recently elders may help murran acquire guns to fight better-armed groups—for instance in conflicts with Somalis and Turkana in the 1990s.

Samburu narratives about their conflicts by and large blame the neighboring groups they have come in conflict with. The standard trope involves peaceful Samburu being harassed by their enemies, until finally they rise up and defeat them. Consider, for instance, the stance of one elder from the Kimaniki age set discussing both past conflicts and their current one with the Pokot:

> There is no community that we have ever invaded and killed people.
> For we have not risen up to go fight with the Boran. It is just the Boran
> who come and fight with us, and we keep fighting with them, keep
> fighting with them until we defeat them straightaway. And we don't
> have fire [arms] ourselves. We only have spears. And the Somalis come
> again, and we fight with them with the spears because we don't have
> guns, and they have guns themselves. [We fight them] until we just
> defeat them, until they just go away. And it has happened again, the
> Pokot are here again. But I think now it is a little bit better, when we
> have a few of these Homeguard sticks [the guns of police reservists]. And
> we were defeating them when we had only spears, so what about now
> when we have those few sticks of the Homeguards? It is now they are
> going to be beaten.

Reality is, of course, far more complex than this Samburu self-portrait as a group that simply minds its own business until the attacks against them become so constant that they must arise, like a sleeping giant, to sweep their enemies away. Though the Samburu have not engaged in large, unprovoked attacks on their neighbors, it is not clear how often their neighbors have done so toward them. Arguably groups like the Turkana and Somalis have at times taken advantage of an uneven situation on the battlefield to raid livestock or gain territory, particularly when favored by such factors as far better access to guns. However, it is important to bear in mind that Samburu murran do regularly engage in small-scale raids on their neighbors. While Samburu are wont to dismiss these lwuamban as the minor transgressions of young men—rather than a major collective action by the Samburu—those who have had their cattle stolen (perhaps with loss of life) may view the situation quite differently. Thus, one Somali man described their attacks on the Samburu in terms not so different from Samburu justifications: "They can't help stealing. So they keep on stealing, keep on stealing until in the end we grow tired of it."

Samburu regularly come into conflict with various groups. To the east, their most common opponents are ethnic Somalis, with whom they have engaged in two major wars since Kenyan independence. To the east they also fight periodically with the Boran, though these conflicts tend to be less epic. To the west their most regular opponents are the Turkana. Although Samburu look disdainfully on the Turkana—referring to them often as "boys" (layiok) because they are uncircumcised—and tend to regard them as not wholly worthy opponents, more often than not Turkana have gotten the better of them in armed conflict and are more often aggressors at least in the larger-scale wars. On the other hand there is significant cooperation and intermarriage between the two groups. Thus, the Turkana may be seen somewhat ironically both as the archenemies (or at least main rivals) of the Samburu—frequently fighting over livestock and pasture, sometimes at considerable loss of life—as well as in many ways their closest friends. Their relationships with Pokot pastoralists and Kikuyu agriculturalists have their own peculiarities. The Pokot and the Samburu have been ritually bonded since before living memory, and have maintained peace through strong belief in a supernatural sanction that would cause death or insanity to anyone who killed a member of the other group. In the past decade, however, this oath has been broken, leading to bitter conflict. Samburu had relatively little contact with Kikuyu agriculturalists in precolonial times but have had diverse peaceful as well as violent interactions in both the colonial and independent periods.

Oscillations between peaceful coexistence and warfare are, then, characteristic of relations between the Samburu and virtually all of their neighbors. How can we account for this? As an ethnographer who has long studied the Samburu, I am inclined, of course, to understand this in Samburu terms. Yet, not surprisingly, other groups explain it in quite different terms. Understanding both sides of these encounters is necessary to render a full understanding of this dynamic.

STUDYING ENEMIES

Samburu memorialize their conflicts in a variety of idioms that—unsurprisingly—cast themselves in a positive, indeed heroic, light. Their interpretations of violence also create identities and meanings dialogically with their neighbors, shaping interethnic relationships during stretches of peace. Turkana, for instance, are admired by Samburu for strength and bravery but are considered largely precultural, reflected in Samburu accounts of brutal patterns of warfare consonant with other "uncouth" Turkana practices, such as not circumcising their youth and eating nearly all wild and domestic animals. Samburu beliefs concerning other groups' characteristics or motivations may, of course, be inaccurate even at a basic level. For instance, Samburu insist that Kikuyu agriculturalists hate them because the Samburu helped the British suppress the Kikuyu-led Mau Mau insurrection in the 1950s. Samburu insist that this Kikuyu grudge from the time of Mau Mau has fueled recent conflicts, yet many Kikuyu are barely aware that the Samburu exist, while those who are their neighbors are bewildered that a conflict which occurred decades before they were born could play any role in recent clashes. The sometimes dubious or arguable factual basis for these interpretations and conceptions of one's neighbors is less important here than the ways both peaceful and violent encounters are shaped through such lenses.

Consequently, the notion that violence emerges through dialogically constructed meanings makes it necessary to account for the engagement of multiple viewpoints, irrespective of the extent to which these viewpoints reflect actual events, motives, or the perceived points of view of opposing groups. Moving back and forth among different ethnic groups has allowed me to employ a genuinely dialogical ethnographic process. In this sense the project problematized the typical anthropological formula in several ways. I took as a starting point my deep engagement with Samburu, with whom I have now worked for roughly two decades. Samburu are my friends—not all Samburu, of course, but many. I am treated as at least an honorary Samburu and regard myself as such. Thus, the conflicts I describe in this book are events that I have been aware of for many years, always viewing them from a Samburu perspective. When Samburu cows were taken, it was almost as if my own cows had been taken, and indeed, when I later came to own about a half-dozen cows, I became all the more acutely aware of the threat posed by enemies.

Friendship is, of course, a pleasurable, necessary, and ambiguous aspect of fieldwork (Rabinow 1977; Grindal and Salamone 1995), given both the gulf of cross-cultural differences that must be traversed and the complications inherent in ostensibly mixing "business and pleasure." As Grindal and Salamone (1995) note, "Friendship is more than a psychological nicety for the anthropologist—it is essential if the work is to succeed" (p. 171). Anthropologists need friends. It is impossible to gain insights into another culture or another way of life without participants who are willing to allow your presence, to share their insights, and to (in varying degrees) let you into their lives. Even in normal fieldwork, there are, of course, complexities to friendship. No matter how much you become an insider in another culture, you are still an outsider. And, of course, you may make the "wrong friends." That marginal people may often be those most attracted to the anthropologist is a well-known pitfall. Beyond this, even under the best of circumstances, good friends can earn you enemies. We are all aware that in fieldwork we make choices (or sometimes they are made for us) about the company we keep. We talk to one person, one clan, or one gender more than another, we choose where we live, and unintentionally or intentionally, we form alliances that open doors to an understanding of our informants' worlds but may at the same time close the doors to other worlds. And in some cases, your good friends can make you enemies.

Beyond normal aspects of fieldwork, this project focuses on deliberately talking with enemies—that is, the enemies of my friends. This can create problems on both sides of the encounter. I was, on one hand, concerned that when talking to the enemies of the Samburu, they might believe that I was a Samburu partisan at heart, though this problem never, in fact, arose. More commonly, I was told that, since I had stayed with Samburu, I must know how insufferable Samburu are and could appreciate the problems of being their neighbors. The Samburu were more suspicious of my dealings with their enemies. "Are you telling them our secrets?" one Samburu friend asked. Of course I was not sharing secrets. Rather, I frequently feigned ignorance with their enemies. "Do you know where Lekeren is these days?" my Pokot friend Simba often asked. I assumed it was just polite conversation, but I kept up my guard, since the first thing I was ever told about Simba was an off-hand comment from Lekeren that he had heard Simba wanted to kill him. Thus, I would reply to Simba's seemingly innocuous queries, "I think he [Lekeren] is in Laikipia. Very far. Almost near Mount Kenya," I would say, even if I had slept at his much closer settlement the night before. "How is Lodokejek these days?" Simba would ask of the area in Samburu where I am mainly based. "It is very good for sheep," I told him. "It just has one problem. There are even more guns than sheep." Pokot knew this was a joke, I think, but one that was not encouraging anyone to undertake expeditions to find out how much of a joke. So, if Samburu asked me if I was telling the Pokot their secrets, I could honestly respond, "I told them there are more guns than sheep here."

But there is also something interesting about working with your friends' enemies, just as there is befriending marginal people in typical anthropological research. Outsiders perceive things that insiders do not. The high school kid who sits at lunch by himself or with a couple of nerdy friends may have a much more critical eye than the captain of the football team, who thinks the world must be great because it seems to worship him. The same is true in contexts where anthropologists work; while we strive to achieve as near insider status as possible, the outsiders may understand a lot of things that insiders never can.

This dynamic is amplified when working with your hosts' mortal enemies. Needless to say, enemies will paint your friends in perhaps rather nasty stereotypes, just as your friends do to them. However, that does not mean what they say is wholly false. Indeed, I believe that I learned things about Samburu by talking to people who *do not like* them that I never learned in trying to get Samburu to *like me*. Samburu, for instance, are wont to point out that their war with the Pokot, their current enemy, is a product of the latter being intrinsically bellicose, having fought with virtually all of their neighbors. When describing this research project to Pokot, they pointed out to me that—as is fundamental to this project—

FIGURE 2. A Pokot man proudly displaying his sheep near a watering point.

Samburu have fought with virtually all of their neighbors too, so perhaps they are the bellicose ones. Samburu always describe themselves as victims, and as their friend it seemed ostensibly true. Just as Samburu don't take seriously the smaller raids of murran, I didn't either. They were just the normal transgressions of youth, pranks at a kegger. Yet their enemies pointed out that they didn't like these thefts that Samburu dismissed as kids' stuff, and that their own attacks were simply retaliation for the initial Samburu ones. They accused the Samburu of being duplicitous and mean spirited. For instance, Pokot insisted that Samburu would kill a Pokot in town, while Pokot would only attack Samburu when cattle and guns were involved. I observed firsthand that Pokot will not bother a

Samburu uninvolved in a conflict, while Samburu were clear about their inclination to take revenge on any Pokot anywhere they were found.

Moving back and forth among different ethnic groups has allowed me to employ a genuinely dialogical ethnographic process. For instance, Samburu take great pride in the fact that they kill only combatants, while others kill women and children. Yet, Pokot showed me houses that had been sprayed indiscriminately by Samburu bullets. For their part, Pokot asserted that the Samburu were uniquely malicious in being the only group that killed women and children, yet I could present to these informants the accounts of Turkana who had admitted to me that the bitterness of war can drive a person to do anything: in this instance, killing Pokot women and children. To some extent this dialogical process has allowed me to critically check differing accounts for plausibility, but perhaps even more importantly it illustrates how the assertions contained in these accounts structure meanings that are relevant to the cultural construction of violence. For instance, Samburu and Pokot give radically different accounts of the role of Kenyan government forces in a massacre of one hundred Samburu raiders in 2007. Samburu claim that their peripheral position in the Kenyan state and the Pokot's favored status is illustrated through claims that they were bombed, in their words, "like people from another country." Pokot, by contrast, insist that they routed their enemies with little assistance, asserting their virility compared to the high-strung and easily panicked Samburu. Both accounts (as described in more detail in chapter 6) likely contain elements of truth and fiction, yet each illuminates the events. Thus, while enemies often lie about their enemies, even lies, exaggerations, and half-truths may help you see things about your friends that you would not ordinarily see.

.   .   .

The structure of the research process, then, has been to take Samburu as the core example, as a literal and interpretive hub of interethnic violence in northern Kenya. I have taken as a baseline the war stories of people I know well, whom I have lived with and studied for over two decades. This focus is both geographically sensible—it creates a reasonably circumscribed study area rather than all of northern Kenya—and creates a certain amount of groundedness at the outset of the project. While

I would not deign to claim anything like "native knowledge" of the Samburu, I can at least say I know them well from basic patterns of behavior studied over an extended period, the many stories I have heard and recorded, and the assumptions and interactions of a Samburu lifestyle and worldview that I have observed over the course of years. And I have long heard stories of the wars with their neighbors. I just also knew that their neighbors would undoubtedly see things quite differently.

This book is largely composed of different versions of the same stories—Samburu stories and the versions told from the other side. These vary from broadly brushed, almost official, narrative to intimate portraits of individuals and their experiences. I focus on four main case studies, highlighting the dynamics of these conflicts and the memories they have forged. I suggest that the memories create understandings of the other, as well as misunderstandings, that are central to the terms of the relationship during times of peace and can form the catalyst for a reemergence of violence.

The book vividly portrays the complex and confusing dynamics of interethnic violence through the lives, words, and intimate experiences of individuals involved in and affected by these conflicts. Yet while this book is an ethnography of a particular people in a particular place, the aim is to enhance our understanding of dynamics that play out across the globe and indeed even in the lives of the Western academics and college students who are most likely to read this book. There is no shortage of case studies of horrific violence around the globe, as well as anthropological studies of violence that can fruitfully be read as comparison, including Daniel's (1996) account of violence in Sri Lanka, Englund's (2001) account of the war-torn Malawi-Mozambique border, Nordstrom and Robben's (1996) collection on anthropological fieldwork in contexts of violence, Aretxaga's (1997) feminist analysis of violence in Northern Ireland, and many others. Gilsenan's (1996) rich account of narratives of violence in Lebanon may provide particularly worthwhile comparison with those in this book, as does Van de Port's (1998) stunning use of the trope of the "world through stories" to elucidate how people in war-torn Serbia used fictive accounts to make sense of their worlds through stories, while knowing all the while that war was the ultimate "certainty that lies beneath all uncertainties" (p. 30).

It would be a fool's errand to even attempt to do justice to all of these comparative examples and worthwhile case studies (or the many others that I haven't mentioned), but my hope is that the description and analysis here can both illuminate the geographically particular events that are the book's primary focus, while helping us reconsider violence much closer to home. I believe we all should care for its own sake about how the time-honored ritual friendship of the Samburu and their Pokot neighbors was broken, leading to a bloody conflict. Yet these events become more meaningful when we consider that they are not simply tales of relatively small, obscure populations in far-off northern Kenya. Thus, I suggest that it is useful to think, for example, about the commonalities and differences between the political dynamics and discourses that led to the Samburu-Pokot conflict and those that led to the latest Iraq War. This is not to reduce one to the other, but rather to consider what case studies can tell us about issues with a global impact as well as about our own lives, in which violence, variously defined and expressed and writ large or small, is a pervasive aspect.

Chapter 1 is organized around a specific incident in which I was tangentially involved—or in which I *may* have been tangentially involved. Through a close reading of the lives and deaths of those directly involved, I consider the extent to which uncertainty is more than a characteristic of fieldwork and of the texts produced by it. Rather, I argue, to a great extent we as ethnographers, particularly working in contexts of violence, in fact *document uncertainty* as the material of our accounts. That I do not know how close I came to being killed in this incident is far less important than the fact that uncertainty about why these events occur, who is responsible, and how and when their lives are affected is intrinsic to the lives of my interlocutors.

Chapter 2 begins a series of interethnic, multivocal case studies focusing on conflicts between the Samburu and their neighbors. I focus here on widespread violence that erupted between Samburu and their pastoralist Pokot neighbors, who had been ritually bonded as friends and allies since beyond living memory. The roots of this conflict emerged in the context of local politics and economy, regional insecurity, and the global trade in small arms. Yet Pokot explanations for casting aside their historically validated friendship focus passionately on a single atrocity—the castration of a Pokot man killed in cold blood in the aftermath of an early skirmish and the impossibility of peace until his testicles were somehow returned. Given the diffuse frictions that appear to have fomented and driven the continuing conflict, this colorful yet one-dimensional explanation resembles classic propaganda—from weapons of mass destruction, to the sinking of the *Maine,* to the accusations against the Tutsi prior to the Rwanda genocide—which Noam Chomsky and others emphasize as crucial to mass mobilization in modern war. Yet despite this partial similarity, there are also differences. First, this "propaganda" drove (or justified) warfare across an area stretching hundreds of miles without mass media, which are portrayed as integral to manufacturing consent for war. Second, in a nonhierarchical society such as the Pokot, individuals decided to fight, rather than merely giving "consent" to violence. In this sense the stories that drove war were told by Pokot combatants to themselves, leading to epistemological questions of how these stories come into being and the relationship between discourse and violence.

Chapter 3 focuses on conflicts between Samburu and Kikuyu agriculturalists, highlighting the role that memories of past violence play in fomenting and structuring violence, and in the discourses used to explain and justify it. I focus in particular on uneven aspects of memory, for conflicts often have roots in memories of past violence that may have tremendous potency for those on one side of the encounter while being forgotten by the other. The focal point of this chapter is a series of clashes that erupted between the two groups in 1998, in which some hundred Kikuyu were massacred, but which also led to continued efforts by the politically dominant Kikuyu to push Samburu from the area. Samburu stridently argue that these conflicts are rooted in the deep-seated hatred Kikuyu bear because of the Samburu's aid to the colonial government in suppressing the Mau Mau uprising in the 1950s. For their part, many Kikuyu today barely know the Samburu exist, and those in close contact are bewildered that events which occurred before most of them were born would have any bearing on present conflicts, focusing instead on the incompatibility of the Samburu as neighbors for those striving toward national and global visions of development. The differing versions of this conflict are, thus, not so much opposed as speaking past each other. The accounts encounter no direct contradiction or misunderstanding, despite forming the shared space of a kind of dialogue, the ultimate outcome of which is violence.

Chapter 4 draws on the interlocking stories of the surviving relatives of a Somali sheik and of Samburu personally involved in killing him in the course of what Samburu see as their greatest military victory in living memory: a massive reprisal raid in 1965. Viewing the sheik as a leader with supernatural powers who had orchestrated a bloody massacre of Samburu, they see his death as emblematic of Samburu resilience in the face of loss—themes that were reinvoked in conflicts in the late 1990s that also began in Samburu defeat and ended in victory. Understandings of these events by the sheik's surviving family and other Somalis, needless to say, differ radically from Samburu views. Yet these differing views are not based on notable differences in the factual accounts of what happened, as both sides of this violent encounter almost entirely agree on the facts. Thus interpretation alone renders groups and individuals righteous warriors, scurrilous murderers, peaceful healers, or evil wizards. Through a close reading of these almost factually identical but radically different accounts, I seek to understand the fundamental misunderstandings through which violence is memorialized, sowing the seeds of future violence.

Chapter 5 takes Sartre's famous declaration that "hell is other people" as a metaphor for the interlocking relationships of the Samburu, Pokot, and Turkana in their shifts between peaceful neighbors and deadly adversaries. In particular, I explore the ironic conundrum that, although Pokot and Samburu have been bonded in ritual friendship since beyond living memory, they have only modest economic and interpersonal interactions, and in fact often describe a strong distaste for one another dating to long before their recent war. In contrast, Samburu and Turkana have long engaged in sporadic and devastating incidents of deadly warfare, yet maintain a close interrelationship and relatively high levels of affection. Narratives and events from each of these groups are critical in defining both Others and themselves. While groups invariably construct themselves as virtuous in peace and in conflict, they define others as friends and partners, as worthy adversaries, or as dehumanized beings toward whom violence is of no moral consequence. Drawing on the differing perspectives of these interlocking groups, I examine the ways peace and war are mediums for refracting identities both of the self and the other, and how these fashion both the terms of peace and the seeds of violence. In doing so, I reconsider the truism in popular culture notions about peace: if people only got to know each other, they would not fight. I suggest that, ironically, sometimes groups fight not because they do not know each other but because they do, and that we must consider the implications of this for hopes for peace.

Chapter 6 focuses on actions and discourses surrounding the Kenyan government, an often-absent player in these northern Kenyan conflicts. By far the most potent military force in northern Kenya, it nonetheless frequently sits on the sidelines, or when entering the fray does so for reasons and in ways that may appear to subvert its defined role as the insurer of peace. The role of the government is particularly important from the standpoint of understanding the cultural construction of violence through a triad of victim-perpetrator-observer, since one important purpose of local narratives regarding violence is to establish legitimacy and bring this most potent observer, the government, onto one side or another. While the government is in principle accepted by local actors as the agent of order among disorder, in practice it is seen as not always approaching this ideal, in some contexts as a perpetrator and occasionally as a victim. Thus, the stories that people on all sides tell to describe, explain or justify the violence are often at least in part stories told most importantly to or for the government, to sculpt legitimacy, to raise the alarm for action, or to deflect blame. The diverse ways local actors understand both the principle of government and its actions, which may contradict this principle, are fundamental to making sense of the conflicts described in this book.

In chapter 7, the book concludes with a reflective essay considering the significance of "Truth" in the conflicting narratives upon which this book is based. On one hand, the importance of these narratives lies less in their objective truthfulness than in the ways they serve—in peace and war—to sow the seeds of violence and permit participants and observers to understand and interpret it. Yet does that push us to a position in which the truth of these stories doesn't matter? How and when do we decide that "what really happened" does matter? Drawing on a diverse set of commentators on violence—author Tim O'Brien's notion of a "true war story," the controversy surrounding Rigoberta Menchú, and German tropes of the *Dachenschlosse* (the "backstabbing" in World War I) used to justify the Holocaust—I consider the extent to which Truth matters. While many of us would agree with O'Brien's assertion that an essential truth may exist apart from what "really happened," we find ourselves likely to accept this proposition when the essential truth is one we agree with (e.g., the underlying message of Menchú), while not always coming to terms to with how the same notion of "an essential truth that exists apart from fact" can be used (for instance, in the Holocaust) to justify the slaughter of millions. Considering these stories from northern Kenya, which contain varying mixtures of truth and falsehood, I suggest that ultimately we are left in the conundrum of unattainable truth, at the same time accepting that clearly truth does matter to the victims of war.

.   .   .

Moving now to the substantive chapters, the book explores narratives of violence in northern Kenya, focusing both on understandings and on misunderstandings that neighbors have of each other. There will be facts, there will be lies, and there will be differing but at least arguably valid interpretations of the same events. All of these will be presented, but it won't always be clear to anyone, myself included, which is which. In working with groups in conflict, there are inherently differing versions and differing valuations of events. In simpler terms, if two groups tell you two different things happened, they can't both be right, but I cannot always tell you who is wrong. In some cases it may be possible to ascertain that one side's version is more plausible than the other, and sometimes it may be apparent that even if neither side is *lying* per se, there are aspects of the interaction that one side clearly did not grasp well. In other cases there are bare contradictions that cannot readily be sorted out. In some cases I attempt to sort through what appears to have happened or not happened, but my emphasis is far more on the stories—on what the stories assert about the other group and about a group itself. That is, whether they are true or not, these stories form the basis for understanding interactions with friends who are also would-be adversaries and adversaries who are also would-be friends.

I

BEING THERE, BEING FRIENDS, BEING UNCERTAIN

It was Saturday, market day in the nearby town of Supilli. In a rural, somewhat out-of-the-way part of northern Kenya, the Saturday market in the nearby medium-size town is like a party of sorts, where people of many ethnic groups gather, socialize, and perhaps spend a bit of their money from livestock sales on beer and roasted meat—a pleasant change of pace from the routines of my fieldwork.

Sammy (my Samburu assistant), Simba (my Pokot host), and I intended to go to the market, but my car, as was often the case, was not in good repair. It only started some of the time, and when it managed to start, an undiagnosed engine problem was causing it to consume ridiculous amounts of fuel. There was public transportation from the little town of Ol Moran, where we were located, but it was unpleasant, usually involving sitting in the back of a truck on a very rough road. So, when I saw the local councilor—an ethnic Kikuyu who was the political representative from this mixed area—with his old Suzuki jeep, I went over to say hello. I struck up a conversation about his car, which filled me with nostalgia since it was identical in make and color to the one I had driven in the course of my doctoral research. He was friendly, and when I inquired about possibly getting a ride to the market he said he probably could give me one if he got some gas, and we could talk later.

I left him and shortly afterward was standing around with Sammy and Simba. I mentioned getting a lift with the councilor as a better option than driving my problematic car or sitting in the back of a truck. Simba responded with disgust, "Pffft! Stay away from that guy!" It wasn't the sort of response that elicited further discussion. Clearly there was some sort of basic disgust with the councilor, so the ride was not going to be an option, and parsing out the reasons for the disgust seemed an awkward conversation.

In the end, we went to Supilli in the back of a bumpy truck, then enjoyed the market with its meat and beer and pineapples, and in the evening I was back in Ol Moran, sitting around reading and relaxing with Sammy. Not long after dusk he went out to use the latrine but returned shortly, looking quite startled. He claimed he had heard gunshots, but I dismissed it as him being jumpy, a nervous Samburu in an area now dominated by their enemies, the Pokot. Just minutes later, however, I realized I had been too quick to shrug Sammy off. The night was filled with keening, wailing, whistles, and chanting as groups of Kikuyu towns-people, angry and forlorn, moved through the streets of the town.

The councilor had been killed—shot dead in the Suzuki I did not ride in.

.   .   .

Ethnography is always personal. It is an odd enterprise in which our authority to convey scholarly knowledge to others is dependent on our "being there." Yet, of course, being there is never a simple thing. As the various iterations of the critique, debate, or exploration of "writing culture" have shown, as much as anthropologists may wish, and at earlier junctures may have claimed, to have our writings serve as objective windows that offer a peek into a reality very different from that of our readers, we are always an integral part of the picture whether we like it or not, and irrespective of the degree to which we acknowledge it or make it a part of our writing. As Borneman and Hammoudi (2009) argue in their thoughtful recent collection on the fieldwork encounter: "Field-work encounters . . . are modes of ethical engagement wherein the ethnographer is arrested in the act of perception. This arrest can lead both to a productive doubt about the ongoing perception of the phenomena in interaction and to the possibility of elaborating shared knowledge"

(p. 27). Put another way, as ethnographers, we are at the center of a strange and complex reality that we can never fully understand, inserting ourselves into this strange reality to convey this imperfect understanding of it to others. Our roles are many. Apart from our explicit one as scholars—which in many cases our interlocutors do not fully grasp—we are, as Hortense Powdermaker (1967) famously called us, "strangers and friends." But we are many other things as well, and our friends (or "research subjects") may construe us to have a host of additional perceived roles. We may, for instance, be suspected of being spies, a common accusation made against anthropologists (e.g., Jarvenpa 1998)—and, fortunately, only rarely true. In the context of working between warring groups, the possibility of being a spy, or the danger of inadvertently acting as one, was very real. I was careful to avoid this role, and despite obvious concern on the part of different warring groups, I was only rarely and mildly suspected of it. One can also be a target. That's a role one can only be cautious about but not prevent.

Thus, while ethnography is always personal, I would contend that this ethnography is particularly (though certainly not uniquely) so. I take this to be neither a singular virtue of this text nor a scourge on its validity. It is simply a statement about the way this text was produced and the kind of knowledge it contains: a kind of uncertainty, indeed a *certainty* of uncertainty. Part of the odd personal nature of this ethnography involved the simple fact of my becoming a kind of conduit between people who never talked, or could once talk but no longer did. Chapter 4, for instance, is to a great extent constituted through the intersection of my conversations with the surviving family of a renowned Somali sheik who was killed by the Samburu, as well as the particular Samburu elder who in his youth drove a spear through their grandfather's chest. The personal dimensions most central to this multisited fieldwork experience revolved around Simba, both in respect to the complexities of that relationship in its own right, and in the strange and coincidental links it created with Lekeren, my longtime host among the Samburu.

Although I formed friendships in all of the communities where I worked in the course of this particular project, as well as in the Samburu ones that predated it, the relationship with Simba was the most important in many ways. He is funny and extroverted, and we enjoyed each other's company a great deal. He cuts a charismatic, larger-than-life figure, and

FIGURE 3. Simba.

by odd coincidence, his personal connections to the Samburu were aligned with my own, having before the war been the neighbor and friend of my longtime Samburu host, Lekeren. Indeed—as noted in the introduction—after I had begun work among Pokot but before I knew Simba, Lekeren asked me if I had met him, characterizing him as a good-natured extrovert who had before the war been his friend but now was reputed to want to kill him. An odd, additional, and coincidental wrinkle to the relationship is that Simba is also the uncle to a Pokot boy, Tinga, whom Lekeren had semi-adopted years earlier, and whom I therefore knew well—a child my own children had grown up playing with. So while through much of my earlier research a childhood Tinga was a fixture at Lekeren's home, a teenage Tinga was now a frequent visitor at Simba's.

.   .   .

Why, when I suggested getting a lift to the market in the councilor's Suzuki, did my friend tell me, "Keep away from that guy!" accompanied by an exclamation of disgust? Clearly he did not like the councilor, but the fact that the man was murdered just hours later in that very car forces other questions. Putting these in context requires a bit more discussion of Simba, my relationship to him, and the ways this bore on fieldwork.

Simba and I shared personal connections (albeit ambiguous ones) through Lekeren and Tinga, as well as genuine affection. We joked and drank and ate meat together, spending days bicycling around the open landscapes of Laikipia. I frequently stayed at his settlement, and to ensure my comfort he bought a thin foam mattress to put atop the traditional Pokot bed composed of thin sticks, providing additional sheets and blankets to keep me warm. One night he went so far as to tuck me in with the new bedding—a rather comical experience as a grown man, particularly given Simba's notable size and reputation as a strong and fierce Pokot warrior. But irrespective of what felt like genuine friendship, could I ever be sure of Simba? The region was violent, and Simba was not a stranger to that. I could never truly know what he was involved in and what he wasn't—and therefore I could never exclude the possibility that what he might or might not be involved in might someday involve me.

As a general rule, in doing fieldwork I aim to avoid getting particularly close to those who are regarded as "important people" in the community. While some people (anthropologists and others) have a tendency to gravitate toward important friends, I am generally guided by the recognition that important friends are likely to have important enemies; by making one set of friends, one risks making enemies of others, or at least suggesting to people that one is aligned with their enemies. While I have not, as a consequence, always avoided important people—my Samburu host, for instance, is a person of prominence within his age set and hence within the community—I have never sought them out, much less deliberately fostered the notion that we were tightly bonded and essentially aligned. Simba is the exception. He is loquacious and fun; once I met him it would have been difficult not to become friends. But it is also the case that his area was certainly the most dangerous that I have ever worked (and at times I had children with me whose safety I needed to consider), with lots of guns, active warfare characterized by intermittent fighting between Pokot and Samburu, and common banditry.

I do not know to what extent, if at all, Simba was directly involved in such activities, particularly banditry. However, I was quite sure that he was highly knowledgeable and highly respected—including by people who might at times be bandits. I believed having it be known that I was friends with Simba offered me protection, irrespective of what direct steps he might actually take (unknown to me) to ensure my safety. Still, I was careful. He sometimes asked to borrow significant sums of money, for instance when he found that calves were available at throwaway prices at a livestock market. I would have trusted him with a loan, as he was wealthy and respected. I was, however, mildly paranoid/concerned that he might be trying to determine if I was carrying significant sums of money—perhaps whether I was worth the while of bandits. Regardless of how much money I had, I would gave the same answer: I had just enough money to buy gas and a few supplies. And—if not quite to the extreme of a prison or spy movie—I always kept money in three or more different places: my official supply, a secure semihidden supply, and an extra hidden supply (perhaps rolled up in a used prescription bottle)—and perhaps another bit hidden somewhere else. In the uncertainties of fieldwork, I believed that trust in Simba would keep me safe. But I did not believe this enough to not take precautions to keep me safe from Simba.

What, then, about the murder of the councilor? Did Simba have foreknowledge? There are three partially overlapping scenarios that could explain why he told me to have nothing to do with the guy in general, and specifically to rid my mind of hitching a ride in his car. And despite the fact that "I was there," I can't offer much guidance on which of these scenarios is true or even most likely. In the most innocent version, he told me to avoid the councilor simply because he (and most likely other Pokot) genuinely disliked him. In this version his dislike is by and large tangential to the fact that other Pokot disliked the councilor enough to kill him (again, in this innocent version, absolutely without my friend's knowledge). In a slightly less innocent version, my friend was protecting me by telling me to avoid the councilor (and more importantly, the car in which he would be killed). Perhaps Simba knew that he was going to be killed, that he was going to be shot in the car where I was hoping to ride. In the least innocent version, my friend knew that I shouldn't be in that car because he had something to do with what happened. We may still interpret it as protecting me, but in this case protecting me from something he had a hand in. How should I know?

.   .   .

What shall we make of the uncertainty of that situation? Of course, it tells us something about the context of fieldwork. I do not, however, intend it principally as the sort of fieldwork adventure story that anthropologists sometimes like to swap with colleagues or share with students. This book isn't about me. It's by me: it could not exist but for the fact that "I was there," and to a certain extent a fair and honest reading of the book and the narratives that principally constitute it need to take account of the uncertainties incumbent in the knowledge that I bring forward. If I do not know why my friend asserted his authority in a way that ensured I did not get shot, I certainly lack the authority to come to definitive conclusions about why, in other scenarios discussed throughout the book, people did get shot. Yet perhaps most importantly, neither do the actors in this book, by and large, know definitively what happened and why it happened—and unlike me, they lack the luxury of being able to get on a plane and fly away. That is to say, uncertainty is central to the texture of the lives of the actors who inhabit this book. Of course some are at times producers of uncertainty—someone knows the truth of what happened in this example and at least some of the others I bring forward, though there may be variations to which the truth may be spun—and they are also consumers of uncertainty. But everyone in this book lives with intense doubt in one sense or another, at one time or another.

.   .   .

In respect to the murder of the councilor, the uncertainties go far beyond why my friend told me to not get into a car that (coincidentally or not) would hours later be sprayed with bullets. The accounts of why it was attacked and by whom are interlocking, conflicting, and unresolved. A semiofficial version was reported in the national media. While acknowledging my limited ability to discern the truth of this situation, I do know that this semiofficial version is almost certainly not true. In the Kenyan national media, the councilor was cited as having been an ardent opponent of the illegal trade in firearms. His murder was consequently painted as the work of criminals whose illegal trade the councilor was stridently fighting to suppress. There were two widely circulating local versions of why he was killed and who killed him, one propagated by Pokot and one by Kikuyu. Based on their commonalities and the extent to which many dimensions are largely agreed upon by local actors, I consider them far closer to what actually happened. Despite sharing many details, however, they cannot both be fully true. These accounts related to the illegal trade in guns, but in neither version was he attempting to stamp out the trade.

Each version claimed that he was acting as an intermediary for Kikuyu who wanted to buy guns from Pokot. He was said to have been given 70,000 Kenya shillings by Kikuyu (approximately $1,000), which he was supposed to use to buy four guns from Pokot. In all local accounts, however, he double-crossed someone. The Kikuyu version maintains that he took the guns from the Pokot but never paid them the money, and the Pokot killed him in revenge. In the Pokot version of the story, he was killed by his own people, by other Kikuyu. He was said to have taken the Kikuyus' money but never gave them the Pokot guns—so the Kikuyu killed him. Of course, it is entirely plausible that he double-crossed *both* the Kikuyu and the Pokot—though it is highly unlikely (based on relations between the groups) that members of the two groups conspired to kill him.

·　　·　　·

Tinga illustrates other personal aspects of this ethnography but, perhaps more significantly, the types of uncertainty that constitute the lived experience of the people whose stories make up this book. As mentioned above, Tinga was a mainstay at the homestead of Lekeren, where I have stayed during most of my time in Samburu from 2001 to the present. When I returned to Kenya in 2001 (after a hiatus following my doctoral research), Tinga was a boy of about seven. He was the son of one of Lekeren's Pokot neighbors at his other settlement in neighboring Laikipia District. There were no good primary schools in that area, so Lekeren agreed to take him in, and he stayed in Samburu, living in the house of one of Lekeren's wives. Tinga became good friends—almost like brothers—with Lekeren's boys, who were around his age. He also played with my children, so I got to know him well.

FIGURE 4. Tinga.

Although everyone recognized that Tinga was Pokot, no one seemed to care much while the Samburu and the Pokot remained on good terms. He had many Samburu friends and learned to speak Samburu. Occasionally someone mentioned that he was Pokot. I recall, for instance, a time when the ball my children were playing with inadvertently went through a crack in Lekeren's house while it was locked and Lekeren was away with the key. Other children called Tinga, and he managed to find a way to squirm into the locked house. Although it was probably simply a matter of his size and dexterity, people joked that being Pokot—who are reputed to be thieves—gave him the skill to break into people's homes. Tinga lived with Lekeren for roughly six years without incident. His father visited him occasionally, but he rarely if ever went to visit his family on school holidays.

When the war between the Samburu and the Pokot began in 2006, nothing changed much at first for Tinga. There was some gossip that a few neighbors were saying things about Tinga behind his back. One woman supposedly talked about wanting to slit his throat, and there were general—if undefined—murmurings that Tinga was an enemy among us, a Pokot. Lekeren and his family defended him, none more vehemently than Lekeren's third wife, Alleni, in whose house he lived. "Tinga is a Samburu! He's not a Pokot!" she would exclaim when she heard rumors that some viewed him as an enemy.

Slowly, however, things deteriorated. In a Pokot raid some distance from Lekeren's home, many cattle were stolen, including many belonging to Alleni's birth family. Many claim that Alleni abruptly shifted her attitude (though I never saw or heard this firsthand). Bitter at the loss of her family's cattle, she reputedly came to see Tinga as symbolic of those who had stolen her livestock and began to hate him as a Pokot. Then he got horribly sick with a stomach ailment so severe that many feared he was going to die. Though he was treated and survived, this spurred more rumors and concerns. Had he been poisoned (perhaps by the woman who cared for him but now was filled with bitterness toward the Pokot)? Tinga himself tells me he just ate some bad food at school that made him sick. Lekeren, however, did not want to take chances, particularly because he had heard that Tinga's mother was inconsolable, crying frequently in fear that the Samburu would kill Tinga. Even if it was a stomach ailment, Lekeren surmised, it was a close call—not just for Tinga, but also for himself. The consequences of being responsible for Tinga's death could be enormous. He arranged to meet with Tinga's father at a peace meeting between the Samburu and the Pokot and returned the boy to his parents.

When I began working intensively with the Pokot, I was surprised to see Tinga. I was unaware at first that he was Simba's nephew, but I met his father, Lokorr, through Simba and then subsequently saw Tinga on several occasions. The boy was saddened to have left his friends in Samburu. He longed to return there—to enter high school, perhaps, at Maralal High School (in the Samburu District headquarters) and rejoin his friends, his brothers. And while he and his friends were always excited to hear news of each other as I traveled back and forth between the areas, he finished his childhood without ever having the liberty to return in safety to the place he regarded as home.

．　　　　．　　　　．

Tinga's story may be read in some ways as similar to my experience with the councilor and his car—though I certainly regard his as more meaningful and more poignant. Tinga lacked the luxury of being a global anthropologist who can leave the world of friends-who-might-be-bandits for places with fewer uncertainties and different human connections. This is Tinga's only world, yet he lives in it precariously and understands it uncertainly. He has inhabited two worlds, Pokot and Samburu, but came to prefer the one in which he was ultimately a sort of foreigner, the one he was forced to leave when tensions arose that were beyond his control but in which he had become unfairly implicated. But more importantly, in my case the dangers were only physical and in my estimation manageable—and I had the choice to not be there. For someone like Tinga, however, the physical dangers were unclear but the emotional dangers real. Although he was defended by those in his adopted home at the time of war, ultimately the person closest to him is reputed to have rejected him. He insists he wasn't—as it was rumored—poisoned. But can he truly know that he simply "ate some bad food" at school, as he explained to me? And is it even possible for him to say or believe the opposite, that he had been poisoned by those to whom he felt close, perhaps even (as vaguely rumored) by a woman who had become his surrogate mother?

The accounts described in this book are complex and can be read in multiple ways depending on one's position and inclinations. Of course they are presented here principally as a mode of scholarship. I aim to use this material to further our understanding of the nature of violence, particularly between intimates, and explain how those involved make sense of violence as they move from peace to war and back again. But the stories are many things, and they involve real people's lives. We read a murder mystery because we are fascinated with intrigue, which leads us to forget that it is also a tragedy, depending on how one looks at it. The friends and family members of the councilor—wailing in the streets of Ol Moran as I pondered the meaning of not having ridden in his car—can tell us clearly about the tragedy in the mystery, as can the many others whose uncertain lives and sometimes uncertain deaths are described in this book.

2

A CASE OF TESTICLES

Manufacturing Consent or an
Ethnography of Lies?

> It's the case of the testicles, that man who was castrated.
> You might shoot a man with a bullet, and you leave
> him. That is fitting for a man. You might stab him with
> a spear. You leave him. He dies. But after killing him,
> [the Samburu] grabbed him and removed the testicles,
> along with the whole genitals. I don't know where they
> take them! The case that is truly bad with the Samburu
> is they need to return those testicles. . . . If they buried
> them, dig them up. If they threw them in the forest, take
> them from the forest. If they were eaten by a hyena,
> bring us that hyena. . . . The cows we take pay for those
> testicles!
>
> KEMELII NYANGALUK, *Pokot elder*

History is rife with examples of "actes de guerre" that make a sufficiently compelling mark on the public consciousness to energize a society to go to war. In some cases these were genuine attacks or compelling threats— for instance, the attack on Pearl Harbor that thrust a previously ambivalent public into backing U.S. entry into World War II—but at least as common are manufactured incidents, such as the destruction of the battleship *Maine,* which justified and garnered public support for the Spanish-American War; the Gulf of Tonkin Incident, which led to the escalation of the Vietnam War; or the assassination of the Rwanda's Hutu president (by other Hutu but blamed on the Tutsi), which justified the Rwandan genocide (Gourevitch 1999). Recent American history offers a vivid example of this in the marketing of the war in Iraq around the theme of weapons of mass destruction. Former undersecretary for defense Paul Wolfowitz (2003), in a remarkably candid interview, elaborates how the Bush administration wanted to invade Iraq for many reasons, but that "the truth is that for reasons that have a lot to do with the U.S. government bureaucracy we settled on the one issue that everyone could agree on, which was weapons of mass destruction as the core reason." Weapons of mass destruction provided a reason that could be sold to the American public (if not the world). We now know, of course, that not merely were the claims untrue—that is, there were no such weapons—but using them as a justification for war was disingenuous. That is to say, whether or not anyone in a decision-making capacity believed there were such weapons is beside the point; this was not the primary motivating factor, but rather a discourse that could be usefully employed by those who wished to wage war.

What, then, do we make of the Pokot elder quoted above in his obsession with the castration of a Pokot killed by Samburu some two years prior to this interview? Possibly slightly tipsy, he used phrasing that was deliberately playful but also filled with deadly anger and serious resolve. For many reasons, it is not conceivable that the castration of a man murdered in revenge lies at the root of a then two-year-old conflict between two groups who were formerly ritually bonded to not kill one another, who had layers of both mutual interest and potential friction, and who embarked on a war in which hundreds have died at the point of AK-47s and similar weaponry. This singular explanation both ignores more basic causes of friction (e.g., chronic theft, competition for land) that informants on both sides of the conflict sometimes invoke, as well as the fact that various acts of provocation in the past failed to start a war. Consequently, it is not simply that this explanation is unlikely to be true; one must wonder to what extent those who invoke it actually believe it to be true. Thus, I ask, is this "case of testicles" in some way similar to the phantom yellow cake uranium that we were told might end up as an Iraq-born mushroom cloud over some American city? Clearly there are many differences. For instance, a Pokot man really was castrated, whereas the yellow cake uranium was a deliberate lie. What they share is the quality of being a simplification, and not necessarily a wholly forthright one, concerning the causes of war.

They share, then, a degree to which discourse—perhaps propaganda—is tied to the genesis or continuation of violence. Yet there are also profound differences. Propaganda is seen as working most importantly through mass media, as governments or people in positions of power create consent for war among the populace (Chomsky 1992). Even in out of the way places, propaganda has been seen as playing an important role in mass mobilization—for instance, radio in the Rwandan genocide (Yanagizawa-Drott 2014). Pokot did not use mass media, but rather spread the news of the killing and dismemberment among themselves. Perhaps the most significant difference, however, lies in the social mechanisms through which the discourses do their work. In the example of the U.S. war on Iraq, discourses concerning weapons of mass destruction created sufficient consent among the voting public to make the mobilization of a complex military apparatus politically viable. In contrast, consider a quote from another Pokot elder: "They [Samburu] castrated a man up in Lorok [Samburu District]. And then the Pokot all awoke, from all the way down there in Churo and Kinyang, and went and attacked Samburu." The key difference, then, is that Pokot do not assert that they allowed a war or consented to a war because of this provocation. Rather, they stood up and did it; they themselves fought and killed. Though there is a social context and likely social pressures to their actions, the decision to fight was largely voluntary and uncoerced; many went to fight, but many didn't, depending on their particular positions and motivations.

I should note here that the testicle story is not the only one in circulation among either the Pokot or the Samburu, though for the former it typically takes center stage. Samburu and Pokot do not agree, needless to say, on culpability or even what the key events might be. Moreover, many of the stories concerning the war lack coherence; like the testicle discourse, there may be significant truth in them, but there is also fiction, and posturing regarding both what happened and its significance. The extent to which these stories reflect genuine feelings, genuine explanations for events, as opposed to posturing, is sometimes unclear. In this chapter, I explore conflicting—and often internally contradictory— accounts given by Pokot and Samburu as to why they went to war. It will not be possible to reach a conclusion regarding the root cause. I will not be able to use the commonplace formula (or perhaps fallacy) where the fact that the surface explanation is unconvincing is used to assert that some other explanation is true. That is, I will not suggest that "since it was not the testicles, it was truly a fight over land," any more than one might argue that "since it was not weapons of mass destruction, it was oil, or the need to relocate American military bases outside of Saudi Arabia, or—well, Saddam was a bad man who tried to kill my daddy." If one motive seems false, presumably there are other motives that are true. However, the simple fact of one explanation being false does not prove that a deeper, hidden motive is any more real. I do not say this out of a failure to ascertain an empirically supportable root cause. Rather, I entertain the possibility that in this instance the actors themselves do not know the root cause, or even with certainty why they are fighting. In this sense discourses concerning why the conflict ignited and why it persists are not so much causal explanations as justifications for events that even the principal actors may not fully understand.

THE SAMBURU-POKOT CONFLICT: A BASIC OUTLINE

Samburu and Pokot are both pastoralist groups living in and around Kenya's northern Rift Valley. Until recently, the two groups were closely allied, bonded by a ritual oath undertaken, by most accounts, before living memory, with the slaughtering of livestock from their respective herds and ritual burying of spears. As will be discussed in more detail in chapter 5, this oath prohibited killing a member of the other group, and anyone who did so was believed to suffer insanity or death. They avoided fighting with one another and occasionally teamed up to raid common enemies. Most recently and notably, in the 1990s the two groups jointly raided the Turkana, with whom the Pokot persistently fight in lowland areas and who were at that point getting the better of the Samburu in a major conflict. Samburu and Pokot sometimes herded together and shared pasture, and intermingled most significantly in areas of Laikipia District that had been opened up in the 1990s to new settlement, with the departure of many European settlers whose colonial-era ninety-nine-year leases on government land were expiring.

Both groups have a significant recent and long-term history of conflict with other groups. The Samburu have fought periodically with such groups as the Turkana, Somali, and Boran. The Pokot also fight with the Turkana, as well as the Marakwet, Lchamus, and other groups. These conflicts are long-standing but often oscillate between warfare and peaceful coexistence. The Samburu and the Pokot alone did not fight with each other, having taken an oath after events that many do not recall with any specificity and others ascribe to a particularly bloody war in perhaps the 1830s. The groups cooperated in violent clashes with the Kikuyu in Laikipia in the 1990s, and against the Turkana in the north about the same time.

Tensions between the two groups began to heighten over the several years leading to the conflict. These mainly involved occasional low-scale clashes between isolated groups or individuals. From the Samburu perspective, the worst of these occurred in 2004, when a Samburu herd boy was wounded and a significant number of Samburu cattle taken. When police went to recover the animals, fighting erupted between Pokot and the police, in which the police chief was killed. For their part, Pokot cite similar types of minor provocation from the same period. However, Samburu and Pokot continued to by and large intermingle, trade together, live side by side in some areas, and herd livestock together in search of dry season grazing even just prior to the conflict.

So what caused the conflict? The ultimate roots of the conflict are difficult to disentangle, as is the precise course of events. Certainly, resource conflicts are readily identifiable. Competition for grazing (particularly given the areas opened up in Laikipia) was certainly a potential issue, and among pastoralists there is always a temptation to steal cattle. All these factors, however, had existed for decades (or longer) before the conflict and cannot fully explain it, even if they came into play as the conflict developed.

Both Samburu and Pokot root the conflict in a series of events in March 2006. Their respective accounts differ somewhat, however, and there is no objective source to clarify what occurred. They agree in most particulars, but not in the exact sequence. Samburu tend to describe the beginning of the war as an unprovoked attack. Some cite two Samburu brothers who had been herding cooperatively with Pokot during the drought but were subsequently killed without provocation by Pokot friends. Others cite an attack on Samburu cattle in which a boy was killed. Pokot fault the Samburu, citing several incidents but focusing predominantly on one in which a Pokot boy was injured by Samburu and brought to the government hospital at the Samburu District headquarters of Maralal. Two relatives of the boy went to visit him and give him aid there, traveling on a local *matatu* (informal public transport). On the way back, the vehicle was stopped and the two Pokot were pulled from the matatu (possibly by relatives of a Samburu killed in the preceding incident). Both men were killed, one castrated, and the bodies dumped off the Rift Valley escarpment.

Following these incidents, the conflict exploded. The major raids early on were by Pokot, mainly in Samburu District but spreading farther south into jointly occupied areas in Laikipia District. Initial Pokot raids involved as many as several hundred fighters, armed mainly with AK-47s, and resulted in the capture of large numbers of livestock. The Samburu launched raids of their own, and the Pokot suffered heavy casualties when they attacked Samburu in an area where—owing to its more central location—a quick Samburu and government response could be organized. Following this, the Pokot started to rely more on smaller raids undertaken with greater stealth. Samburu have relied both on small-scale raids (though usually with less effectiveness) and major attacks that range from qualified successes to dismal failures. Conflict continued well after the most intense warfare, though usually in low-grade hostility, such as fighting between "patrols" meeting in advance of grazing cattle seeking pasture in border zones between the two groups.[1] Though both sides are heavily armed with military-style weaponry, over years of conflict the number of people killed is not especially high. Though an actual figure would be difficult to ascertain, it is likely less than three hundred or four hundred, with these deaths having mostly occurred in a few major raids.

None of this serves to explain the conflict, even if it highlights some main events. Individuals on both sides continue to cite a variety of causes, sometimes structural, sometimes quite immediate. Samburu assert, as do Pokot, the duplicity of the other in government-organized peace meetings, suggesting that whenever there is a meeting, the other side attacks. Sometimes a recent wrong is noted: some animals were stolen or some individuals killed. Pokot assert that the Samburu want to grab their land, and Samburu similarly assert that the Pokot (or possibly other figures using the Pokot as mercenaries) want to grab Samburu land. Samburu say that the Pokot are impossible to live with because they steal even trivial, ridiculous things. One Samburu man asserted that a Pokot man will visit your home, steal a spoon, and then disappear to his home area in neighboring Baringo District for ten years. Pokot have similar stories about the Samburu. Individuals from both sides sometimes assert that they are simply "paying for the bullets"—inflicting causalities to avenge their own causalities.

MOTIVATING WAR IN NONHIERARCHICAL CONTEXTS

It is important to consider the significance of these discourses, particularly in the context of warfare between groups without hierarchical political or military structures. These discourses in many instances bear a close resemblance to what we regard as propaganda, yet the context and dynamics are quite different in northern Kenya. In a society like the United States, the fundamental role of propaganda is to get the voting public on your side. The role of propaganda was exemplified in the latest Iraq War, where politicians used the media to market the war like any other product through what Paul Rutherford (2004) termed "weapons of mass persuasion"—less sympathetically termed "weapons of mass deception" by Rampton and Stauber (2003). Noam Chomsky has long been outspoken on the role of the media in "manufacturing consent" in regard to war (Chomsky and Herman 1988; Chomsky 1992): "In a totalitarian state, it doesn't matter what people think, since the government can control people by force using a bludgeon. But when you can't control people by force, you have to control what people think, and the standard way to do this is via propaganda (manufacture of consent, creation of necessary illusions), marginalizing the general public or reducing them to apathy of some fashion" (1992).

If the stories that Samburu and Pokot tell concerning the war bear some similarity to classic propaganda (insofar as they contain a high degree of falsehood, but persuasive falsehood), there are important differences. For instance, there is no power elite behind the mobilization. More importantly, what is required of the consumers of these stories is not merely consent (and certainly not apathy), but rather enthusiastic participation. Ferguson (1995) suggests that war occurs when those with decision-making power decide it is in their interest to wage it. Yet in nonhierarchical contexts, no one may actually have the status, authority, and power to make that decision and bring others to act in accordance with it (even if they might encourage, provoke, exert pressure, or provide rewards). Thus, Chomsky's contrast between totalitarian regimes and democratic ones becomes more dramatic. Among groups such as the Samburu and the Pokot, there is neither a tyrant who can coerce his subjects to war nor a democratic structure to convince or trick its citizens. Nor is there a freestanding military apparatus that is simply activated when the decision-making process is complete. Rather, violence must be born organically, through a system that may be collective but is to varying degrees voluntary. That is, the decision to commit violence principally lies with individuals who engage in it by all accounts voluntarily.

The difference between hierarchical societies and this voluntary, self-motivated form of violence is vividly illustrated by an aborted Samburu reprisal raid on the Pokot, which followed the theft of an estimated three thousand head of cattle in 2006. A party of approximately one thousand Samburu—perhaps half of them bearing guns—gathered near the area where the animals were stolen, on the edge of the Rift Valley escarpment. Their intent was to recover their livestock or else sweep through the Pokot lowlands, collecting whatever livestock they could find. Certainly there was a social and political dimension to this: although participation was voluntary, it did not occur in a social vacuum. People (especially gun owners) were encouraged to participate, and wealthy Samburu (including those with political influence) supplied weapons, ammunition, and food. Support could be given openly, since this was regarded as an effort to recover livestock—a legitimate policing action—rather than an offensive raid (though it could turn into a commonplace cattle raid, particularly if the missing cattle were not found). Participation was, however, voluntary, and individuals were motivated predominantly by the desire to either recover their stolen animals or (among those not affected by the Pokot raid) to gain livestock. As this formidable party began its descent into the valley, however, it began to rain. Additionally, the Pokot (not surprisingly) began to shoot at them. Although no one was killed, six Samburu were injured and the group retreated, aborting the reprisal raid.

Such an occurrence is difficult to imagine in the context of a disciplined, hierarchical military such as that found in state societies. While certainly commanders may respond to the possibility of casualties or other tactical concerns and call for a retreat, the explanation given to me by Samburu for halting the raid—"It was raining and they were shooting at us"—would hardly pass muster in a formal, hierarchically organized military group. Soldiers are expected to follow the commands of their superiors, even in the face of likely death. In a context such as the Samburu-Pokot conflict, however, participation is to a high degree voluntary, not simply in joining a raid but in continuing to participate as a raid progresses.

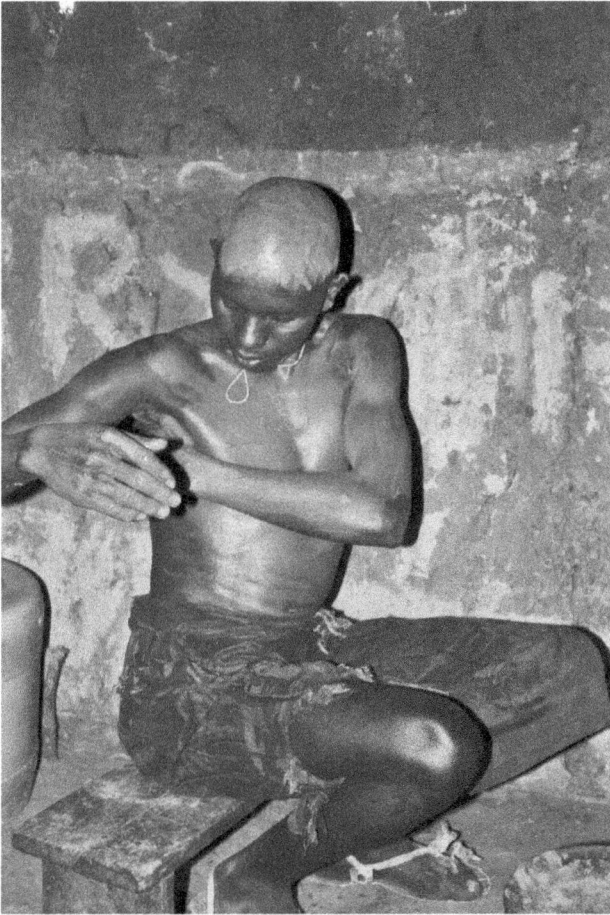

FIGURE 5.   A Samburu *murran* decorating his body with
red ochre.

This arrangement is not restricted to the Samburu, but rather is characteristic of conflicts in any context where states, or fairly disciplined and organized nonstate actors, are not the principal players. Moving even farther from state-organized violence, one may think of the comical scene in the classic ethnographic film *Dead Birds* (Gardner 1961), focusing on warfare among the Dani of New Guinea, in which a battle is called for the day when it starts to rain and the combatants do not want to get their decorative feathers wet. Yet we may see this phenomenon, or consider the degree of the voluntary nature of violence, in a range of contexts. It is easy to forget the extent to which war as we know it is a product of organization and discipline; who knows what percentage of American soldiers would have stormed Fallujah, for instance, if they had the option of relaxing in their barracks or going home to their families.[2] Widespread tropes depicting war-torn regions as "chaotic" and violence as "senseless" may distract us from the fact that the ability to cause such seeming chaos requires discipline, order, and hierarchy. This is not to say that there are no pressures to engage in violence—whether financial, social, or political—or that there is no continuum from the combatant with virtually no independent agency to those (such as the Samburu described above) who as individuals determine to an extremely high degree both when to attack and when to stop. Whether a specific context is more like a disciplined army or a sortie of potentially wavering Samburu is debatable. For instance, in the early days of the Iraq War, the insurgency was likely more akin to the Samburu. As the war continued, insurgents became increasingly organized into formalized militias in the face of long-term occupation and competition or conflict among themselves. Other well-known events—the wars in the former Yugoslavia, the genocide in Rwanda—might be analyzed in similar terms.

To the extent that individuals are making their own decisions about whether to participate in violence, one has to consider the persuasive discourses that may convince them to fight. This is not to reduce the motivations for violence to discourse—clearly material or other interests are often also involved. But to some extent they are necessarily motivated by the stories that are told, and the stories that are told to varying degrees create the social space that allows violence.

METHODOLOGICAL ISSUES

The point of looking at these discourses is to understand what motivates actors to engage in organized violence in the absence of a political structure that compels them to do so. This, however, poses a methodological problem as the researcher (in this case, me) seeks to understand whom these discourses are intended for. Obviously I am the conduit through which the discourses are transmitted from Pokot and Samburu to this page, but I clearly am an imperfect conduit in many ways. Most notably, it is difficult to ascertain the extent to which the discourses provided to me are isomorphic with those they share with each other, or whether what they say is what they truly believe. That is, one confronts three levels of understanding that may or may not coincide:

1. What people actually believe about why they are fighting.
2. What peers say to one another about why they are fighting.
3. What members of a particular group say to me about why they are fighting.

The difference between the first two, for instance, could occur if someone really just wanted to steal cows or to kill an enemy but felt it more socially acceptable even to his or her peers to give an explanation grounded in a higher moral purpose, whether self-defense or avenging a wrong. Individual motivation may be different from the social construction of a space for action. This is classically illustrated in *Anna Karenina* (Tolstoi 1877), where the soldiers going off to fight the war with the Turks all claim to be doing so for reasons of patriotism and defending Christianity, but all in fact have life situations (e.g., financial problems, bad family situations, the desire to find a socially acceptable means to commit suicide) that compel them to go. Sociologist C. Wright Mills (1940; Campbell 1994) discusses this as a "vocabulary of motives"—or as the financier J. P. Morgan once quipped, there are always two reasons for any action: a good reason and the real reason. Yet, as Mills argues, these justifications—whether true or false—frequently play an important role in constructing behavior. As he notes, "Often anticipations of acceptable justifications will control conduct. ('If I did this, what could I say? What would they say?')" (p. 443). A vocabulary of motives provides a socially acceptable set of explanations that may be drawn upon to explain action, and consequently has direct effects on behavior.

One example is seen in political riots. Although they are generally spurred by some type of populist furor—as in, for instance, the violence that followed the disputed 2007 Kenyan elections—this doesn't mean that everyone participating in a riot is equally motivated by politics. Some, perhaps disheartened by the structural violence that leaves them impoverished and vulnerable in everyday life, just feel like throwing a brick at something or someone. Political riots give them an opportunity to do that. It may also give license, even to people motivated in large part by political outrage, to perhaps steal a radio that they had previously admired in a shop window. Thus it would be misguided to expect that the finest, most accurate rendering of conscious, collective motivations for or explanations of violence would actually reflect why people fight. At the same time, these discourses, situated within and also constructing a social context, sculpt an acceptable social space for exercising individual motivations for violence, even if the outwardly stated motivation is not always the most compelling internal motivation.

In some ways, then, an attempt to understand motivations is not wholly possible—perhaps even participants themselves do not fully grasp them, much less their peers and even less an outside researcher. Nevertheless, these discourses are the best thing we have, and consequently it is important to understand some of the factors that influence the discourses recounted to me. While the stories that individuals and groups use to explain or justify violence are important (presuming they reflect some type of broader reality), it is important to examine the factors that may introduce a gap between them and actual motivations. That is, what factors influence the kinds of explanations and the contours of the stories I have collected?

One overriding factor is that it is rare for anyone to disclose that they fight without reluctance. Combatants do not want to portray themselves as aggressors, at least to me. As Bauman (1986) artfully conveys, there is an essence of performance in any narrative, and this is especially prominent in the narratives and explanations presented to me in a time of war. In some senses I become a kind of moral node, a place where my interlocutors voice how they are righteous in the context of the conflict. Some of these discourses have taken on a semiofficial status. There are numerous official "peace meetings" organized not by the warring groups but by government agencies, peace NGOs, and sometimes private parties. At such meetings both parties air their grievances and state what they believe is needed to resolve the conflict. Needless to say, they paint themselves in a favorable light. To some extent, then, informants may reiterate to me the kinds of statements they make at these meetings, which is to say, prepackaged positions concerning their innocence. Impression management in Goffman's (1959) sense surely played a central role, one way or another, in the type and tone of explanations. Some who do not know me well viewed me as actually having a role within the "peace process," in general or in regard to specific individuals. For instance, on one day of interviews I was accompanied by a worker from a local European ranch and may have thus appeared to be associated with the local white ranchers (though I, of course, was not), and on that day informants' responses seemed to be more tailored for that audience. The extent to which discourses are massaged to fit the particular circumstances of conflict are clearly exacerbated in a context of ongoing violence, as compared to instances where the events are historically distant.

The issues are somewhat different in regard to individuals or groups I know well. For instance, I have greater confidence that Samburu discourses concerning the causes of conflict reflect a correspondence between what individuals believe, what they say to one another, and what they say to me. Based on long-term research, including work on issues of violence, I have a far greater understanding of the dynamics of violence, greater linguistic competence, deeper cultural knowledge, and more diffuse interpersonal interactions and ties. What I glean about Samburu motivations and discourses can to a far greater extent be triangulated against differing data points and differing types of data points. On the other hand, close personal ties can create other forms of distortion. Individuals may have greater concern regarding their presentation of self (in Goffman's [1959] terms). They may be less likely to make statements that they feel could adversely affect my view of them, because I am not a stranger. They also know that their views might have implications for others with whom I also have a close relationship.

There is really no way to correct for these completely. However, what I aim to do is to provide some of these stories—some public, some personal—to illuminate the factors that shape the social context of violence, as well as the factors that influence how those get related to me and the bearing that has on our interpretation of their import. At a minimum these stories create a social space in which violence is possible. Valorizing stories may motivate some, while less virtuous renderings might be seen as having the effect of turning the will of others against them, whether that be co-ethnics who do not want violence, or external forces (e.g., the government, NGOs) that attempt to stop it or to take sides, either in conflict or in setting the terms of its resolution. It is difficult, sometimes impossible, to separate truth from "spin," but each has a role in the social context that creates and allows violence.

TRUTH AND SPIN: PERSONAL PERSPECTIVES

I will start a discussion of gauging truth, "spin," and their importance with a close reading of a personal relationship, a triad of which I was a part. Here, despite my close relationship to all the parties (or perhaps partially because of it), the veracity of the stories I was told was difficult to determine. That the stories did not present the whole truth, however, seemed apparent from the extent to which the informants in question changed their stories, albeit subtly, over time.

This particular case involved two of my closest friends among the Samburu and Pokot, Simba—a Pokot elder who became my central contact, best friend, and key informant there—and Lekeren, my long-time Samburu host. These two men were friends before the war, yet over time I heard several different versions of their current relationship and their attitudes toward one another. Most notably, as my research progressed, the attitudes they expressed about one another shifted to a more positive portrayal, though not an entirely consistent one. Part of this, I believe, reflects the extent to which I was increasingly insinuated in their relationship. While I was not involved in actual interactions between them, I was now close to two men who previously had been friends but were now (to an extent that was difficult to determine) official enemies.

The key issue here is a specific but shifting claim that, despite their past friendship, Simba now wanted to kill Lekeren. I began work on this project already knowing Lekeren well—having lived in his settlement in Samburu over the course of seven years at that point—before ever having met Simba. My first hint of Simba's existence came in the form of a casual question from Lekeren, relatively early in my research with the Pokot. "Have you met someone named Simba?" he asked with a mix of curiosity and jocularity. "We used to be great friends. He likes to talk and laugh a lot. I hear he says he wants to kill me."

This was not the only version of the state of their relationship that I heard over the next two years. I have no way of confirming which is the most forthright version of events, but my best guess it that the first one was the most honest representation of Lekeren's views, though his perception certainly may have also shifted over time. I had not yet even met Simba, so Lekeren had no motive for casting aspersions on someone I was yet to encounter. This does not, of course, mean that his description truly reflected Simba's intentions, but it appeared to be Lekeren's genuine perception of them.

This assertion changed over time, by and large softening in tone. The next version of this story from Lekeren contained more specifics but maintained Simba's desire to kill him. In that version Lekeren was giving a lift on his motorcycle to a local chief at a time when hostilities had begun but movement between areas was still possible. Simba was said to have stopped Lekeren's motorcycle by the side of the road in a border zone with intermittent conflict and told him never to pass that road again. The implication was that he would be killed if he returned. Months later Lekeren produced a third, softer version. Now he claimed he wasn't the one Simba wanted to kill. Simba had been standing with two other Pokot elders, who seemed unwilling to even exchange basic polite greetings with him and his passenger. In this version Lekeren guesses that he was not the target; rather it was the chief he was carrying, who was perceived as a ringleader in attacks on the Pokot. Thus, the warning was not directed toward Lekeren, but toward his passenger, seemingly exonerating Simba of any desire to harm him personally (and he even opened the possibility that it was Simba's companions who were making the threats, and Simba merely conveyed them, perhaps even helpfully, to Lekeren). Still, he admitted, even after recounting the final version, that he had heard from other sources that Simba wanted to kill him, but he characterized it as the "rumblings of people." Simba was a real "bull" among the Pokot—a strong, charismatic leader—so people liked to talk about him; perhaps, Lekeren mused, he himself was viewed the same way, as a bull of the Samburu. So perhaps it was just idle gossip, which Lekeren had no way of confirming.

Simba dealt with the same question somewhat differently. He never voiced ill will or suspicion against Lekeren. In fact, he often made explicit statements to the contrary, suggesting that even if hotheaded youths or poor people were fighting, two wealthy and well-mannered elders like him and Lekeren could just sit down together peacefully and respectfully. At other times, however, he implied sentiments that were less than fully friendly. One of the first times I slept at Simba's settlement, I showed him some photographs that I had recently taken at Lekeren's home. Simba seemed pleased, and as he gazed smiling at one of Lekeren with his favorite bull, I asked him what sort of person Lekeren was. "He was one of our guys in the past," he asserted. "And now?" I asked. "He's a hyena!" laughed Simba. Simba often commented, "The ones who were friends before are the ones who are the worst enemies now. But the people who didn't know each other, they don't have any issues." When asked to explain, Simba noted that your friends know all your secrets—your whereabouts, your wealth in livestock—a significant fact for someone whose entire herd of over two hundred cattle was stolen by Samburu the day after he returned to the apparent safety of Laikipia from his land near Mount Kenya. Although Simba never said as much, one could easily infer that Lekeren was one of the "friends" who could have betrayed Simba's secrets, including the number of his livestock and their location. And indeed, that particular attack was launched in part from a *lorrora*—a large ritual settlement built for initiating Samburu youth—that Lekeren was a key figure in organizing. This is not to say that he planned the attack or provided information on Simba, but certainly he had the knowledge to do so.

Simba's explicit statements about Lekeren were usually, however, high minded and friendly. Despite signs that he may have been well connected to Pokot involved in violence, Simba asserted that fighting was for young, poor rabble-rousers rather than stately elders such as himself and Lekeren. For various reasons—not least the rumblings about his desire to kill Lekeren—I never fully trusted that this truly reflected Simba's intentions. Simba often asked me about Lekeren—particularly where he was living—and I was deliberately vague or inaccurate, claiming lack of knowledge about his exact location or suggesting he was living farther away than he truly was. These ruses may have been wholly unnecessary, but it seemed unwise to provide anything that could potentially be used as "actionable intelligence" by Simba or other Pokot raiders.

Both men, but Simba particularly, offered varying views on the virtue of peace returning between the two groups. Lekeren generally expressed a strong, unequivocal desire for peace. He was in some ways distant from the world of raiding, partially because he was an elder while warfare was mostly the purview of murran, but also as the *launoni* (ritual leader) of his age set, distanced from warfare by virtue of his position. Even as murran, launoni are forbidden from taking part in raids, since the death of their ritual leader would be extremely unpropitious for the age set as a whole. Lekeren did not suffer any losses in livestock from the war, though he did lose access to land for which he had bought a title deed. He was, however, more likely to regain his land from peace than conflict. While sometimes he would express the sentiment that all Samburu wanted peace, at other times he admitted that those who had suffered losses felt bitterness and wanted revenge. And although I do not know if he was involved in planning raids against the Pokot, he was certainly to some extent aware of these plans, since he alluded to some impending raids before they occurred, albeit in vague terms, which could have reflected either imperfect knowledge or reluctance to share specifics with me. Consequently, in some cases I had a good idea that raids were going to happen before they did. A well-positioned Samburu elder certainly had far deeper knowledge than a foreign anthropologist.

Simba is a different case. Simba frequently offered a stock answer expressing a desire for peace: "We just want peace. It's only poor people who benefit from war." Yet other times he took a different tack. One day when I was staying at his settlement, he came home and, for no apparent reason, began a new humorous spiel (as Lekeren first told me, it is true that Simba likes to joke a lot, so maybe it was just a spiel) that he seemed to find very amusing. "One day," he mused, "I want to shoot a Samburu right in the head. I've shot them every other place, here and here in the body, but the head not yet. So, one day I want to just aim well and shoot one right in the head," motioning right between the eyes. In the same conversation he expressed his desire—a desire held by all reasonable men, and particularly by wealthy ones such as himself—for peace. But later he continued: "As for me, I have no guilt about killing Samburu. I will just kill completely until they die. Those cows that they took, Jon . . . ehhhhhh. I had gone to Nyahururu to get money. Four hundred thousand shillings. I went to buy one hundred bulls. Now that money just went. I still am suffering that loss completely." It is difficult to interpret either of these personas—the Simba who yearns for peace and the Simba who asserts that killing Samburu is no different from killing a dog or a gazelle—or to reconcile perspectives that stand in stark contrast. Either could be genuine and either could be false. He certainly could see the benefits of peace, particularly as someone who has suffered through Samburu raids and who might benefit from the opportunity to practice peaceful pastoralism. On the other hand, he knows that a desire for peace is the standard audience pleaser. No one goes to one of the many peace meetings organized by the government, churches, or NGOs and expresses a desire for war, except perhaps in response to the (real or alleged) intransigence of the other party. On the other hand, it is possible that his stated wish to "kill! kill! kill!" stems from a source other than bitterness over the theft of his 239 cattle, a number he repeats often. He likes to joke, and violence is certainly within the scope of his jests. He was beside himself laughing when, with my video camera rolling, he pretended to stalk and hunt down one of his friends and neighbors. As he mused on his desire to one day shoot a Samburu in the head—it didn't matter if it was a man, woman, whatever—he said it with humorous bravado. Maybe he didn't really mean it. Though I find it unlikely that he would have said it if he didn't at least kind of mean it, not as serious intent but as the sort of thing that someone like him—a Pokot man of unusual physical strength, well respected by his co-ethnics and feared, admired, and often hated by Samburu for his skill with a gun, which he had allegedly used to kill many of them—could readily say. It was, more-over, something he might find funny.

How do we get to the truth of the matter? If people I know extremely well are less than forthright, what would I expect from people who less clearly fit the mold of key informant or even confidante or close friend? On the one hand, it seems to make truth impossible. On the other hand, perhaps in some ways the closeness of the relationship creates an incentive to be less than truthful for reasons of impression management. Lekeren may be motivated to *not* say negative things about Simba if he thinks I like Simba, not wishing to alienate me by saying bad things about my friend. He also may be more careful knowing that information might be passed through me to Simba (although it wasn't). The same can be said of Simba: he might think I would see him in a more negative light if he stated an intention to kill my friend and could presume that I might well tell the friend.

This dynamic can also be seen in other relationships. Kijana, a young Samburu man, was the first to bring me to Ol Moran, and although he was not there with me more than a couple of times, he happened to introduce me to Simba. He appeared to be on good terms with Simba—

even when fighting between Pokot and Samburu was at its worst—and Simba typically had positive things to say about him. However, Kijana clearly did not feel safe in the area. He had purchased a farm, for which he had a title deed, but abandoned it in 2006, though he occasionally came to the area. Simba never had bad things to say about Kijana, repeatedly insisting that Kijana was safe when he came to his home. I assumed that for whatever reason Kijana's standing with the Pokot in the area was not bad and suspected that he was playing both sides of the conflict. For instance, one Pokot implied that he was selling ammunition to the Pokot (a suspicion that was never confirmed, but which other Samburu suggested was quite plausible and not even that bad: "It's just business and Kijana is a businessman").

Given Kijana's apparent good relations with the Pokot, I was surprised one day at the vitriol expressed concerning him, when I talked with one of Simba's neighbors about how those with title deeds to land in the area were unable to return to their farms. I suggested that the Samburu might have legitimate grievances, since some had purchased farms in the area but could not safely reside or raise crops there. He denied that Samburu were unable to safely return to their farms until I cited specific examples. Then, when I mentioned Kijana, he responded:

> There is no person who is as terrible an enemy, as terrible as that guy. . . . If the Samburu come—if Kijana should come here, the next day Samburu will arrive [to raid], God's truth, God's truth. That guy is the enemy above all others, above all others. He should not set foot here again. . . . Tell him not to come here and look at the wealth of people and say, 'This guy has such and such, this guy has such and such.' That one is an enemy. He comes with a lorry. He comes with a lorry full of Samburu. Like when they killed at Rattia. He comes to get the secrets of Pokot. That is his problem. He can't come back. Others can come back but he can't. He'll be the last person [allowed] to come back.

His vitriol certainly appeared genuine, but it is unclear how to reconcile this speech with Simba's seemingly positive attitude toward Kijana. If Kijana had been responsible for spilling secrets about Pokot, Simba should have been more bitter than anyone. This elder was claiming that Kijana had passed secrets prior to the raid on Rattia, in which Simba's cattle were taken. Possibly Simba was feigning respect and affection out of regard for me, though their relationship clearly predated me—it was through Kijana that I met Simba. Perhaps Kijana was useful to Simba, a double agent who played both sides. There is no way to tell.

Or perhaps the elder who proclaimed that Kijana was the "enemy above all others" was lying. Indeed, he may have had other motivations for having ill will toward Kijana. Both men were closely affiliated with the wealthy white owners of a local ranch, which was now mainly used for wildlife preservation and high-end tourism. Kijana was one of their main Samburu contacts, while this Pokot elder was one of their main Pokot ones. His motive, then, could be less genuine bitterness toward Kijana because of the war than a desire to eliminate Kijana from the picture as far as their white mutual benefactors were concerned. Or he may have envied Kijana from those days. I am speculating, of course, but speculation is warranted when there is no self-evident way to reconcile those perspectives—one man says that Kijana is the enemy above all others, yet the person who should hate him most (were this true) seems to be his friend.

"IT'S ALL ABOUT THE CONSERVANCY"

Consider another lie, or set of lies, in which personal relationships are implicated. Most of my interviews were conducted on the east side of the Ol Moran area, working with Pokot assistants whom I found and hired in the local community. One day, however, I decided to go to the west side of Ol Moran (a white-owned farm dividing the two sides) with a man who regularly worked on research for the white ranchers. When asked about the cause of the war, several individuals focused on a proposed wildlife conservancy in the Amaya area, somewhat to the north. Amaya is on the dividing line between Samburu and Pokot, technically in Samburu District but disproportionately populated by Pokot. I had heard rumors about this conservancy, which was said to be a brainchild/ conspiracy between Samburu politicians and a prominent white rancher who had a large private game ranch near Nanyuki. In the views of the Pokot I was interviewing, the goal of this conservancy (which as far as I knew existed only in the minds of Pokot conspiracy theorists) was to alienate the Pokot from their traditional lands around Amaya. Pokot rights to this land were ostensibly confirmed by an obscure early twenti-eth-century map that no one had evidently seen and whose existence I cannot confirm. I also have no way of knowing whether this map shows what it is claimed to show, for that matter, nor is there any logical reason that a map by an early twentieth-century colonialist has any bearing on early twenty-first-century realities, whatever crypto-religious significance the Pokot attributed to it. Thus I seemed to have been provided with a whole set of rather dubious propositions:

1. The cause of the war is a conservancy that may not even be a serious proposal.
2. The main purpose of the conservancy is to alienate Pokot land.
3. It will also enrich a white man and perhaps wealthy Samburu.
4. An obscure map proves that this potentially alienated land is truly Pokot land.

Much of this could be dismissed out of hand. At that point I could not say anything about the conservancy; I'd heard rumors, but it was impos-sible to say if they were anything other than rumors. If the conservancy was a serious proposal, it was a fair assumption—given the nature of Kenyan politics—that enriching wealthy figures probably figured in somewhere, but this seemed to be getting ahead of the game. And the map, however passionately it was clung to, seemed to be nothing more than a talking point. Even if such a map existed, it wouldn't prove any-thing of import to contemporary realities. And the crux of my ques-tion—why did this war start?—did not seem connected to rumored con-servancies and secret maps, since the matter of the conservancy seemed to have arisen well after the war had started.

So why tell this story? A few points were apparent. Possibly the most important one is that the story was told to me in the company of someone in the employ of a white rancher. Though she was not the one allegedly involved in the conservancy (and from what she said to me, not sympa-thetic to any alleged proposal for one), the informants likely presumed that I would pass this information back to people in a position to oppose such a proposal. That is, the message was tailored to the audience. Geography was probably also important. I got this story from individuals living in an area closer to the allegedly proposed conservancy, who might feel it directly affected them. It thus reflected not so much a statement of what *caused* the war as a negotiating point in discussing the terms of peace. In that vein, whether this was a cause of the fighting now, or whether it was even possible to negotiate an end to fighting, was hardly relevant. That the conservancy was rhetorically defined as a cause of fighting meant that the fighting could be used to negotiate away the conservancy, even if the conservancy could not be used to negotiate away the fighting.

Somewhat later I had an opportunity to talk with a well-placed Samburu friend who is close to the Samburu politician named in relation to the conservancy and is himself involved in conservation issues. Somewhat to my surprise—as I had supposed the Pokot discussions of the conservancy might be a baseless conspiracy theory—he expounded on the virtues of the proposed conservancy. He thought it was a great use of land that belonged to the Samburu but could not be utilized because of hostilities with the Pokot. He did not mention that the Pokot might use this land. He believed that it was a great way to protect wildlife. That the area was mostly devoid of wildlife (Pokot eat them) was apparently irrelevant. Perhaps, he suggested, the Pokot should also make a conservancy on their side (the area of the proposed conservancy being, in his view, clearly on Samburu land, since it was in Samburu District, irrespective of who lived there), as it would create a buffer between the groups. So his story also contained misrepresentations, albeit different ones, and they put the Pokot representations in a somewhat different light. He had asserted that this was, indeed, Samburu land, a conservancy would protect wildlife (albeit nonexistent wildlife), and it would prevent war (all the more so if the Pokot expanded the conservancy onto what he agreed was their land). The Pokot story (or at least many elements) remained dubious, but their fears and their desire to establish talking points and negotiating points were grounded in proposals by Samburu and others that genuinely aimed to alienate them from land they used.

SPIN AND COUNTERSPIN

Let us turn now to some broader narratives. I would not take a biased perspective that Samburu accounts are necessarily more reflective of accurate events, but I have seen fewer obvious inconsistencies in them. Samburu narratives concerning the general course of the war follow a fairly consistent pattern. There were initially small-scale, though lethal, conflicts (the blame for which is disputed), followed by large-scale Pokot attacks, which were eventually repulsed. Following this, Pokot engaged in small-scale raids to which Samburu retaliated on a grand scale, until the matter settled into mutual small-scale conflict. Pokot narratives often absolve them of all blame but in a way that necessarily creates inconsistency.

Pokot narratives generally are composed of several propositions that deflect guilt from themselves but fail to construct a coherent narrative. In particular, the Pokot attribute the cause of the war—that is, the breakdown of the oath between them—to Samburu actions. Here again it comes down to the testicles. Samburu broke the oath by killing a Pokot and mutilating him in what is portrayed as a humiliation to not only him but all Pokot. Consequently, any actions that follow, any intransigence Pokot have in putting a stop to the war, is directly attributable to the actions of Samburu. This position, though not entirely consistent with what may be established concerning the precise genesis of the war and its longevity, paints a plausible and reasonably virtuous portrayal of Pokot engaging in righteous warfare against the Samburu until such point as the case of the testicles is somehow resolved. As another man complained, "We are still owed those potatoes [i.e., testicles]," meaning that peace is not possible until some way is found for them to be repaid.

This statement on its own is reasonable, irrespective of its full veracity. What makes this assertion problematic, however, is that at the same time Pokot deny all aggression. As one Pokot elder asserted, "Because from [the beginning of the war] until now, no person has come out from Pokot to go and attack in the morning. There is none. From this side. But from theirs, they've come to Rattia, they've come to Lorumurum, they went to Magadi, Refu. How many times? Four. And no person has come from here to go there."

Thus, there is an apparent inconsistency. They make a claim to righteous anger, anger that they assert has inspired revenge and renders peace a distant prospect. At the same time, they deny participating in any vengeful acts. Thus, it is unclear what acts of revenge they admit to committing. The two virtuous subjectivities that the Pokot (often the same Pokot individual) take are thus contradictory: acting in righteous vengeance and not engaging in aggression at all.

This inconsistency can partially be explained by two subtle aspects of this quote. Part of the latter claim—that Pokot do not engage in raiding as Samburu do—may be viewed through the lens of what I term "collective irresponsibility," which I will discuss in more detail in chapter 4. Collective *ir*responsibility is the inverse of aspects of what Evans-Pritchard (1940) famously described as collective responsibility: an action by a group member is the action of a group, and an attack on an individual group member is an attack on the group. In contrast, one may assert that things done by members of our group do not reflect collective actions (although what is done by members of other ethnic groups can be subject to collective blame). In this case, Pokot I have spoken with are principally residents of Laikipia, while the large-scale Pokot attacks occurred predominantly to the north. The informant quoted above qualified his statement by saying that no one has come out "from this side." Thus, these Laikipia Pokot could plausibly portray themselves as being victims of attacks rather than perpetrators, since Samburu had launched several large-scale raids in Laikipia, while large Pokot raids occurred earlier in the conflict and in other areas.

Secondly, Pokot did not deny that some co-ethnics from their area were engaged in theft of livestock, but aimed to paint it both ways: as the righteous action of people revenging the loss of testicles—"The cows we take pay for those testicles!"—but also as the action of simple thieves. As a man who minutes earlier had made a passionate case for righteous vengeance contended, "If there are cows that were taken, those were thieves. Those were thieves. Not [like] those people [i.e., the Samburu] coming with weapons. This is just stealing. If I go and steal a chicken, isn't it just said that *I* stole a chicken? It isn't *Pokot* who stole the chicken. And other times it is other tribes. Other times if you follow those cows they aren't here, they've gone a different direction." Thus, he places individual responsibility on the particular people who stole cows. Even if it concerned Pokot from this area, he dismisses the idea that it was collective action, and thus rejects the notion that the Pokot as a collective body bear responsibility.

Pokot, when they do admit to aggression against the Samburu, take pains to differentiate their attacks from those of the Samburu. As one Pokot man asserted, "There is no time that people have come out to attack Samburu in the morning." He is essentially distinguishing between two sorts of raids. His claim is that Samburu raiding involves attacks that

FIGURE 6. Pokot girls decorated for dancing.

are aimed not just at taking animals but at killing people who have no chance of defense. Settlements are surrounded, attacks take place at dawn while the residents are unaware, and the killing involves defenseless people, women and children alike. In contrast, the Pokot are said to steal livestock in the afternoon, with relatively little violence. Individuals have the opportunity to defend themselves, and relatively few casualties are said to occur.

There are several problems with this assertion. The first is that traditional Pokot raiding is said to follow almost precisely the pattern for which they blame the Samburu. As Schneider (1967) describes it, traditional Pokot raiding involved "attacking a corral at sunrise, kill all who get in their way, women and children included, and make off with the cattle" (p. 280). While this described raids in the distant past—Schneider was recording folklore concerning raids that he presumed had occurred prior to British pacification, hence before my informants were born—it is instructive that the normative pattern did not involve "warriors meeting in battle and seeing who would be defeated and who would be the victor," as the same informant claimed. That is to say, there does not appear to be a deeply rooted, historically validated Pokot taboo on the behaviors they attribute to Samburu. Moreover, several informants described small-scale raids/theft occurring in the afternoon as an effective strategy, rather than as having a moral purpose. Large raids draw attention, both from Samburu and from the government. As one Pokot man asserted dismissively, "Usually it's on the big raids that you don't get anything [i.e., livestock]." Another, explaining strategy in detail, suggested that by stealing livestock from the pastures late in the day, the missing cattle might not even at first be noticed, pursuit by the owners might be difficult, and police would not begin to follow the livestock until the next day, when the trail was already cold.

Other issues belie Pokot assertions that the Samburu are uniquely bad insofar as they kill women and children. One is that Pokot insisted that *only* Samburu engaged in this practice, asserting that the Turkana, for instance, do not. This created an interesting dialogue, since the Turkana are the only group that admits killing children in the heat of battle, suggesting that the bitterness of war will drive you to do most anything. Pokot claimed that only Samburu were child-killers, but were forced to hem and haw when faced with the assertions of my Turkana informants that Turkana kill Pokot children.

An important further point, particularly relevant to spin and counterspin, is that Samburu assert that they (unlike Pokot) do not kill children, claiming that it is contrary to their core cultural beliefs. In contrast, long before the recent war, Samburu told me how on their joint raids against the Turkana, Pokot (unlike themselves) did kill children, which Samburu viewed as a shocking and barbaric act. These stories predominantly centered on the Samburu-Pokot attack on Turkana at Lokorkor in 1996, when Samburu asserted that Pokot (their then friends) killed women and did horrific acts such as tossing babies into boiling pots. While there is no way to prove the truth of these claims, it is important to note that they were made about their friends, not about their enemies.

TWO SIDES OF SEVERAL STORIES

There are, then, a variety of ways in which Pokot and Samburu stories differ, and on the part of one or both stray some distance from the truth. In other stories, however, the facts are almost wholly agreed upon even though the interpretations and the meanings pertaining to the opposing group may differ significantly. These are particularly interesting because they highlight how more than self-interest or deliberate misinterpretation fuels violence, as different cultural readings feed enmity and stereotypes between groups.

CASE STUDY I: BURNING A LORRY

Samburu described an incident in which Pokot burned a lorry belonging to a Samburu chief. The lorry was in the forest in a border zone between the two groups. Pokot evidently simply happened upon it and set it ablaze, though without harming its owners, who safely fled. Samburu offered descriptions of this attack as evidence of two deficiencies among the Pokot. First, it demonstrated that, despite statements at peace meetings and elsewhere, the Pokot didn't really want peace, since they were still engaging in attacks—and on peaceful people no less, not combatants. Second, it was portrayed as a bizarre and random crime. Why would someone destroy a lorry? It was one thing to steal cows, but to engage in property destruction from which they did not benefit demonstrated how crazy the Pokot truly were.

I was not able to glean much information from Pokot about this incident because it occurred in an area distant from the home areas of my Pokot informants. However, as I heard the story, something about it—I wasn't at first sure what—did not seem entirely right. One day, while another Samburu man who lived in that area was relating this story, it struck me: "What was the lorry doing in the forest?" I asked. After some discussion it became apparent that the lorry was there to illegally harvest timber—which Samburu in this area do regularly, but Pokot do not. The man conceded that the Pokot, who use this forest for grazing their cattle, may not have wished the forest to be destroyed. Consequently, what was portrayed as a random act of destruction might, the Samburu man agreed, have been a rational act to prevent the illegal destruction of resources utilized by the Pokot.

I had no opportunity to interview knowledgeable Pokot on this incident (which occurred at some distance from my main research areas), so it is not possible to get their views on precisely what happened or why. However, it is clear that the initial Samburu description was intended to create an impression of the Pokot that may not be wholly accurate. The fact that there were no cattle and that they didn't kill people seemed to exemplify bizarre, random, destructive behavior, the behavior of crazy people or even wild animals. However, when taken in the context of what the lorry was doing, their behavior makes perfect sense. This "senseless act of destruction" was, in fact, enforcing the laws of Kenya. Although it may be a stretch to infer that the Pokot were acting as lawful forest guards or even ecoterrorists in this incident, their behavior is perfectly consistent with a desire to preserve a forest they use for their cattle from wanton and illegal destruction.

CASE STUDY 2: A STOLEN GUN

An incident that occurred in 2009 and the contrasting explanations for it shed light on the ways subtle differences in descriptions and attitudes can affect interpretations. The incident occurred at the market in Malasso, in Samburu District overlooking the Rift Valley escarpment. Despite ongoing conflict between the two groups, in this area the conflict had cooled enough that for a time Samburu allowed Pokot to make their way up from the valley floor on market days. At the market Pokot could purchase basic foodstuffs and also engage in trade of their own—including arms sales.

The first report of the incident I received was from Samburu, who told me that at the market Pokot had gone berserk, shooting randomly, killing a couple of people and wounding many others. Soon it became apparent, however—based on Samburu accounts—that Samburu had instigated the violence. Two murran had been negotiating with a Pokot for the purchase of a gun. The murran conferred in their own language as to whether one was strong enough to take the gun by force, and when one was testing the gun the other grabbed the Pokot, who in the ensuing fight was killed along with his Pokot companion. In response, other Pokot at the market began shooting in revenge, killing several and wounding others. Thus, while the initial Samburu description placed culpability mainly on Pokot who had gone on a crazy shooting spree, it now appeared that the Samburu who instigated the incident were principally to blame.

As the story unfolded, however, additional details again cast the incident in a different light. The gun that started the fight was, my Samburu informants asserted, a Samburu gun. At first I was dubious of this detail, since it seemed that a mass-produced item—such as a gun—would be difficult to identify as "Samburu" or "Pokot." Samburu were insistent, however, that the gun had been identified. First, it was a European-made G3, a heavier weapon favored by Samburu and generally not used by the Pokot, who prefer the lightweight Russian-designed AK-47. Moreover, particularities of the weapon purportedly identified it as having belonged to a specific individual who had been killed in fighting with the Pokot, who had then taken his gun. From this standpoint, the attack on the Pokot, which had initially seemed like an unprovoked act of violent theft, was in fact revenge against someone who may have been involved in killing their friend, the killer then having the audacity to attempt to sell back the weapon to the survivors. Seen in this light, the attack by the Samburu murran on the Pokot gun seller seemed like an understandable act of violence, though I still doubted the details, particularly the alleged provenance of the gun.

A short while later, I had the opportunity to discuss this incident with Pokot, who wholeheartedly blamed Samburu for instigating the violence by attacking the gun dealer. "But Samburu said the gun belonged to their friend who was killed," I pointed out. My expectation—given that I thought the claim to have identified the gun sounded dubious—was that Pokot would deny this as a ridiculous lie. To my surprise, they did not. "We have so many guns taken from their people who were killed, and even they have guns taken from our people who were killed. If you fight and you lose the gun, you have been defeated, and you should leave the matter." Thus, rather than deny the Samburu version of events, they confirmed but reinterpreted them. This incident proved that Samburu were small-minded people, petty and bitter people, who did not accept the consequences of war. If men fought, then the spoils of the victors were the spoils of the victors and the matter was finished, except to continue another day perhaps on the field of battle. Blame did not lie with the Pokot for killing their friend (both sides kill people, after all) nor for having his gun (it's a prize of war), nor even in trying to sell it. It lay in the unmanly pettiness of Samburu. Samburu were simply unwilling to accept defeat and move on as Pokot expected of real men, a theme consistent with the next case study.

CASE STUDY 3: "SIXTEEN YEARS"
Pokot broadly portray Samburu as people who, rather childishly, never let go of their bitterness, and they claim that this tendency toward

small-minded bitterness is a cause of continuing war. As one man asserted in comparing the Samburu with the Turkana: "Turkana are real men, even if you fought yesterday and meet together today, they can't be angry. They will just sit together as usual. But Samburu can kill someone even in town. They are people of petty anger. That way, indeed, is how Samburu are." This pettiness, holding onto anger, is exemplified in the assertion that Samburu insist the war will continue for sixteen years. When I asked one Pokot man when there will be peace between the two groups, he replied, "It will take some time, a period of like sixteen years. Because Samburu say even the child who is nursing, even the small child who is nursing right now—'We will fight until even that child is fighting.' Sixteen years. There you have it. It will reach sixteen years because they [Samburu] are the ones who said that, not us. [For us] if it is men, men will fight and it will be finished. But for children to be pulled along—those [Samburu] people are selfish." Pokot thus claim that Samburu are intent on continuing the war, not just in the near term but on an ongoing basis—until even babies who are now suckling at their mothers' breasts take up arms against the Pokot. Pokot read this as a bizarre act of bitterness and selfishness. War takes place between men, and men should fight and finish the fight. The same informant compared their wars with the Turkana: "You know our war with the Turkana—that was the first of all. That was a good one. We meet, and we see who will be beaten and who will be the victor. But this one of Samburu . . . it is like the one of children."

This trope of "sixteen years" was not simply concocted by Pokot and attributed to the Samburu. Samburu have made to me on multiple occasions precisely this assertion, that the war will continue for sixteen years, until today's babies become warriors fighting the Pokot. Their reading of this statement is, however, utterly different from that of the Pokot. This statement is made in reference to the duplicity that Samburu assert Pokot bring to peace negotiations. "They agree to peace and then the next day they attack. Or even we are at a meeting and an attack occurs while we are there." Thus, Samburu assertions of "sixteen years" are not intended to convey a mindless, petty desire to continue war indefinitely. Rather, it is a statement that they will not give up the fight until the Pokot are serious about the fight ending, until the Pokot cease attacks and resolve to honestly settle their differences.

While Pokot criticize the Samburu for clinging to petty bitterness, they pick and choose what it is appropriate to remain bitter about. Samburu should not be bitter about guns lost in battle (even if there are attempts to resell them to surviving family members). They also should not be bitter about farms they purchased that are now occupied by Pokot. Since some Pokot also lost farms to the east of Laikipia, they assert that it was simply a more or less fair swap. Yet Simba still feels entitled to express bitterness at the loss of his 239 cows the morning of the Samburu raid on Rattia, feels that it is still reasonable (at least in rhetoric) to one day shoot a Samburu right between the eyes, that perhaps when he has killed five Samburu he will feel that the debt has been paid. And as for bitterness, there is still the matter of the testicles.

THE CASE OF TESTICLES

To conclude these excursions through the spin, counterspin, explanations, and half-truths of why the Pokot and the Samburu are at war, let us return to where we started: the "case of testicles." When I asked another Pokot man to explain the war, he replied:

> If you want to get to this exactly, go and ask this question to Samburu. Go and find them today and ask this question. Ask them what? This question. Before you were [our] friends and then you kill a person. Samburu killed a person. They killed a Pokot. They removed his testicles. They took them away. So would you [Jon] agree to be killed and have your genitals cut? That's where it started. It is really bad. That is where it started. Killing a person and cutting the genitals. Would you agree to [someone doing] that? [Jon: No.] There you have it. That's where the problem came from.

Following this Pokot man's suggestion, I went and asked some Samburu about the castration incident. "They said what?" was the confused response of one murran, as if he had never even heard of this issue before. Another man responded with similar bafflement. "They are worried about that? Pokot have done so many other things to us. They've even cut people's faces off," he continued with incredulity. Their response was, then, not really to deny that the incident had occurred, though many seemed unaware that it had. Rather, it was disbelief born of a sense that the event had so little to do with anything in their world that its veracity was irrelevant. When I mentioned this Pokot claim—that they are fighting because of those testicles, that those testicles should somehow be returned or paid for—Samburu were utterly baffled.

How do we read this discourse, and other discourses that I have engaged with in this chapter? Who are these discourses intended for? To what extent do they reflect factual events and actual motivations?

One approach to such discourses is to recognize—following the theoretical groundings in the introduction—that violence is always part of a cultural system, but one that inherently lacks shared meanings. This cultural system is always composed of perpetrators, victims, and observers, with each of these roughly hewn positions composed of heterogeneous groups and actors, with movement between the basic positions often shifting rapidly, and even at any particular point being ambiguously defined. Understanding violence as a cultural system points, nonetheless, to the fact that both violent acts and the discourses surrounding violent acts contain communicative elements. An attack, a theft, a mutilation says something in and of itself—or is intended to say something, though it may be passively read in a very different way in the first instance, and then subsequently rewritten by myriads of actors in myriads of ways as it enters the realm of discourse. Both Pokot and Samburu characterize their violent acts as at times explicitly designed to "send a message." Each at times expresses a desire to make the other "feel pain." This pain is not simple revenge; rather, it is framed as demonstrating the consequences of continued violence. When you take cattle in response to the theft of your cattle, or you kill people when your people have been killed, you are not simply enacting a cerebral model of "an eye for an eye" justice. You are expressing to your adversaries that they live in a world in which "an eye for an eye" is the model of justice, and that they need to be careful about what they do because they can expect retribution—that is, watch what you do when you take an eye (or testicles, or cows, or a life) because you also have eyes and more.

Clearly, however, there are serious limitations on what can be explained through this model. Most notably, however deliberate and clear these communicative acts might be to the Samburu or the Pokot, the communication is exceptionally imperfect. The imperfection is evidenced by the fact that Samburu do not simply disagree with key Pokot discourses concerning the cause and continuation of the conflict, nor are they simply unaware that these discourses exist, but when confronted with them by the anthropological intermediary, they are baffled by the notion that such discourses could exist in the mind of another human being. At a more basic level, the stated tit-for-tat "message" of attacks that is asserted by both sides is never understood as such, since without fail it is possible to reinterpret or extend the timeline so that one's own attack is the "tit" (i.e., the act of revenge) and their adversary's is always the "tat" (i.e., the provoking act). Consequently, every attack framed as a message of righteous vengeance will be read as unprovoked, and hence justify an act of vengeance that will itself be read as unprovoked.

It is also necessary to consider the communicative acts directed at those defined as "observers": mainly the government, but also others who through organizations or as individuals organize peace meetings between the warring parties or otherwise aim to influence events. It is difficult to discern any impact of these peace meetings; meetings are held, and then fighting continues. One Pokot man sardonically suggested that maybe these efforts would be successful if I brought Jesse Jackson from America to hold a peace meeting, but otherwise fighting would continue. Sometimes at smaller meetings individuals are paid to attend. At larger meetings it is unclear why people participate, except to make sure that their grievances are heard and heard equally. Notably, however—to return to the discourse of the testicles—this issue of the castration had not appeared in causes of conflict or outstanding grievances at official peace meetings, at least those I attended and those informants have described. These tend to focus on thefts of cattle (particularly whatever thefts preceded a particular meeting) or recent killings (for which "the bullets must be paid"). The absence of the testicles discourse suggests that it is intended for other Pokot, to construct righteous anger on their part rather than as either an official accusation or a basis for reparations. Indeed, it is notable that such a discourse would be utterly out of place at a peace meeting, in which means and terms of settlement are the focus of the agenda. As one man professed, "Those testicles will be paid for by God, when Samburu die," framing it as an unforgivable debt that can never be repaid, at least in this world. Suggestions that it might be repaid by seeking out the testicles in the forest where perhaps they were thrown or bringing the hyena that perhaps ate them similarly frames it as something that can never actually be corrected.

Should we, then, ultimately read it simply as propaganda? Is "the case of the testicles" really no more and no less than a Pokot version of the Gulf of Tonkin Incident or any other half-true, half-false rationalization for fighting a war? There may be something useful in a comparative project of anthropology that finds exactly the same thing in the remote stretches of northern Kenya as one finds in Washington, DC, the Kremlin, or on either side of Gaza. At the same time, one might wonder why we need to know about the remote stretches of northern Kenya if they are just like us anyway. And indeed, I would argue that there are important ways in which this example may tell us something else—things that may inform our understandings of similar situations while also illuminating important differences.

Perhaps key to what is distinctive in this case study is the question of whether it is "true"—that is, how do we gauge the veracity of the assertion that the Pokot are fighting because a man several years before was killed, his legs held apart, and castrated as one would a sheep? I would argue that it is neither true nor a lie. Those things happened, yet they can't explain the war. They cannot, I would argue, even explain Pokot motivations for war—yet at the same time, subjectively, I do not doubt that many Pokot sincerely experienced this event as providing the motivation to attack and kill their enemies and to capture their cattle. If it may be read in one sense as a falsehood, it is a falsehood told to oneself; when it is shared with others, it is with peers, not in the top-down sense of classic state-centered propaganda. Ultimately it is a story one tells to oneself, because in this instance those who fought—those who "all awoke" when they heard of the taking of the testicles—themselves chose to fight.

3

GREEN STOMACHS, MAU MAU, AND THE GOVERNMENT OF WOMEN

UGARTE: You despise me, don't you Rick?
RICK: If I gave you any thought I probably would.
PETER LORRE AND HUMPHREY BOGART
in *Casablanca*

In mid-January of 1998 a party of Samburu met a large group of lightly armed Kikuyu—the latter, from what can be pieced together, on a mission of revenge—and massacred them. This was the culmination of a series of back-and-forth provocations near the Ol Moran area of Laikipia, which had become an area of increasing tension between Kikuyu agriculturalists and various pastoralist groups, all of whom had begun to occupy the area as many of the ninety-nine-year leases issued to white settlers expired. The events leading up to the massacre of the Kikuyu vigilantes, as well as the event itself, are murky, but Samburu attest that the conflict was driven by the Kikuyu's will to drive them off land that they felt they had rightfully earned through their leadership in Mau Mau during the fight for independence, a conflict in which the Samburu had largely assisted the British colonial government.

.   .   .

Our images of conflict frequently revolve around the concept of mortal enemies. We can easily come up with lists of groups paired up by shared and (at least in common portrayals) ancient hatred: Jews and Arabs, Hutu and Tutsi, Sunnis and Shiites, Serbs and Croats. Needless to say, the enmity portrayed is usually far more historically contingent than what commonplace portrayals suggest. The broader point is that we tend to think of hatred as a thing that is matched: hatred occurs between enemies who hate each other in a way that largely mirrors the enmity on the other side. Yet this may sometimes be far from the case. A war or conflict may linger in the cultural memory of one group long after the recollections carry little or no emotional weight for the other party, if they are still remembered at all. They may or may not despise the other, but to despise them they first would have to give them at least a bit of thought.

One need not go far afield to find an especially vivid portrayal of this. In the northern United States, the Civil War holds no particular emotional grip over the historical imagination. In elementary school, children learn about Abraham Lincoln, the freeing of the slaves, and perhaps some key dates and explanations for the conflict. Yet there is typically little visceral, emotional immediacy. It is like everything else one learns in history class, long and interesting to some, less so to others— perhaps more compelling than the Huguenots, less so than the civil rights movement.

Yet travel from my home in Kalamazoo to, say, Mississippi, and you enter a different postwar environment. Take a drive down Jefferson Davis Avenue, and you may recall a man who would be despised in the North if anyone cared to remember him at all. Take that drive on his birthday if you like, for it is a public holiday. The South (or, I should say, many in the South, at the risk of essentializing) does not view the Civil War in the same way as those in the North do. Though the war is long over, in the South the sediments remain. While it may be the case that northerners harbor stereotypes about the South, the idea that southerners are still living the Civil War is one more layer of mockery in their attitudes toward them. Yet to many southerners, "the South" and "the North" do still exist as collective bodies, which remain opposed even if the armed conflict is long since over.

In this chapter I consider similar circumstances involving Samburu and their Kikuyu neighbors. Their history is long and varied, at times intense and at other times peripheral. More than anything else, colonialism and then postcolonialism brought them together—the most notable feature of this to Samburu being their opposition in Mau Mau. While the Kikuyu—Kenya's largest ethnic group, and the one to have their lands most intensely colonized by the British—led the Mau Mau insurrection against the British colonial regime in the 1950s, the Samburu sided with and assisted the colonial government. Samburu firmly believe that the Kikuyu, who have dominated the economy and politics of Kenya since independence, continue to bear a grudge for the Samburu role in Mau Mau. This enmity has, in their view, been expressed both in government bias against them and in basic (if perhaps veiled) antagonism toward them by Kikuyu more generally as contact between the two groups has increased in independent Kenya. Yet many Kikuyu do not even know that the Samburu—a relatively small ethnic group—even exist. And just as in the United States it would never occur to northerners that the Civil War should in any way shape their views of the South 150 years later, Kikuyu living in areas where they have butted up against Samburu express sincere bewilderment at the idea that a conflict of fifty years past could in any way be a basis for current conflicts, looking instead at contemporary on-the-ground conditions. While I believe that Kikuyu lack of concern for memory is genuine, I also consider the extent to which this may be regarded not simply as a lack of memory but as a deliberate erasure of memory—or perhaps an intentional stance in which the types of claims they make are better served by debates in which the grounds are ahistorical, or even antihistorical, in nature.

PEOPLE WITH GREEN STOMACHS, IF PEOPLE AT ALL

In the precolonial era, Samburu contact with the Kikuyu was not markedly intense, since they did not typically live in close proximity. Samburu tended to be farther north than they are today—living as far north as southern Ethiopia until the defeat of the Laikipiak Maasai in the late nineteenth century—while the Kikuyu resided in the Mount Kenya area and Kenya's central highlands. Although both Samburu oral history and written colonial accounts report significant trade with the Meru—a group closely related to the Kikuyu—in regard to the acquisition of grain in particular, the Kikuyu are not mentioned. One explanation is that the Meru are significantly more pastoral than the Kikuyu, descending from the slopes of Mount Kenya to make use of dry lands pasture below.

Samburu did, however, have enough contact with the Kikuyu to form significant (and not favorable) attitudes concerning them. They regarded them not only as cowards but as not even fully human. The basis for this "less than human" status is the assertion that they have "green stomachs." This discovery was made while raiding and subsequently killing Kikuyu. To prevent bloating during decomposition, Samburu traditionally slit the stomach of those they killed. In the case of Kikuyu, they discovered the contents inside to be green—because of the inclusion of green vegetables in their diet—resembling the stomach contents of goats, certainly not of human beings. This characterization construes them in one sense as not fully human, since their stomachs had physical characteristics that Samburu do not associate with human beings— viewing them instead much like Westerners view Martians, as little green men. Beyond this, the stomach and the color green have important symbolic connotations for Samburu. Among Samburu, the stomach is the seat of emotion, such that someone who is being encouraged to be stalwart or stoic is encouraged to have a strong stomach. A bad person is said to have a black stomach and a good person a white one. In humans, the color green is associated with weakness, such that a green stomach implies a lack of bravery and an inability to withstand adversity (Straight 2006).

Samburu interactions and contact with Kikuyu increased markedly in the colonial era. Kikuyu were the first Kenyan ethnic group to be truly and intensely colonized. Their lands in central Kenya were the most desirable to white settlers, who seized them for coffee and tea plantations or for other agricultural activities. Kikuyu became the principal colonial workforce, not least because working for money in the colonial system provided an alternative livelihood for those displaced from their land. As settlers moved from the central highlands to the plains, the Kikuyu remained the ethnic group that provided herders and other workers on farms and ranches, a situation that moved them into proximity with the Samburu. This was particularly the case in Laikipia, a plateau of rich grasslands that had been cleared of Maasai in the first decades of the twentieth century to open it for white settlement. Samburu neighbored Laikipia to the north, and it was a relatively easy trek from their home areas to white ranches.

There was no particular conflict between Kikuyu and Samburu at that time. Samburu, however, maintained the tradition of killing enemies during their time as murran as a means to establish manhood. Killing an enemy was traditionally seen as a key rite of passage. As one Samburu Kimaniki elder explains, "You know before, in Samburu culture, when a warrior had not killed he would just go and look for a person to kill. It was not so much that they needed animals [from livestock raids]. It is that you kill a man. You kill a man first. And then you cut his genitals and you come and you are going to be praised. . . . And that person is then praised. That man, then, it was that one who is a man." In a similar vein, Lelenguya, an elder of the Lkishilli age set, explains: "A warrior who had not killed, it is like he was always branded a *laroi* [coward or person of no consequence]. So even if he was a warrior, with red ochre in his hair and plaited braids, it was still like he wasn't really a warrior, because he had not killed and he did not wear the copper bracelets on his wrists."

The person killed need not belong to a group toward whom Samburu had particular animosity. Anyone who was not Samburu was placed into the category of *lmangatti,* or enemies, and was hence a legitimate target. Removing the genitals was a means of proving that the person you killed was in fact a man rather than a woman or child. Men who had killed were permitted to wear copper bracelets on their wrists, and some say that in earlier eras a man was not allowed to marry unless he had killed and earned these bracelets. Today these bracelets are rarely found, however, partially because it may be undesirable to display to the government that you have murdered someone, but more commonly because they can understandably lead to tension when entering multiethnic towns for shopping or livestock marketing, where you might run into the co-ethnics (or even relatives) of the person you killed.

Within this tradition of killing enemies to attain manhood, Kikuyu farmworkers provided Samburu with a convenient and easy target. They were readily available and not hard to kill. Thus, in the 1920s there were a number of incidents in which Samburu murran of the Lkileku age set murdered Kikuyu on white farms. While these killings were not rampant, they were sufficiently frequent to draw the attention of white settlers, and they continued until the crackdown following the alleged murder by Samburu of the white settler Ted Powys in 1931 (Holtzman and Straight 2005; Fratkin 2015).

Following the death of Powys, there was a marked crackdown on the Samburu, including forced labor of the murran and colonial attempts to dismantle the age set system, which seemed to foster a group of idle young men preoccupied with killing enemies. Alongside these measures, murran were no longer allowed to carry spears unless they were issued a special "spear chit" by the colonial administration for a limited time under special circumstances—for instance if a lion was troubling the herds. They were thus deprived of the means to continue killing Kikuyu, even if the other measures did not abate their desire to do so.

Over the next two decades, contact between the Samburu and the Kikuyu was less notable. Because Samburu was a closed district, Samburu could not leave without special permission for purposes of employment, although significant numbers did so to serve in the colonial army or police, or to work as herders on white ranches. These jobs were typically of limited duration, however. Similarly, the closed status of the district meant that few Kikuyu entered, although a limited number did, mainly as employees of the colonial administration. Based on oral accounts and colonial records, these few Kikuyu appear to have been on friendly terms with the Samburu, and there is no evidence of animosity between Samburu and Kikuyu during that time period, though that was shortly to change.

SAMBURU AND MAU MAU

A kilometer or so from my house at my main Samburu research site are the almost vanished remains of a detention camp where Kikuyu were held during the Mau Mau insurrection. Little remains of the camp. Though Samburu tell me that there are graves of many Kikuyu who died there, the only obvious feature on the landscape is a green, low-lying depression where fifty years ago Kikuyu hand-dug a large reservoir, since filled in with sediment. Samburu was selected as a fitting locale for detaining Mau Mau insurgents because of the presumed hostility of the local population, and perhaps the inhospitable climate for anyone trying to escape. There were other sites for Mau Mau detainees elsewhere in Samburu; for instance, near Baragoi there is a place now called Soit lo Kikoyo, "Stones of the Kikuyu," where Mau Mau detainees did quarry work, and the district headquarters, Maralal, served as a site to imprison important Kikuyu leaders, including Kenya's first president, Jomo Kenyatta. Conditions at the old camp near my house are said to have been particularly brutal, and neighbors recall the screams of Mau Mau who were beaten or even, Samburu claim, castrated by the British. Yet Samburu report being largely indifferent to this brutality, even to some extent supportive of the torture. When Mau Mau insurgents launched attacks on British farmsteads, African workers were sometimes killed—including some Samburu. Consequently, because of the Samburu herdsmen killed by Kikuyu on white ranches, local Samburu viewed the Mau Mau detainees at the nearby camp with antagonism. This is illustrated in an exchange with one Samburu elder of the Mekuri age set, who neighbored the camp and expressed support for the ill treatment:

LEPARIYO: Oh, we hated the Kikuyu because of the way they killed our herders. They killed our people who looked after the white people's cows.

JON: So you even liked it when they were castrated?

LEPARIYO: They killed our herders.

The Mau Mau insurrection of the early 1950s, based mainly among the Kikuyu, aimed at liberating Kenya from colonial rule. The Kikuyu were the obvious group to instigate rebellion for several reasons. They were subjected to colonialism earliest and most intensely. The central highlands that make up their home area was particularly desirable for white settlement, its high altitude particularly suitable for growing cash crops such as coffee and tea, and also mostly free of malaria. Thus, disproportionate numbers of Kikuyu were displaced from their land and forced to turn to wage work on the now-white farms that had been taken from them. The Kikuyu were also the earliest group to have significant Western education and to develop a clear consciousness of their colonial predicament. This is exemplified in the leader of the independence movement, Jomo Kenyatta, who while petitioning in England for Kikuyu land rights, studied anthropology at the London School of Economics under Bronislaw Malinowski. His thesis was later revised into the well-received ethnography of the Kikuyu, *Facing Mount Kenya* (Kenyatta 1962). The insurrection was a period of brutal violence, with deaths numbering into the tens of thousands (though there is no single agreed-upon count). Most of these were Africans, predominantly Kikuyu, who died both at the hands of British forces and in conflicts between Mau Mau and loyalist African groups. The threat and reality of violence were sufficient for the colonial government to declare the Mau Mau Emergency, beginning in 1952, taking both military and civilian action to suppress the rebellion (see Anderson 2005).

Samburu did not support Mau Mau—indeed, they aided the colonial government. There were a few pre-Emergency contacts between Samburu and Kikuyu politicians, mainly stemming from the Samburu desire to get rid of the highly unpopular system of grazing control, but these did not translate into either support for the Kikuyu or a marked desire for the British government to leave. This can be attributed to a number of factors. First, Samburu had a markedly ambivalent attitude toward the white government. Certainly they hated some aspects of colonial rule—grazing control, periods of forced labor, and hangings in the 1920s and 1930s of individuals who killed members of other tribes. But there were also aspects that Samburu saw (and retrospectively see) as positive. For instance, colonial rule brought the cessation of widespread warfare, such that people lived free of anxiety from attack. As one man describes it, "The old people said that a very good life had come because even a dog could relax [and not guard the settlement]. Because you couldn't fear anything while the white people were here. There was nothing you could fear. So that's what they meant by 'a good life even a dog could enjoy.'" Moreover, Samburu describe considerable admiration for the power of the white government. Lekadaa, one of the first Samburu to acquire a Western education in the 1930s, describes with modest contempt the attitude of the then almost universally uneducated Samburu toward the British: "They considered the whites to be next to God. . . . They only trusted in God and the white man. When you wanted to attempt a difficult task, people would ask you, 'Are you God or a white man?'"

This attitude contributed to a sense that suggesting the Kikuyu would drive away the British was, as well as being perhaps undesirable, a ridiculous impossibility. The British took steps to further foster that attitude among Samburu and to abate any rise in Mau Mau sympathies among them. A distinct effort was made, for instance, to keep the Samburu from what was termed Mau Mau "infection." They felt the Samburu were mainly a loyal tribe, but also simple people who might be turned against the government. Consequently, it became official policy to avoid sentencing Samburu criminals to hard labor, so that they did not come into contact with Kikuyu (CPK 1952), while unofficial efforts were made to keep even murderers out of prison for the same reasons (Ramon Good-win, personal communication).[1] In Maralal (the Samburu District head-quarters), Mau Mau were publicly belittled for the benefit of the Samb-uru, as one Samburu describes:

> The DC [district commissioner] used to stand up and tell us, "You Mau Mau want to chase away the government but you are like rats." He asked us, "Can your spear pierce a rat? Then how can the Kikuyus say they don't fear bullets?" They continued despising the Kikuyu. There was a time they brought a senior Mau Mau called Paul Ngei. It was market day and the DC said, "Have you ever seen a thing called a Mau Mau?" "No!" Then he said, "Do you want to see?" "Yes!" He brought Ngei, then he said, "Have you seen?" "Yes!" Then the DC told him to stand up and he was a short man. The DC said, "His mind is as short as his size. No brains!"

Apart from these factors, some aspects of the Mau Mau insurrection encouraged Samburu to participate alongside the colonial government. As noted above, Samburu were angered by the Mau Mau killing their herders on white farms (a notable reversal of Samburu killing Kikuyu herders twenty or so years before). Following the murder in neighboring Laikipia District of eight Samburu herders working on European-owned ranches, hundreds of Samburu volunteered as trackers or soldiers, fight-ing with the British against the Mau Mau (CPK 1952). Various Samburu give slightly different reasons for this. Some express a degree of coercion on the part of the colonial government, but generally they describe vary-ing motivations for voluntary participation. Partially there was a desire for revenge, as Lepariyo, a Mekuri elder, describes it: "It was announced that people were wanted for employment to fight the Mau Mau. So many people went. . . . The Samburu hated the Mau Mau because they killed our people who were working in those ranches. They used to try to take the white people's cows, and the Samburu herders who would try to defend them would get killed."

Fighting Mau Mau also provided an opportunity to reverse restrictions on key aspects of warriorhood that had been banned for a generation: carrying spears and using them to kill enemies. As one man describes it, "There were people who wanted to go [fight Mau Mau] because they were given spears. . . . People were not interested in employment then, but some wanted the job because they were given spears."

Thus, Mau Mau provided an opportunity for murran to be issued spears with a license to kill—which they apparently did enthusiastically. One participant in these operations boasted to me, "We killed so many Kikuyu at that time." Chenevix-Trench (1993) suggests an almost excessive exuberance, to the point of Samburu hunting down and capturing an undercover anti–Mau Mau police unit in the Mathews Range in eastern Samburu.

IN MAU MAU'S AFTERMATH

Samburu, of course, chose more or less the losing side. By the mid-1950s, Mau Mau was largely defeated as a military movement, but it set the stage for a peaceful transition to independence in 1963. And like the Mau Mau movement, independent Kenya was quickly dominated by Kikuyu, from the presidency of Jomo Kenyatta through all levels of government and the bulk of the economic sector. Samburu thus found themselves marginalized in independent Kenya. Whether they were, in fact, deliberately marginalized is an open question. That is, whether the Kikuyu as a whole or the particular figures who dominated the government acted out of deliberate animosity toward the Samburu is unknown. Nonetheless, Samburu certainly perceived that to be the case.

Samburu see themselves as having been marginalized or exploited by the Kikuyu in various ways since independence. In general, they view their district as having been underdeveloped, for the most part deliberately. They believe that because they were on the losing side in Mau Mau, they were denied the fruits of independence. At other times they see themselves as having been deliberately targeted. One example is the Ngoroko bandits (for more detail, see chapter 6) who plagued Samburu during the 1970s and early 1980s. The Ngoroko were a well-armed paramilitary group of Turkana from whom Samburu suffered significantly, as did other neighboring groups (including other Turkana). Among the Samburu, however, it was suspected that some Ngoroko attacks were not Ngoroko at all. Rather, they looked to the Anti-Livestock Theft Unit of the Kenya Police, which was stationed in Samburu for the purpose of repelling Ngoroko attacks. It was, thus, widely rumored that Kikuyu leading the Anti-Livestock Theft Unit were actually stealing Samburu cows, largely because of antipathy stemming from Mau Mau.

Other Samburu, though not ruling out a Kikuyu grudge, emphasize other factors regarding perceived marginalization in a post-independence Kenya dominated by the Kikuyu. Samburu perceive Kikuyu as extremely greedy people—comparing them to hyenas, who are said to eat their own intestines if their stomach is pierced. Thus, many Kikuyu actions in postcolonial Kenya are perceived as stemming from a general Kikuyu desire to get rich off the resources of Kenya in the same way as the whites they ousted had done. One Samburu, for instance, cites a case (likely apocryphal) elsewhere in Kenya: "People in Mombasa said that they needed tractors [for farming]. So [the first president] Kenyatta told them, 'Okay, I will send you tractors.' The next day there were truckloads of Kikuyu sent to farm the land [displacing those who wanted tractors]."

Older Samburu in particular contrast the Kikuyu-dominated government to the British colonial government in markedly unfavorable terms. The British were viewed as deeply masculine figures. This virility could be unfavorable when it turned into brutality but was also admirable. Some colonial officers are referred to as being real *laingoni,* or bulls, in the same way that strong and brave Samburu are characterized. In contrast, Samburu portray the Kikuyu as utterly demasculinized figures. They are considered extremely cowardly; even if they are clever with money and know how to get rich through both legitimate and corrupt means, they lack the courage to defend their property. With this demasculinization comes the notion of unreliability that Samburu men attribute to their own women. In the views of Samburu men, if a man says he will do something he must do it, but the word of women means very little. Thus, for instance, Lempirikany, a Kimaniki elder, expounded on some roadwork that was scheduled to be completed by a particular date in 2008 but had not yet been done. He remarked on how different the Kikuyu-dominated government was from the colonial one: "This government of women, they say they will do something sometime but there is nothing that they do. If the whites said they would do something on a particular day it would be done on a particular day." Another man, remarking on the heightened insecurity since independence, similarly put this in gendered terms: "It [the white government] was good because no one could attack another by then. People lived peacefully because they feared the whites. But things have changed now because people are fighting everywhere. Even women are in charge of themselves now. So this is a government of women."

Thus, the ills that Samburu attribute to their position in postcolonial Kenya are not simply a result of a Kikuyu grudge stemming from Mau Mau. Samburu also believe that the Kikuyu want to get rich off all communities, their community included. Moreover, the Kikuyu are seen to lack the masculine qualities that would allow them to govern in a straightforward, meaningful, effective way. Yet the backdrop of Mau Mau remains.

MEMORIES OF MAU MAU? THE 1998 CLASHES IN LAIKIPIA

In January 1998, a series of clashes erupted between Samburu (along with their Pokot allies) and Kikuyu agriculturalists, resulting in the deaths of a significant number of Kikuyu. The Samburu had been expanding southward and the Kikuyu northward, as fertile areas of Laikipia became available. Laikipia had been taken by the British as an area of European settlement in the colonial period, and the ninety-nine-year leases granted to settlers were by and large honored after independence. As the leases began to expire in the 1990s, however, these areas became available for African settlement, leading to friction between previously separated groups. The opening of these areas both removed the zone separating the Kikuyu from northern pastoralists and created a valuable and disputed resource—high-quality grazing for pastoralists and land with some potential for farming by agriculturalists. While Kikuyu have increasingly occupied these lands from the south, pastoralists from the north found rich new pastures that provided a welcome alternative to the increasingly congested grazing found in the higher-productivity zones of their home areas. The area had been relatively peaceful prior to these clashes, forming a multiethnic zone with Kikuyu and Samburu, as well as smaller numbers of Pokot and Turkana. Kikuyu by and large purchased small farms that they cultivated in the area, while pastoralists came on a more peripatetic basis. While conditions were largely peaceful, some minor disputes—involving small-scale theft and violence—arose prior to the 1998 clashes.

Precisely what happened in the 1998 clashes is impossible to determine. However, based on accounts by Samburu and Kikuyu informants (some of whom from each group were directly involved in the clashes) and the Akiwumi Report (Government of the Republic of Kenya 2003), compiled by a judicial commission appointed to inquire into a variety of "tribal clashes" in Kenya, a reasonably—if not wholly—clear picture can be gleaned. Needless to say, each group is prone to label the other as aggressors, but the accounts do not differ radically. The clashes in Laikipia began on January 11, 1998, when an unidentified group of pastoralists (probably Pokot) stole fourteen goats from a Kikuyu widow. A group of her Kikuyu neighbors set out after the thieves and recovered ten of the goats. In the same evening a group of Kikuyu (possibly the same neighbors) launched a revenge raid on the homestead of a nearby Pokot elder, killing and maiming a substantial number of his goats and cattle. When government efforts to bring reconciliation failed, Pokot teamed with Samburu began a series of revenge attacks on Kikuyu homes in the area over the nights of January 14–16, resulting in the death of two Kikuyu.

In response, Kikuyu organized a large reprisal force numbering up to three hundred men, armed with sticks, machetes, and bows and arrows. This group was apparently composed at least partially of Kikuyu from outside the area, driven in by truck and minibus along with women to cook for them. As one Kikuyu elder explained to me, "People who were killed, they came to fight, to help their people. When they heard there was a war people came from those other areas to help their people here." The goals of this party are not wholly clear: perhaps revenge, self-defense, or (as some Samburu claim) to drive pastoralists off valuable disputed land. The party, however, met with a well-armed group of Samburu and Pokot, who routed them, leaving at least forty Kikuyu dead (and perhaps many more) with few if any Pokot and Samburu casualties. While a few isolated incidents occurred shortly after this, the massacre marked the end of large-scale conflict in the area.

Why did these clashes occur, how were they explained by both parties, and how did they affect future relations among the parties involved? Initial reports, found in local media and picked up by human rights organizations (e.g., Daily Nation 1998a, 1998b, 1998c, 1998d; Amnesty International 1998), couched the conflict in terms of politically motivated ethnic violence. Specifically, Kikuyu had aligned in the recent election against the party of then president Daniel arap Moi, and some suggested that they were being punished for their opposition or that this was an attempt at ethnic cleansing before future elections. These reports, however, do not appear to have a sound basis. Neither Kikuyu nor Samburu whom I interviewed cite this as a factor, nor is the pattern of deaths consistent with such motivation. The vast majority of dead were armed Kikuyu apparently seeking revenge, and with their deaths the violence abated. The Akiwumi Report—although confirming the political basis of ethnic clashes elsewhere in Kenya—found no evidence for political motivation in the violence near Ol Moran.

Samburu explanations of the events agree that the conflict was instigated by the Kikuyu, but explanations of Kikuyu motives differ. Two Samburu men who participated in the clashes characterized it as self-defense, but without a clear understanding of why it occurred. "The Kikuyu are the ones who attacked us. Their neighbors told them not to go, but they insisted and so they were told, 'Then you go and be wiped out.' . . . The Kikuyu were just interested in killing people—they were not even after livestock. They mutilated cows and burned houses. When they got a house like this one, they just set it ablaze. But there was no previous grudge. The fight just started there and we don't know the motive behind it." A firsthand account like this, by young, uneducated men, forms an interesting comparison with more widespread accounts. Their straightforward, not especially reflective description characterizes their own reactions to events without the spin that was added by those more distant in time and space or those with various political motivations. Other young, uneducated men—born long after Mau Mau—note, however, a general Kikuyu hatred of the Samburu. As one man commented on a disarmament campaign that seemed likely to take guns from Samburu but not their neighbors, "You know the leader in power is a Kikuyu.[2] So he wants us to be finished." Indeed, by and large Samburu attribute the clashes directly to Kikuyu animosity toward the Samburu stemming from Mau Mau. As one elder asserted, "They just don't like us. But they cannot do anything to us. They don't like us, they say that we were not with them, we used to attack them, because of those Samburu who used to go attack them [during Mau Mau]." In a similar vein, another added, "The Kikuyu hate the Samburu, because didn't they attack people in Rumuruti [i.e., near Ol Moran]. They killed people with machetes.

And then they also got killed. Samburu and Kikuyu don't like each other up until now. It is just that Mau Mau grudge that is continuing."

Alongside this Kikuyu animosity toward the Samburu, most Samburu claim Kikuyu were driven by a hunger for land. To some extent this is portrayed as part and parcel of a general desire to enrich themselves wherever the opportunity arises in Kenya. Beyond this desire for resources, however, Samburu assert that the Kikuyu claim entitlement because of their leadership in Mau Mau. "They say that this land is theirs because they drove off the whites and we helped them stay" were the characteristic words of one young elder, echoed by numerous others. Samburu point to the fact that many Kikuyu were brought in from out-side the region, suggesting that this was not a simple local dispute but widely orchestrated—with Kikuyu arriving on trucks and minibuses from as far as a hundred miles away.

Samburu thus largely view these clashes through memories of Mau Mau, but largely in the motivations they attribute to their adversaries. That is, they assert that Kikuyu hate the Samburu because of Mau Mau. The Kikuyu believe they are entitled to Laikipia because in Mau Mau they drove off the whites. Discussions with Kikuyu, however, present quite a different picture.

ABOUT A GOAT

> It was about a goat. That is, the Samburu stole a goat. So
> when the Samburu stole the goat, Kikuyu followed
> them, and when they entered the settlement, they cut a
> goat and a cow. So people began to fight. They began to
> kill each other.
>
> JAMES KAMAU (pseudonym), KIKUYU elder

Whereas Samburu provide an account of the 1998 clashes that is imbued with deep collective memory, Kikuyu wholeheartedly deny the influ-ence of the past—indeed, they even find the suggestion nonsensical. As one Kikuyu man remarked to me, "Were you even born during that time? Was I born during that time? How could people be fighting about something that occurred before they were even born?"

Kikuyu provide an account of events that is highly uniform and, in fact, largely consistent with Samburu descriptions. Kikuyu agree that tensions existed before the clashes, but they were based in the practicalities of everyday life: pastoralists (particularly Samburu) had a broad tendency to steal livestock from Kikuyu. Samburu, and other pastoralists, do not deny that they did so, and continue to do so when provided the opportunity. Stealing livestock is (unlike other forms of theft) highly valued culturally. Pastoralists like to have cows, and the demasculinized Kikuyu are seen as easy targets. This joking exchange between a Kikuyu and a pastoralist at a recent livestock market is highly illustrative:

S: You guys [Kikuyu] should forget about livestock and stick to stuff like metal work.

K: What do you mean?

S: Metal work, like fixing bicycles, radios, stuff like that.

K: Well, what's the reason that you guys have to steal goats at night?

S: What's the reason that nobody defends them?

Though spoken in jest between two men on friendly terms, it illustrates the attitude of many in this interethnic zone that, on one hand, pastoralists are brazen thieves and, on the other hand, Kikuyu are cowards who really don't deserve to have livestock that they are not men enough to defend. Thus, Kikuyu descriptions of tensions that occurred prior to the clashes were centered almost universally on livestock theft, a tendency that—if somewhat stereotyped—is essentially accurate. As one Kikuyu man explained, "Those clashes just came from those guys, from Samburu. It came from that thievery, that thievery. They came to steal cows and drive them to the places they live. So they came to steal from us but Kikuyu didn't go steal from them because we don't have guns. So they come they steal and leave with our things. So Kikuyu, seeing their wealth has been stolen, they followed, and when they followed, the war started."

Kikuyu deny significant aggression in the conflict. Though not included in all accounts I gathered, it is generally agreed that Kikuyu did retaliate to an act of theft by attacking a home (whether Pokot or Samburu) and maiming livestock. They also agree that they gathered, armed with sticks and machetes, as tensions increased. They differ from Samburu, however, in intent. Where Samburu insist that the Kikuyu were intent on driving them away, Kikuyu explanations are considerably more benign, ranging from gathering to help their fellows to merely attempting to survey the situation. These accounts may, however, be colored by the consequences. As one Kikuyu man described the events, "Those people gathered to follow their livestock. They gathered because elsewhere our people were killed, our livestock was stolen, so it is a must that you gather to follow your livestock. So there, when they went to follow their livestock, death was found there, because those guys had guns. Guns. And like I said, if one guy has a gun and one guy has a machete, that war—it's not even a war. It's just like coming to finish people." Another Kikuyu man specifically denies that the group which gathered had any will to fight:

> You have to gather together, because you want to know, "What is this war like?" So when you leave, it's necessary you carry something to defend yourself. . . . When they reached there, they found it wasn't a good war, so they just wanted to run away. So you go to look things over, but it turns out you just go to get finished. Because those guys who got finished there, they weren't finished while they were fighting. They went and saw those guys had guns and then they started to mow them down. . . . They went to the bush to try to help the people who had been attacked. But then they were surrounded by those enemies and there was no place at all to escape. So they were surrounded and they were attacked. They were killed. Sixty people.

It is difficult to determine whether these retrospective accounts of the motivations of the losing group are wholly accurate. The circumstances do give cause to think that they may have been more aggressive than the above accounts indicate. There is something, after all, about a large group of people going out with clubs and machetes that suggests they are looking for trouble. And there is also reason to claim that you weren't really looking for trouble if you end up being routed. One saves face by asserting that one was attacked rather than being trounced in a fight that had been sought out.

To some extent that is tangential, however, to the issue Samburu often bring to the fore: that Kikuyu wanted to drive them away because of a grudge remaining from Mau Mau. Perhaps the Kikuyu did want to drive the Samburu away, perhaps some did, or perhaps they were angry. But there is no indication that it had anything to Mau Mau.

OTHER MEMORIES

If Kikuyu insist that their motivations were in no way driven by either grudges against the Samburu or claims to Laikipia derived from their own role in Mau Mau, many Samburu do, in fact, make the case that they have a historically validated claim to Laikipia. This assertion is based on Laikipia's seizure from the Maasai by the British during the colonial period. Until the late nineteenth century it had been populated by a now extinct Maasai group, the Laikipiak, who were vanquished by an alliance of Maa-speaking and non-Maa-speaking groups, purportedly because of their excessive aggression. It was then inhabited by Purko Maasai, who were forced out during the Second Maasai Move in 1911, which allowed all Maasai groups to live in contiguous areas and opened the rich pastures of Laikipia for white settlement.

It is not clear to what extent the Samburu lived in Laikipia. Some Samburu describe Laikipia as "a place that people just pass through" rather than truly inhabit. Informants intend this statement less as a description of what the history of Laikipia has actually been, though it may be based on inferences from observed events. Rather, it alludes to vaguely perceived supernatural aspects of the place, which for some reason do not lend themselves to a group really making it home, so it is destined to be perpetually "of the bush." In recent history Samburu likely did not spend much time in Laikipia prior to the Second Maasai Move, though oral migration histories do mention time in what is now Laikipia. Moreover, the group most closely related to the Samburu—the Lchamus, Maa-speakers who live near Lake Baringo—does present evidence of Samburu having lived in roughly the Laikipia region. The Lchamus are closely enough related to the Samburu that not only do they share clans (though these are in somewhat different segmentary groupings) but some families have lineages in both ethnic groups. However, when Laikipia was populated by the Laikipiak and later the Purko Maasai, Samburu would not have had significant access to these areas, since these groups were more powerful militarily.

The opportunity for Samburu to move south came at the expense of those two groups, in the wake of the defeat of the Laikipiak and the forced migration of the Purko. In the time between these events and the widespread influx of white settlers, Samburu appear to have made some use of Laikipia. Reliable informants, for instance, assert that the Kileku age set (circumcised in 1921) was initiated in Laikipia. And given its proximity, this area certainly was utilized for pasture. However, claims to Laikipia do not rely particularly on Samburu use, but rather through reference to a kind of pan-Maasai identity. It certainly is accurate that Laikipia was a Maasai area in precolonial times. Apart from the fact that this is known historically, Maa-language place names still dominate the landscape, interspersed with the occasional English word or Kikuyu names for villages or areas that they have populated for a few decades.

There is an important difference between the Samburu belief that the Kikuyu want to drive them away because of Mau Mau, and their belief that they are entitled to Laikipia because of its Maasai history. Though the Kikuyu deny any deeper historical validation, some Samburu assert that Laikipia should be theirs. It is not evident how serious Samburu are in this assertion—it may well be little more than a counterpoint to perceived Kikuyu claims to entitlement—and despite years of living with Samburu, I have seen no indication that it was a serious motivation for clashes with the Kikuyu. Yet these memory claims are important not only to Samburu but also to Kikuyu, who are aware of these claims but deny their validity.

"I AM A KENYAN—WE ARE ALL KENYANS": MODERNITY AS THE ERASURE OF MEMORY

A young Samburu elder laughed derisively at the Kikuyu who had come, he claimed, to drive the Samburu out of Laikipia during the 1998 clashes. They were not even all locals, he asserted, not the farmers who are fit and tightly muscled from agricultural work even if Samburu hold them to be cowardly. Some were big-bellied town people, he insisted, brought in from as far as Nyeri on the slopes of Mount Kenya, aiming to fight but totally incapable of carrying out their mission. "Some of them were wearing suits," he asserted, barely controlling his laughter as he mockingly mimicked a Kikuyu who had been killed there, holding out his hand as if it contained a fistful of Kenya shillings: "Please don't kill me! I'll give you money!"

His callousness is somewhat chilling—finding humor in a massacre, even of enemies—and whether his story reflects anything that actually occurred is far from certain. He did not participate in the violence nor was he even in Laikipia at the time. His description is, however, consistent with other accounts suggesting that the Kikuyu might have organized themselves to fight but ended up offering little resistance. They were seen as weak and cowardly, and although a few Samburu had guns, they assert that, finding their opponents unworthy, unmanly, and not worth the bullets—about one dollar per round—they killed them using only spears. Yet this mocking of their victims contains a second important element: the notion that their opponents included a Kikuyu man in a suit offering money to save his life. Where this is obviously mockery of this (perhaps apocryphal) man's lack of preparedness and cowardice, it also speaks to a positive image the Samburu hold of the Kikuyu: they are rich, and they are clever with money.

Alongside their derision, Samburu hold positive views of Kikuyu. One man noted, for instance, how different his home area in Samburu would be if it were occupied by Kikuyu: instead of a dry, overgrazed plain, it would be "full of food" (Holtzman 2009). Other Samburu ostensibly emulate everyday habits associated with the Kikuyu, particularly those who have lived side by side with them in Laikipia. My Samburu host, Lekeren, for instance, takes his tea with very little sugar. This is a stark contrast to most Samburu, who typically drink their tea extremely sweet, a habit that some "developed" Samburu associate with being very "local" (Holtzman 2004) or unenlightened. While Lekeren does not admit that his Kikuyu-like tea preferences involve acting more like a developed Kikuyu, this is a common example cited by his friends and neighbors, and not in wholly negative terms. While Samburu typically look down on the Kikuyu in most ways, few do not admire or even covet their wealth (even if they are seen to have acquired it through largely dishonest means).

Some Samburu have also started to emulate Kikuyu in less subtle ways. For instance, in Laikipia, after a period in which they were mainly squatters, Samburu began to purchase the title deeds to farms to secure access to land on which they often make efforts to practice some agriculture. At points the purchase of title deeds has led such land-owning Samburu to be in some ways more closely aligned to their Kikuyu neighbors, who support government-sponsored efforts to evict non-land-owning pastoralists from Laikipia, than to support Samburu peers making use of pastures without title deeds. In some ways, then, the Kikuyu serve as a discursive replacement for whites as the symbol of modernity in postcolonial Kenya. However, they differ from Samburu images of colonial whites in several ways. The British were seen as orderly and impartial, and although they could also be brutally harsh, this was an index of their strength. As Lekadaa noted above, during the colonial period the Samburu mused that "the white man follows God"—that only God was more powerful and more capable than the British. The Kikuyu, in contrast, are seen as unmanly and focused only on their own enrichment. Yet even if this is in some ways looked down upon—the image of a people exceeded only by God being replaced by a hyena that would greedily eat even its own intestines if they were hanging out—Kikuyu are nonetheless admired for their cleverness and success in getting wealthy. Thus, while Samburu do not want to *be* Kikuyu, some will nonetheless copy them in certain ways to the extent that they represent models for modernity, models for gaining wealth in contemporary Kenya.

These varieties of Samburu experience are largely lost upon Kikuyu. If the Kikuyu replaced the British as a model for what it means to be modern, they largely took on European colonial stereotypes of pastoral peoples as being backward livestock thieves unable to change their ways because of their traditional values. The following characterization by a Kikuyu elder is typical: "It is hard for herders like Samburu to leave stealing because that is their measure, they hold to livestock as their measure, just like we value farming. And they can't leave stealing because they want to increase their livestock. Even if they have a hundred cows, they want to add one of yours." A key aspect of Kikuyu discourses regarding the clashes is Samburu lack of education. Kikuyu even attribute their defeat partially to their differences with uneducated people. "Kikuyu aren't warriors so much," one man stated. "They just pay attention to their own work, they go to school. But these bush people, their work is just war. There isn't any other work that they do." Indeed, the Kikuyu attribute various aspects of the problems the Samburu are said to have caused to a lack of education. Their singular focus on livestock is attributed to being uneducated, a discourse that echoes white colonial discourses concerning pastoralists that date back more than a century. Samburu lack of respect for title deeds—illustrated by the view that they want to seize, or at least graze their animals on, land owned rightfully owned by another—is also attributed to a deficiency of education. One Kikuyu man explained Samburu attacks on them: "They saw that farms take up a lot of space, and if we weren't there they would have a big place to herd their animals. But the thing is, these farms were bought. So how would a person move away? You have bought it. You can't leave. So instead you would die here." Kikuyu, for their part, assert that they would never have tried to drive away Samburu, at least those with legitimate title deeds. When asked if the Kikuyu had tried to drive people away, one young man was emphatic: "No! Kikuyu believe that if someone has bought a farm it is theirs." He continues, "You know [Samburu], instead of coming here to follow the law they come here to break the law. They come to steal. They come to bother the people who farm here."

Perhaps the most significant negative outcome of a lack of education is, according to the Kikuyu, tribalism. As one elder asserts, "You know if you haven't gone to school you will just be a fool. You know those [Samburu] haven't studied. They don't have schools. Their children are just fools, they just herd. . . . If a person hasn't studied, he doesn't see how people stay. He just believes in his own tribe. So if you haven't studied, you look at other people and say, 'They aren't my tribe.' But if you've studied you know there is no tribalism."

This theme that a lack of education produces tribalism reverberates in Kikuyu perspectives on Samburu assertions that they are entitled to Laikipia because of precolonial history. As one Kikuyu elder claimed,

> You know Samburu believe this area is theirs. They want to steal it, like the place is theirs, but people have bought [these farms]. So it's things like that that bring these problems. They believe this because of Maasai. . . . Because you know in the past, during the time of colonialism, these ranches belonged to the white people, the British. They chased the Maasai from here, those whites. Now they believe the area is theirs. They hold together and say, "Maasai and Maasai" [i.e., Samburu are Maasai]. But if they awakened, if they studied, they would know it isn't theirs.

Whether or not this Samburu interpretation of their historically based claim to Laikipia is factually accurate—which is debatable—the Kikuyu do not merely assert that this claim is wrong. Rather at several levels they maintain that such claims are in general invalid, backward, tribalist. To even assert that a group has a right to the land based on a historical claim is inherently premodern, based on a traditional ethnic affiliation rather than laws of land ownership associated with the modern state. A push to end tribalism became a prominent theme in the wake of the controversial 2007 elections, which was characterized by significant violence, much of it directed against Kikuyu. In that context there was a movement among Kikuyu in particular—though taken up to some extent by others—to erase tribal identity: instead of saying, "I am a Kikuyu," to say, "I am a Kenyan." That is, everyone is a member of a nation-state, a modern state in which all should be treated equally and other forms of identity are meaningless. Just as it is backward to attack someone because they are of a different tribe, it is also backward to assert that you are entitled to resources by virtue of belonging to a particular ethnic group.

While such a view is positive in some ways—ostensibly saying that you shouldn't harm your neighbor because of ethnic identity—its use by Kikuyu was somewhat disingenuous. First, in the particular electoral and postelectoral context in which the assertion "I am a Kenyan" became prominent, divisions were largely tribally based, and the Kikuyu were no exception. They voted as a bloc for their candidate and took to the streets in postelection violence just like backers of other candidates did. More germane to the issue of Laikipia, however, an assertion that tribalism is inherently bad erases memory. There is no question that over the history of postcolonial Kenya, Kikuyu, as largely the heirs of the colonial state, benefited from favoritism among their co-ethnics. While it is true, as Kikuyu claim, that they bought the farms that Samburu are said to invade, steal from, or contest the rightful ownership of, their ability to buy these farms was a consequence of "tribalism," whether in gaining the means to purchase the farms or in being offered the opportunity to purchase them at all. It is convenient, then, after having gained advantages to a great extent through their own tribalism, to then adopt a discourse that tribalism is the province of the primitive and the uneducated, like the Samburu; identity politics is good if it helps you to become a "have," but it loses its allure when used by "have-nots" to threaten your position. These Kikuyu, consequently, asserted that through education one learns to both dispense with tribalism and respect the laws that protect the property rights of the legitimate owners of land—themselves—even if this discourse ignores that these property rights may have been acquired at least partially through tribal favoritism.

Like tribalism, memory from this perspective involves living in the past, while being an educated, modern citizen of a nation state means you understand that property rights are conferred by laws, rather than by memory claims. Irrespective, then, of the truth of the memory claims that Samburu assert are at the center of conflicts with Kikuyu in Laikipia—that the Kikuyu want to drive them out because of Mau Mau, that the Samburu are actually entitled to the land because of precolonial Maasai occupation—it is not in Kikuyu interests to frame the debate around competing memory claims. Modernity erases memory. If Maasai lived there one hundred years ago, or Mau Mau fought the British there fifty years ago, or Kikuyu got favored access to the land thirty years ago makes no difference in regard to the situation now, which is that (mostly Kikuyu) farmers occupy land that they rightfully own, that they have rightfully purchased and cannot be taken away.

.　　　.　　　.

The relationship between the Samburu and the Kikuyu today, in violence and in peace, has been shaped by a long history of which a series of violent interactions are an integral part. Whether early colonial violence of Samburu against Kikuyu farmworkers just for the sake of killing, the killing of Samburu farmworkers by Mau Mau rebels in the 1950s and the killing of Mau Mau by Samburu aiding the colonial government, or attacks on Samburu in the 1970s and 1980s that they claim Kikuyu instigated, this violent history forms a backdrop against which ongoing conflicts over Laikipia take place. Yet the role these incidents take in the minds of Kikuyu and Samburu is not even remotely similar. Samburu frame recent clashes through the deeply historicized lens of a past in which the two groups were great opponents, in which the Kikuyu fought them because of the "grudge of Mau Mau." In this view, Samburu underdevelopment is a remnant of the role they took in aiding the British, leaving them suffering now at the hands of unworthy heirs to colonial power.

Yet as I have shown, there is a major imbalance in memory. Kikuyu do not perceive themselves as enemies of the Samburu going back to

Mau Mau. In Kenya at large, Kikuyu are often nearly unaware of the existence of the Samburu—certainly scant on details—and definitely do not cast the Samburu as their great and ancient enemies. Where they do interact, in this case in the border areas of Laikipia, Kikuyu frame the conflict in terms of the everyday difficulty of living near backward pastoralists. Where Samburu insist that there is an epic clash of competing memory claims, Kikuyu suggest that there was a simple conflict about a goat that escalated into a horrific, if transient, massacre. They recognize that there is more to the conflict, but it is not about memory.

Indeed, the fact that Samburu suggest it is about memory is construed as a symptom of the very backwardness that in a Kikuyu view makes them such difficult neighbors. Memory is a domain of the backward, a refuge for people who cannot understand the laws. People who steal your livestock because they measure their worth by cows alone, or who want to graze their cattle in your fields of maize—these are the sort of people who justify their actions through memory. They are the sort of people, uneducated people, who hate you because of your tribe. They are not the sort of people who can understand that land is something that is purchased, that it is subject to laws, that rights to it are not determined by passionate memory claims, much less by violence, but by the cold and impartial execution of governmentality in the nation-state, with rights and laws that all share. And how things came to be divided as they are, how one group has the land and the other doesn't, is better erased; it is not to relevant to remember as you live in the modern present.

4

KILLING THE SHEIK

We arrived and saw the fires, the fires where the Somalis
had set the settlement ablaze. And we said that there
was no point in sitting there watching the fires that
were burning the deserted settlement, while people
were lying in the cattle enclosure dead, and they were
being eaten by vultures and others were lying dead
outside. So we asked ourselves, "Why should we keep
watching the bones of the people who are being eaten
by vultures?" and so we continued on past them. Do
you know about the loibon in charge of the Shiftas? It
was then [that we pursued the Somalis and] that loibon
was killed.

LELENGUYA, SAMBURU *elder*

This story of the celebrated war with the Somalis begins, as the war stories of Samburu herders often do, with an ignominious defeat. Over forty
years ago at this telling, ethnic Somalis raided a large Samburu settlement
while the murran were away at a wedding, killing women, children, and
old men, and stealing thousands of livestock.[1] When the murran returned,
they pursued the livestock but were gunned down by their heavily armed
adversaries. The area had originally been named Lpusi, "Gray,"—a common name for places with little vegetation and light, sandy soil—but has
since been renamed Lpusi Lampasion, "Lpusi of the Disaster," and the
songs of the dead warriors are said to still haunt the area at night.

The "War of Lpusi" did not, however, end with this disaster. Samburu
massed from miles around and crossed the Uaso Ngiro River seeking
revenge. Though the Samburu carried only spears, they confronted the
heavily armed Somalis and—despite the disparity in weaponry—routed
their enemies until coming upon the man said to be the architect of their
defeat, a man widely referred to simply as "the Sheik." Viewed by Samburu as a Somali *loibon*—the seers who offer talismans and guidance to
aid Samburu in various endeavors, including battle (Fratkin 2011; Spen-

cer 1965; Straight 2006)—he was met at his home, where Samburu speared him to death and then drove the Somali invaders from their homelands for a generation.

.   .   .

Thus the story goes. Samburu widely regard the War of Lpusi as their greatest victory in living memory, with the killing of "the Sheik" celebrated as its crowning achievement, a defeated underdog rising from the ashes of ignominy to righteous victory. Yet, needless to say, there are other stories. It is unsurprising that Somali accounts of this episode differ radically from Samburu ones—unsurprising, perhaps, except in the sense that Somalis generally agree with Samburu on almost all the key facts of the incident, while gleaning wildly different conclusions. Beyond this, the story that has been told and retold of these events takes on the character of a cardboard cutout morality tale. Both the subtleties of the events and interactions and how they bore on the lives of the real individuals involved in them are lost in such an epic rendering. And yet, as I aim to show in this chapter, these are the aspects that can be most crucial in understanding both the broad implications of these events and the discourses about them, as well as interpreting their meanings for actors on both sides of the interaction

This chapter focuses on a single event, seen from several different Samburu and Somali gazes, as a collective mythos and as an intimately meaningful event. My goal is neither to merely show that different people see things differently, nor to definitively determine what "really happened," though each of these play a role. Rather, using a multivocal style of presentation and analysis, I aim to understand how these varying perspectives, interpretations, and discourses construct a single social space, a social space that is ostensibly shared while it leads actors to very different courses of action and to very different meanings. I argue that this specific event both epitomizes and catalyzes joint understandings and misunderstandings that Samburu and Somalis have of the Other, views that are crucial to understanding not only interactions, attitudes, and relationships in the past but ones that resonate into the present.

"THE GOVERNMENT OF KENYA IS BEHIND *EVERYTHING!*"

Somalis living in Isiolo District (Kenya) on the borders of Samburu concur with many of the basic elements in the Samburu account of the War of Lpusi. They agree that the Samburu were attacked and routed in a brutal manner, and that the Samburu successfully avenged that defeat. While there are some elements of significant contradiction, the differences in Somali and Samburu versions are principally of emphasis and interpretation rather than facts. First, while Samburu uniformly remember it as an epic war ending with the death of "the Sheik," only older Somalis remember the Sheik at all. Most strikingly, even those Somalis who remember the events well tend to deny or ignore that what could be construed as a war with the Samburu even occurred at that time. Somalis from the Isiolo area claim they were not involved in the violence, and neither were the Samburu at war with them. As one Somali elder who was resident in the area at the time concurs, some Somalis—not they themselves—did decimate the Samburu settlement, but "those are from another district, not Isiolo District. They [the Samburu] were beaten, but not [by people] from this area." He thus agrees that ethnic Somalis were the aggressors, but Somalis from a distant place unaffiliated with Somalis from the local area. Moreover, while there was a war at that time, he and many others emphasize that it was not with the Samburu, the events of Lpusi being a minor and largely unrelated affair.

I will turn to the largely unremembered Samburu role shortly, but first will address the question of who the attackers are held to be, if not Isiolo Somalis. "If" is key word, for just as victims are prone to apply what Evans-Pritchard (1940) described as "collective responsibility," perpetrators frequently adopt a stance of "collective *ir*responsibility": the killers are people *like* us but not *actually* us. Somalis recognize at least three distinct groups among the residents or sometimes-residents of the Isiolo area where these events occurred, and they assert that it is not the Somalis of Isiolo who are responsible. Samburu, in contrast, see them all as Somalis, though sometimes they make contrasts to construct more pejorative categories, while also tending to apply these pejorative terms to the group as a whole.

Somalis in the Isiolo area distinguish at least three major categories (along with differences on matters such as clan affiliation that are less

FIGURE 7.   Milking time at a Somali camel camp.

central here). First, there are pastoralist Somalis, living a nomadic lifestyle raising camels, cattle, and small stock. Somalis were indigenous to Kenya at the beginning of British colonialism, and by some accounts continued to expand to the south and east before the British halted their movement. Somali pastoralists continue to migrate extensively in northeastern Kenya, sometimes moving as far south as Isiolo and eastern Laikipia, where they encounter Samburu.

The primary group of Somalis around Isiolo does not, however, belong to this indigenous pastoralist group; they were relocated by the British to the Isiolo area during the colonial period, as retired soldiers from the colonial army who had been transplanted from British Somaliland. As one Somali elder explains, "Originally, you know, they settled the Somalis, they were ex-servicemen. When they were finished, accomplished with their mission, they discharged all of them. Some of them settled in Naivasha, some in Nairobi, the rest here in Isiolo. Instead of sending them back to British Somaliland where they came from, they stashed them here in Kenya. So Somalis were settled here in Isiolo long before any other tribe." For the most part, they were soldiers in the colonial regime, fighting for the British against the Germans in Tanganyika during World War I.

Following the war they were discharged, and as compensation were given land in various parts of Kenya. Somalis local to Isiolo are principally the descendants of those ex-soldiers and can be at odds with the pastoral Somalis. While the local Somalis keep livestock, they do not generally migrate out of the area as the nomadic Somalis do, though they may send their livestock considerable distances with hired herders.

A third category (now largely defunct) is what has been termed the "Shifta." I will discuss this category in more detail shortly, but name derives from a Somali term for "bandit," though they were originally a movement to counter the colonial British refusal (later backed by the independent Kenyan government) to allow ethnic Somalis, who dominated what had been the Northern Frontier District in colonial Kenya, to join the Republic of Somalia. Recognition of Shifta as a third, distinct category shifts culpability for the attack on Lpusi in several ways. First, the Shifta had close ties to Somalia—perhaps actually coming from there—such that *Shifta* is often used by Somalis to distinguish "bad Somalis" from good ones. That is, the people responsible for attacking Lpusi were Shifta, meaning that typical Somalis should not be blamed. However, these "bad Somalis" may be understood even by local Somalis principally as freedom fighters.

Thus, whereas Samburu see the attack on Lpusi as being the work of "Somalis," Somalis attribute it to "Shifta." They are construed as not being residents of the area (at least for the most part) and are in the Somali view not even from Kenya. Thus, though there are many complexities to this distinction, Hassan, a Somali native of Isiolo in his sixties, asserts: "They were not the locals. They used to be called, you know, Shiftas. . . . The Shifta War was part of a political background. Somalia was claiming this part of Kenya. It was called NFD [Northern Frontier District]. So they armed these people. They trained them over there. They send them here to fight, to kill the armed forces. Came here without laws. And eventually they made that mistake [of massacring Samburu]." Attributing the attack to Shifta transforms issues of culpability in important ways. Clearly it diverts blame from "good Isiolo Somalis" to "bad Shifta." As Hjort (1979) describes in his detailed ethnography of Isiolo town and its environs, the extent to which town Somalis supported the Shifta is unclear, may have changed over time, and may have been driven by coercion on both the Somali and Kenyan sides of the conflict. The uncharitable line between "good Somalis" and "bad Shifta" fosters ambiguity to the extent that Shifta violence may be afforded a degree of legitimacy when directed against their principal opponent in this war: the Kenyan government.

Who were the Shifta, construed as both bandits and freedom fighters?[2] The label emerged in the context of a low-level conflict in northern Kenya in the mid-1960s and was rooted in the political mess that commonly emerged in Africa when political boundaries did not coincide with ethnic ones, though this one was handled with uncommon ineptitude. As Africa was carved up by European colonial powers in the late nineteenth century, little attention was paid to the boundaries of the native African populations; lines were drawn from convenience or even caprice, most famously illustrated by the jut in the Kenya-Tanzania border drawn so that Queen Victoria's cousin, the German kaiser, could have the equatorial snow-capped peak of Mount Kilimanjaro just as she had Mount Kenya. Consequently, across Africa one finds ethnic groups spread across national boundaries, and nomadic populations frequently move back and forth without much regard to borders at all.

In the 1940s the Somali people were spread across five separate entities: French Somaliland (now Djibouti), Italian Somaliland, British Somaliland, the Ogaden region of Ethiopia, and the Northern Frontier District of the Kenya Colony. After World War II, the British foreign secretary, Ernest Bevin, proposed the creation in 1946 of a Greater Somalia, encompassing British Somaliland, Italian Somaliland (captured during the war), and parts of Ethiopia, a proposal that was announced to enthusiastic response in British Somaliland. While British and Italian Somaliland fused to form the independent Republic of Somalia in 1960, the soon-to-depart colonial government in Kenya began to negotiate the status of Kenyan Somalis, located mainly in Northeastern Province. Initially colonial authorities proposed to subject the question to a referendum, with the local population deciding whether to remain with an independent Kenya or join Somalia. The secessionist option held almost universal sway among Kenyan Somalis, but when it became apparent that ceding almost a fifth of Kenya's land mass to Somalia would be unacceptable to the new Kenyan government— and that the departing colonial power had no real legitimacy in negotiating such a transfer—the proposal was withdrawn. The onset of violence in northern Kenya was the ultimate result (Reisman 1983). While Somalia clearly played a role at least in training and supplying Shifta, the extent of their support is unclear. There was, moreover, a deliberate effort by the Kenyan government to depoliticize the conflict, portraying the violence as solely the work of lawless criminals, masking both the desire of their own citizens for secession and an unacknowledged border conflict with another nation (Whitaker 2008).[3]

The conflict in northern Kenya began with ill-defined lines, which over time became even blurrier. There was no direct military contact between Kenya and Somalia, but Somalia (with training and materials provided by the Soviet bloc) lent direct assistance to the insurgents. Precisely how much direction they may have given is not clear. Nor is it clear to what extent armed Shifta infiltrated from Somalia or were simply drawn from the local population. Moreover one cannot determine to what extent the local population—though certainly sympathetic to the political goals of the Shifta—themselves joined the movement (see Hjort 1979). Added to this already complex situation is the fact that there were many divisions among Somalis (e.g., various clans, tribes) with their own internal conflicts, such that even politically based militias could be used to settle scores in local disputes over power or resources.

This situation was made increasingly turbid by two conjoined though partially unrelated factors. First, as just mentioned, the Kenya government deliberately masked any political motivations behind the conflict. Rather than acknowledging that at its roots were political issues of self-determination and a border dispute with a neighboring state, the government construed the insecurity strictly in terms of lawlessness. Shifta were thus branded as simple bandits. Related to this was a confounding factor: many *really were* bandits. If you give a bunch of guys guns in a poorly policed region with valuable resources, it is not surprising that they might turn to more lucrative pursuits than mere freedom fighting. Thus, Shifta became heavily involved in livestock theft (from neighboring tribes as well as rival Somalis), poaching that decimated herds of elephants and left rhinos largely extinct in northern Kenya, and simple highway banditry—all pursuits that continued long after the secessionist struggle had ceased. The consequence is that the masking of political motivations that accompanied the label "Shifta" took root in the cultural landscape of northern Kenya. As Whitaker (2008) notes, the government essentially treated all Somalis as Shifta, sometimes taking cattle from ethnic Somalis who were not related to the conflict in any way.

If Shifta were defined as nothing more than criminals, all Kenyan ethnic Somalis conversely came to be treated as real or potential Shifta. Isiolo Somalis don't deny that there may have been Shifta among them, but they insist that this was not the dominant sentiment. As one man asserts, "They weren't all Shifta, even Shifta sympathizers. They were not. There were some supporters. [But] quite a lot of them didn't even know, didn't care. They simply wanted peace." Nevertheless, the government treated all Somalis as Shifta (Whitaker 2008), such that Isiolo Somalis now emphasize their oppression at the hands of the British and the independent government, including the killing of people and livestock in collective punishment (see also Hjort 1979): "Over five thousand cattle were gunned here. 1967. Sixteenth of May. No Somali must own even one cow. . . . It was because of secession. . . . Sixteenth of May—eleven old men were killed in this mosque."[4]

Even the enmity with the Samburu, when it is acknowledged at all, tends to be blamed on the government. Somalis assert that the government incited Samburu hatred against Somalis and encouraged them to steal livestock: "The British government maneuvered. They killed a district commissioner and a chief so that enmity would ever be there. They went to Samburu District, and Samburu were told, 'This now is your land. Never allow a Somali to come.'" Somalis were concentrated into camps to lessen the risk of infiltration by Shifta, and some claim that the Samburu were told to take advantage of Somalis' now poorly guarded livestock: "The government took the owners of the livestock [and concentrated them in camps]. So the livestock just stayed at the settlement without anyone guarding them properly. So the government told Samburu, 'There is a place where the cattle [are] gathered and there is no one watching them, go and take that livestock.' So the Samburu came and found there was no one to defend the livestock and took it."

In the end, Somalis read themselves as the ultimate victims. Ex-soldiers who were resettled by the colonial government in a policy that one man described as "use and dump" were subsequently persecuted by the government in the context of the secessionist movement. As one Somali elder described his peers, "They don't even want to come back here because of the suffering they felt here. People being driven out of their house early in the morning—five o'clock. You can't even do your business. Everything collapsed."

Thus, he maintains, the Somali community that had lived around Isiolo for almost half a century ceased to be vibrant. Some left for Nairobi; children of families with resources sought school or work abroad. Thus, whereas Samburu see the attack on Lpusi and their avenging raid as a war with an expansionist and unified ethnic Somali people, Somalis portray it as a minor episode in a wider secessionist struggle with the Kenyan government, a war in which they lost almost everything.

AND THE PRAISE SONGS WERE SUNG

> The blow of the horn went out and passed across the highlands, and the blow of the horn passed from there and the wind of these hills took it to Baragoi. . . . The blow of the horn went through all of the Samburu lands, whether we were in the highlands or the lowlands. It went to all Samburu and it was said that people had been attacked and the whole place had been destroyed. And with the blow of the horn, anyone who can be called a warrior, all of the warriors, they got up at once, all of them.
>
> LENGALA, SAMBURU *elder*

The Somali reading of Lpusi and the killing of the Sheik are wholly alien to Samburu accounts of these events. No Samburu I have ever encountered gives the slightest hint of a political context behind the conflict, nor do they see it as anything other than righteous revenge for a vicious attack. The description of one elder is typical: "That battle of Lpusi, we were killed ourselves and we went to revenge it. So we went to pursue our livestock and even take theirs, and went and burnt the houses at Lowuan Ngiro. And so we had to go and attack the Shifta, and pushed them beyond Isiolo. And since that time the Shifta have never come again."

As Samburu recall it, Lpusi was attacked without provocation, and across their lands people were called to gather with the blow of the kudu horn (*mowuo*), kept by age set leaders to call their fellows.[5] Samburu quickly massed an impressive group of several hundred warriors and crossed the Uaso Ngiro River. Since the Somalis had guns and the Samburu did not, Samburu employed tactics to draw fire, emptying the magazines of the older-style Somali guns, then swarming and overcoming them with their greater numbers. For many, defeating the better-armed Somalis using only spears is an important aspect of their achievement. While Samburu accounts differ on how many Somalis fled and how many stayed to fight, one person they agree did not flee was Sheik Ahmed Yassin, or as Samburu commonly refer to him, "the Sheik."

Samburu viewed the Sheik as having been paramount to the Somali success. He was construed as the equivalent of a Samburu loibon—a seer who engages in everything from healing, to foretelling the future, to creating magic for success in war or any endeavor (Fratkin 2011). As one man exclaimed of the Sheik's importance:

> He was a complete loibon. The Somalis believed in him completely. He
> was like a God to them. . . . He helped the Somalis to attack Samburu
> for a long time. At the time when he[6] hadn't killed the Sheik, Samburu
> could not retrieve the cows the Somalis had taken. They couldn't
> retrieve them. Because of that loibon. Because that loibon gave them
> many [magical] things to see the places the Samburu lived. So then if the
> cows were taken they could never be found. So then to kill the Sheik,
> for this guy to kill the Sheik, Somalis couldn't come near. These days
> they can't come near the places Samburu live.

These assertions of the Sheik's mystical status are reinforced by various details surrounding his death. Oddly, he simply awaited the impending onslaught while reading the Koran underneath a tree—perhaps, Samburu conjecture, because he felt protected by his sorcery—and surrounded by his livestock, which behaved in an unworldly way. Another man describes the scene:

> We went to the big settlement and the loibon was there under a tree.
> He was praying to their God, like they usually do in the mosque, and he
> was just wearing white robes. And as we asked each other, "What is this,
> warriors?" as we didn't know then that he was a loibon. And with the
> cows and the camels, they all squatted that direction, all the cows were
> also facing that direction—that direction that the Somalis usually face
> when they pray to God. That one that they usually call Mecca. It was
> there that each cow faced, and instead of lying down as cows usually do,
> they were squatting like camels. And then a cow stuck out its tongue
> and it was incredibly long. . . . And the cow could extend its tongue so

that it could sweep the soil. And it made this sound, not like loudly mooing, just the tongue going "hee, hee," just the tongue sweeping the soil.

When the raiders finally managed to drive off the cattle, the animals still acted not like normal livestock but like wild animals. They were exceptionally difficult to herd away, and many were lost in the bush owing to the magical powers of the Sheik. As Samburu elder Leshornai describes it, "His cows were wild animals, some were like buffalo, others eland, others those ones with teeth like trees [i.e., elephants]. Even his camels wouldn't go. Even the goats didn't go. They were just like another kind of animal, animals of the bush."

A further bizarre detail highlighted in many Samburu accounts is an assertion that the Sheik was accompanied by a woman—or perhaps a woman, perhaps a hermaphrodite—presumed to be his daughter, who also had magical powers. She had red hair and bizarre secondary sex characteristics: "Even that girl was a loibon. And this girl had only one breast, the other had never grown. It had never grown and the chest was just flat like that of a man." When the Sheik was killed, the "girl" became crazed, leaping on the chest of one of the warriors, until she was eventually beaten to death with clubs.

This victory over the Somalis was memorialized then and now. As one man describes the immediate aftermath, "The praise songs were sung, 'We have killed a loibon of whom the Somalis are proud,'" marking the accomplishments of the warriors as Samburu typically do, in songs at collective dances where girls and murran extol their accomplishments. And indeed, this accomplishment—defeating the Somalis and killing the Sheik—is memorialized to this day as a great military victory when the odds were against them, a victory that preserved the lands and livelihood of the Samburu. One elder describes the consequences of this victory: "And then since the time that loibon was killed, Somalis have come to hate that area of Lowuan Ngiro [where the Sheik lived], from that time up until now. And still the Somalis have not stepped in that area, and put a house post in that area up until now. And before that it had been their place since way back. And so if we hadn't gotten them on that night, by now the Somalis would have spread out and reached on top of Laikipia, it was just that they wanted to grab land from us during that time."

There are, then, areas where Samburu and Somali accounts mesh and places where they do not. Both sides agree that the Samburu responded to a largely unprovoked attack and that the Sheik was killed, after which Somalis vacated the area, but many of the motives and key details differ significantly. Where Samburu see the work of a hostile ethnic group that they subsequently defeated, Somalis see the Samburu as accidental victims in a bigger struggle. Perhaps killing Samburu was the mistake of an undisciplined militia, but many maintain that the Samburu had become pawns of what one Isiolo elder terms "the kingmakers" in the British and then Kenyan government.

Yet apart from some of these discrepancies, this account is still partial. Though the Samburu paint the Sheik in a manner befitting an evil wizard in some pulp fantasy novel, he was of course a man—Sheik Ahmed Yassin—seen by Somalis in quite different ways than Samburu saw him. And conversely, even if his death occurred in a massive raid by a large group of Samburu, he was killed by a man—a particular man whose life has been shaped in important ways by that act.

TWO FAMILIES

I arrived at his settlement to meet this man, in his midsixties, heavily bearded unlike most Samburu men, drawing perfect little white circles of dust all up and down his thighs using a random piece of scrap he had found lying on the ground. Later, his son sat beside him, proudly extolling his father's achievements and boasting how through his bravery he had saved the Samburu and vanquished the Somali aggressors. "Because of *him*," he emphasized, pointing to his father. "Because of him. He indeed killed the Sheik. They fled completely. They didn't return again, even up until now." The Samburu hero clapped once and put his hands over his face, then into his lap like a shy child. He babbled incoherently in Kiswahili, occasionally repeating in English, "Tomorrow, tomorrow, tomorrow, tomorrow," and repeating the motions with his hands again and again. Looking over at his father's bizarre speech and movements, his son chuckled. "He just fathered me while he was like this."

Move perhaps sixty miles to the southeast, and I am sitting with two women, one quite old, the other, Fatuma, a vigorous fifty, their heads covered in the scarves of their Islamic faith. Fatuma passionately exhorts,

FIGURE 8.   Amina (right) and Fatuma (left).

"Samburu say complete lies. He was a holy man. He was a sheik. He would treat patients, he would look after people. He didn't know anything about the affairs of the Shifta, he just stayed with his cattle by himself. . . . He was a person of God. He was a holy man. Sheikh Ahmed Yassin. He was known throughout East Africa. He wasn't a bad person. Therefore, Samburu say lies."

Though this reflects the general Somali view, it is not surprising that it would be held with special passion by his surviving family: Fatuma, a granddaughter, who as a young child was wounded during the Samburu counterraid in which the Sheik was killed, and Amina, a now-elderly daughter who had fled before the attack. Where the Samburu paint an evil wizard directing a murderous onslaught against them, Somalis see a simple and peaceful holy man. Born in British Somaliland, he was resettled in Kenya with his father, who had served the British in World War I. And there he lived peacefully, raising livestock, studying the Koran, and teaching. He did indeed have powers, but they were used for healing, and he helped members of many tribes, including Samburu, and once even a British settler's wife who had been unable to give birth.[7]

Samburu and Somalis agree that the Sheik had extraordinary powers but differ markedly on their nature and how they were used. These disagreements figure not only in key contrasts in the interpretation of these particular events, but also in the fundamental ways Samburu and Somalis understand each other in times of both war and peace. A central example of these diverging interpretations surrounds the consequences for those directly involved in his killing. Although many Samburu participated in the raid, many bypassed the Sheik, largely out of fear, before a man I will refer to as "L" killed him.[8] Consider this exchange, with L and his son:

SON: Others feared to kill.

L: Even I feared.

SON: He rose up to kill him.

L: *[Babbling incoherently.]*

SON: Because people were afraid that if they killed him, they would just die then and there. Only this guy could handle this matter.

L: *[Babbling in English]* Blood, blood, blood, blood . . .

SON: How many people were there? Six hundred. And only he could kill. He alone killed. He was able to kill. Other people just passed [the Sheik] and left him. They went and killed others and left the Sheik.

According to this description, other Samburu were reticent to kill the Sheik, and one fellow warrior even tried to stop L, causing him to badly cut his hand on his own spear blade as his fellow grasped the shaft of the spear while his hand thrust forward. And indeed L—beginning that very day—suffered from his heroism. L pantomimed, and occasionally chimed in, as his son recounted the killing of the Sheik and his first exposure to his witchcraft:

Just he, himself, speared the Sheik. And then the Sheik dropped the book [the Koran] he was holding in that way. So as the Sheik died this way [mimicking falling backward], he dropped the book like that. He dropped it on this guy [L]. When the book was dropped on him, it made it so his eyes—there was nothing he could see. So then his guy, his [L's] second, grabbed him by the hand this way and ran him off, because you know the war was continuing. He ran with him, he ran with him to the bush. He hid him. He hid him because now there was nothing he could see. He had no eyes then. [L: No eyes then.] Then they went to a place with water. He rubbed his eyes with water then until he healed. [L: And I healed.] He healed there. At the river there, he healed. Then he went back to kill people. He killed people, he killed people, then he drove off the cattle.

Although his eyes healed, he never fully recovered from the sorcery of the Sheik. While he has led a productive life, marrying, siring many children, and becoming relatively wealthy, he is by all accounts a madman. The insanity comes and goes. When I met him, he was said to be at an in-between stage, incoherent and behaving as one might expect from a five-year-old: sometimes playful, sometimes shy. At other times he is verbally abusive and violent, and other times again he is like any normal Samburu elder. The warrior who assisted him is said to have fared worse, having gone completely insane and died without marrying.

The fate of these men is taken by Samburu generally and by L himself as conclusive evidence of the sorcery of the Sheik. In killing him—a noble and necessary act to save the Samburu people—they exposed themselves to magical powers that have governed their lives ever since. Yet where Samburu see these men's madness as proof of the Sheik's malevolence, Somalis portray it as incontrovertible proof of the Sheik's innocence. Fatuma explains: "You know a witch is a bad person. You know, they [those Samburu men] killed, and then they continued on and became crazy. And why? If he had been a witch, they wouldn't have, they would have just stayed like normal people. You see, if you kill a witch you kill a bad person, you kill a person of demons. Isn't it? Those Samburu wouldn't have gone crazy if he was a witch. His cows wouldn't have gone wild. Therefore he was not a witch. He was not a witch. He was a person of God." Along these same lines, Fatuma explains that the type of acts Samburu attribute to the Sheik are unforgivable sins within his Islamic faith, in contrast to the Samburu and their own holy men:

You know, in this tribe [Somalis] if you go [to someone like the Sheik] and say, "Destroy the family of Jon," that is a sin. [Amina: A total sin!] It is like you are making a person be killed. And in the Islamic faith, it says if you shed the blood of a human being, that is a huge sin, bigger than any other sin in the whole world. God cannot forgive you if you kill a person. No matter where you go, no matter how many times you ask. If you kill a person, there is no being forgiven. . . . You know the loibons of Samburu, they don't have religion, they don't have the Bible, they don't have the Koran. So with their loibons, the warriors come and say we want to fight with such and such people. So he does what? Witchcraft perhaps. People go to that loibon, he tells them they will win that war. He does witchcraft. But God doesn't like it. [Amina: God doesn't like it!] It's like you have made people be killed. You know there might be children who will be killed, women who will be killed. Innocent people. So it is a very big sin.

Thus, where Samburu see the consequences of the killing of the Sheik, the wildness of his cattle, and the insanity of his killers as being proof of his wizardry, Somalis take exactly the opposite view. These were punishments from God for the sin of shedding innocent blood, which the Sheik, as a pious Muslim, would never have done.

REMEMBERING THE SHEIK, FORGETTING THE SAMBURU

The war in which the Sheik was killed was not the last of conflict with Somalis. Occasional clashes continued for many years, and in the 1990s large-scale conflict broke out that largely parallels the earlier war stories of both groups. It began with small-scale conflict in the early 1990s, escalating into full-blown war in 1996. As in the War of Lpusi, Samburu emphasize the aggressiveness of the well-armed Somalis, who were eventually routed by determined Samburu—this time after acquiring comparable weaponry. Many Samburu, in fact, make explicit comparisons to the earlier war. As one elder describes it: "When Lpusi was attacked, [the Samburu] all came together and attacked those Somalis up to Isiolo. . . . When those Somalis went, they organized a bigger raid and attacked the Samburu again [in the 1990s]. So when the Somalis were attacked again, they were chased beyond Isiolo. . . . Didn't the Somalis go to Nanyuki? They were chased from Isiolo again, just like they were when the Sheik was killed."

As with the earlier conflict, Samburu emphasize both the ignominy of their first defeat and the brutality with which they exacted their final triumph. In the war in the 1990s, Samburu also perceived themselves to have been humiliated at the beginning of the conflict. One young man sang for me a taunting song that girls had used to mock him and other warriors to spur them to action: "No drought has been terrible enough to drive us from [the] Uaso [River area] / And now we have been chased away by people whose skin is just black like ours."

This defeat led Samburu to acquire new weapons and use them without mercy, which young men proudly recount. One group of murran laughed as they bragged to me of routing the Somalis, firing a black-market Russian rocket-propelled grenade (RPG) into a mosque. In a separate discussion a Samburu elder extolled the value of RPGs in response to my doubts concerning the wisdom of a borderline subsistence population spending four hundred dollars on a single-use weapon. "It is very expensive, but it's completely worth it," he assured me. "You know that is what finished the Somalis. We fired it into the middle of their large settlement, and that is what finished the Somalis."

Somalis, of course, give a very different reading of this conflict—one that also parallels the War of Lpusi, though lacking references to the earlier war. The absence of Samburu is perhaps unsurprising since even in the earlier war the Samburu were minor players, pests perhaps but not memorable. In the 1990s the Samburu were painted in similar terms. Though Somalis acknowledge attacking them because of the Samburu's persistent cattle theft, they were not the main opponents. Whereas in the 1960s the government was their main adversary, in the 1990s it was the Boran. The Boran are a neighboring group competing with the Somalis for dominance in Isiolo District at various levels. Isiolo town itself is largely mixed between Boran and Somalis, such that they compete there for economic and political privilege. In respect to pasture, Boran pastoralists' main territory is to the north, while Somalis live more in the northeast, butting up against each other to the east and west, as well as the south where they both border the Samburu. Somalis see them as competition for domination of the district, mainly in regard to electoral politics—the member of Parliament (MP) is a Boran, and he can consolidate his electoral hold by keeping Somalis out of the district. Thus, Somalis argue, the war in the 1990s was the result mainly of the Boran MP inciting his constituents, arming them, and flooding the district with weapons and armed men from as far away as Ethiopia. The Samburu are seen as having served as allies of the Boran but were not the main opponent. While some victims of Samburu attacks recount with bitterness the brutality exacted upon them, the Samburu are remembered only as minor allies of the Boran in a bigger struggle.[9]

As in the 1960s, then, Somali and Samburu readings of the conflict are quite different. Samburu paint themselves in both conflicts as heroes, overcoming well-armed aggressors to emerge victorious against difficult odds. Somalis, on the other hand, are pressed to place the Samburu in either conflict at all, while construing themselves as victims when larger forces aimed—largely successfully—to chase Somalis from Isiolo District.

STRANGE FRIENDS, STRANGE ENEMIES, AND MEMORIES OF VIOLENCE

Understanding violence as part of a cultural system is significant because of the ways violence shapes and crystallizes the relationships between groups in both war and peace. Key facets of the story of the Sheik highlight Somali and Samburu understandings of one another, though other aspects that are not fully foregrounded paint a more complex picture. Perhaps the most notable lacuna in accounts of the wars is that Samburu and Somali are not always enemies. Samburu are sometime friends with Somalis, while maintaining the general premise that Somalis are terrible, aggressive enemies. Somalis are also friends with Samburu, though they tend to view them as lowly, primitive, heathen cattle thieves. These attitudes were illustrated and reinforced by the War of Lpusi and reverberate into the present.

The Samburu relationship with Somalis has historically been quite different from that with other neighboring pastoralist groups, such as the Turkana, Pokot, and Rendille, with whom economic cooperation and in some cases intermarriage is common. Somalis and Samburu do not herd together, and Somalis view Samburu women as heathen and unclean. Samburu men occasionally marry Somalis, though this is typically considered unpropitious, leading to unexplained early deaths. As the Samburu elder Lekutaas observes, "A Somali is never good with us. A man dies if he takes a woman from Somali. More than ten people have brought a girl from the Somalis and they are no longer there [i.e., they died young]."

Interactions between Samburu and Somalis mainly occur in varying forms of trade, armed conflict, or a curious mix of the two. Most of the earliest traders in Samburu were Somalis, beginning with the early colonial caravan trade and shops established in trading centers as British rule became solidified. Several major Somali families now have a multigenerational presence in Samburu towns as traders or businesspeople. At the same time, conflict has been rife, during the Somali expansionist period before British rule and particularly in conflicts since independence. Yet ironically these roles—trader and enemy—can be oddly intertwined. In the 1970s and 1980s, for instance, Somalis were heavily involved in poaching, and despite frequent fighting with the Samburu, they also served as middlemen for ivory and rhino horn that Samburu poached (see also Hjort 1979). More recently, firearm proliferation has added a further twist to the intertwined roles of raider and trader. While Samburu characterize their acquisition of guns as being forced upon them by Somali aggression, the Samburu elder Lekirimpoto succinctly describes the role of Somalis in both supply and demand: "These Somalis who attack us, they bring us guns," expressing a widely held belief that Somalis use guns on Samburu as well as sell them to Samburu. Another elder, Lembas Letoole, describes it in a different way, emphasizing the role of Somalis in both demand and supply: "Those Somalis who attack us, they have guns. So they sell them to us. So we have those who bring the guns. And sell them to us. They just ask us if you want, and if you say 'Yes,' then you ask about the price, then they tell you its price, then they tell you, 'It's five cows.' Then you give him the cows and he gives you the gun, then others will buy. Then the Somalis can go bring more guns."

Of course, it is likely not that simple. The Somalis who sell guns to Samburu and the ones who attack may not be the same individuals, though it is plausible that the two are not so distant. Samburu and Somalis are not sworn, constant enemies with clear battle lines, but rather groups that intermingle in both conflict and trade.

The logic of this intermingling differs according to the perspective of the group. Samburu, while concerned with ethnic purity in limited situations (e.g., ritual occasions), are typically open to interethnic friendship with neighboring groups, particularly friendships that are contextually useful. For their part, Somalis do not appear to take Samburu seriously enough to truly despise them, viewing them less as enemies than as pests whose persistent petty cattle theft might provoke Somalis to action or who may occasionally serve as an inconsequential target from whom to gain additional pasture or livestock. Somalis characterize the minimal aggression on their part during the War of Lpusi as retaliation for Samburu livestock theft (allegedly undertaken with government support) or a result of poverty induced by Samburu theft while the Somali herd owners were concentrated in government camps. One Somali man fused a government conspiracy against them with Samburu lust for livestock: "So the government told Samburu, 'There is a place where the cattle [are] gathered and there is no one watching them, go and take that livestock.' So the Samburu came and found there was no one to defend the livestock and took [them]. So then the people came, they found the livestock were finished. Those guys joined the Shifta."

These accounts may have both truth and spin to them. By and large they paint Somalis as peaceful victims. Yet this is not consistent with widespread events in Kenya or elsewhere, the reputation of Somalis, or even their own self-representations. Somalis have the reputation—to some extent even among themselves—of being aggressive and expansionist. One vivid symbol of this is the Somalian flag, which portrays the five stars of the Somali people, representing iconic places that Somalis inhabit. Unfortunately—for both themselves and their neighbors—four of these stars are located outside of the borders of Somalia, representing dreams of a united Somalia that can only come at the expense of neighboring nations. This has led to border conflicts with neighboring countries, such as Kenya and Ethiopia. In their everyday interactions, Somalis can be aggressive and quick to anger, particularly if their honor has been challenged. Men carry short daggers, and Somali friends indicated to me that it is not uncommon for acquaintances to stab one another with little provocation. Boys are trained in the use of guns from an early age. In a Somali camel camp one day I heard shots ring out repeatedly, and as I sought with a little concern to determine where they were coming from—although we were in a fairly safe area, it is usually a good idea to know who is shooting at whom—a friend pointed out two figures in the distance, one small and one large. It was a Somali man guiding his small son (perhaps eight or ten) in target practice.

Somalis, however, can construe the alleged aggression as righteously finishing fights rather than provoking them. And Samburu are viewed as inherently provocative, owing partially to their perceived primitiveness and partially to their mean-spiritedness, which can also be construed as a kind of savage xenophobia. Their primitive mindset is seen in a single-minded focus on cattle, a characteristic that contributed to the war in which the Sheik was killed as well as more recent conflicts. As Ahmed, one Somali man, described it:

> According to their culture, all the cattle, every cow is theirs. So Somali have a lot of cattle when they are staying there. . . . People bring cattle to market, camels to market, hides and skins to market. And they [Samburu] don't have any other income-generating source. So Samburu don't like to see someone else with cattle. In their culture once they are circumcised, once they are initiated, they must go fight for cattle. They must bring cattle. So that's how Samburu started that war. That was 1996, '97. They killed a lot of people, took their cattle, sheep, goats.

Having been engaged in fieldwork with Samburu around that time period, I know firsthand that this characterization is not wholly accurate. While I was not in the field during the most intense period of the war that Ahmed recounts, there was chronic small-scale conflict with the Somalis during my doctoral research in 1992–94. At that time Samburu had few guns, while Somalis were well armed, having obtained military weaponry in cross-border trade from the recently destabilized Somalia, ranging from AK-47s, to machine guns, to rocket-propelled grenades. Samburu certainly still took Somali livestock—on more than one occasion I was fed meat from what I strongly suspected were stolen Somali camels—but by and large very well-armed Somalis were making use of pasture that was Samburu land and moving to the edges of core Samburu territory.

A second theme regarding primitiveness that structures Samburu-Somali relations regards the Somali attribution to Samburu of small-minded xenophobia in which all non-Samburu are ultimately construed as enemies irrespective of any history of positive interaction. This is seen directly in the story of the Sheik, where the Samburu man who was accused by Somalis of killing him (albeit falsely) was a friend of the Sheik and visited him often to sell cattle or seek treatment.[10] Fatuma, the Sheik's granddaughter, explains Samburu attitudes:

> Let me tell you something about Samburu. They could take a small child like this one, and raise her. You see? She stays in their place, they

feed her, they send her to school. But suppose, for example, a Somali killed someone. When Samburu pass that child and they say "enemy," they say "mangatti."[11] . . . Samburu, you give them milk, you feed them, and then at night they come and kill you. Because they say, "You are not my tribe." They say you are an enemy, "mangatti." We stayed with them, we were raised with them, we went to school with them. Those young men we went to school with—how many times did they break into our house, wanting to finish us?—and it was just my class-mates. And they came to kill us, until we had to move away. . . . They said, "This is not your place. Go, all of you." . . . You could be together for years. But if they see you are a different person, you are an enemy.

Samburu, then, are in the Somali view mean spirited, because they have a primitive mindset with strict lines between "us" and "them." You are Samburu or you are the enemy; if you are a Somali, to Samburu you are a Shifta. Even if you have lived together your entire lives, you will always be "mangatti."

PEOPLE OF DEMONS

Lekutaas, my closest Samburu neighbor, scoffed when I told him the Sheik's family looked down on the Samburu because their godlessness led them to commit acts unthinkable to followers of the Muslim faith:

[We Samburu] *are* people of demons, it is true, but Samburu don't kill women, Samburu don't cut people's throats.[12] You hear? And why do Somalis cut people's throats like they are goats? They are people of demons more so than Samburu. Samburu don't do things like that. . . . But Somalis, they cut people's throats like goats, they do a lot of things that aren't proper to do. Their religion: useless. You hear? Their religion isn't holy. They find people inside of settlements and burn their houses until they burn to death inside. Such people have religion? And they say it is because of their religion? Their religion. Why do they burn people? Those are religious people?

Who, then, Lekutaas asks, are the people of demons? In many ways this gets to the root of the ethnographic question of how Somalis and

Samburu understand their relationship in peace and war. It speaks, as well, to the broader theoretical goal of understanding the ways violence emerges dialogically within a cultural system that is by its very nature rooted in contradictions, as well as the analytical goals of how we as anthropologists might attempt to deal with the potent multivocality inherent in such contexts, and indeed in a vast arena of contexts that constitute the social worlds we humans inhabit. As Lekutaas illustrates, reflecting on the words of Fatuma, Somalis blame their conflicts on the primitiveness of the Samburu, who are neither Muslim nor Christian; who are unclean and do not dress properly, their murran running about, as Somalis mockingly assert, "with their buttocks hanging out"; who steal cattle because of their primitive culture and who killed the Sheik because their small-minded xenophobia labels anyone outside their own culture an enemy because they cannot distinguish between a scholar, a holy man, and their own witch doctors. Fatuma and others may be right about many of these facts and their tangible import. Nevertheless, it was unarmed Samburu who were massacred and their houses burned at Lpusi.

Lekutaas is the kind of figure who is in a position to speak to some of the unresolved contradictions in Samburu and Somali accounts. He is a Samburu—and therefore partisan—but also introspective, enabling him to speak critically of both Somalis and his own fellows. And indeed, he nimbly lays out the contradiction at the heart of the understandings and misunderstandings between the two groups. It is axiomatic that opponents in war demonize the other to justify their killing. Here Lekutaas suggests not so much that either side is wrong to demonize the other, but that ostensibly both sides are right.

Lekutaas took part in the War of Lpusi but not in killing Sheik Ahmed Yassin. An elder in his early forties at the time, he had military experience in a Kenyan unit of the British army fighting communist insurgents in the jungles of Malaysia, and consequently was able to offer advice to his peers on how to fight people armed with guns. He asserts that the raiding party of which he was a part—there were several groups, divided mainly according to clan membership—had the opportunity to raid the Sheik themselves but decided not to. What was the point in killing such an old man, he asked? And besides, since his livestock were too few to satisfy all the raiders, quarrels would naturally arise in dividing the spoils. He acknowledged that the Sheik had been friends with Samburu, that he had known him personally, and that he treated patients from all ethnic groups using powers that Lekutaas does describe as sorcery, though he doesn't know if these powers were used to aid the Shifta.

There are a few notable factual discrepancies between common Samburu and Somali narratives of the events. Particularly enigmatic is the Samburu emphasis on the presence of the red-haired hermaphrodite daughter, a sorcerer like her father, who does not appear to have ever existed. Somalis were baffled at questions about such a figure, some stating that perhaps there was a male bodyguard present but no one else—possibly his hair was died red with henna, as older Somalis sometimes do. Although it appears to be an embellishment to the narrative, it is meaningful (e.g., White 2000) to the extent that it emphasizes the abnormal, otherworldly powers of the Sheik. Other events are deemed by some to be largely unreadable. For instance, even Somalis close to the Sheik are uncertain why he did not flee, since the Somalis knew the Samburu attack was coming and most of them sought to escape toward Isiolo town before the raiders arrived. Somalis and Samburu sometimes offer explanations that are quite similar in some respects but become mirror opposites by virtue of interpretation. Samburu suggest that he did not flee because he had no fear, that he was not afraid because he felt that his sorcery would protect him. Indeed, in L's account, many Samburu did not take the opportunity to kill him because they feared his supernatural powers. As L and his son indicated, some Samburu feared that if they killed the Sheik they would die then and there, as a consequence of his sorcery. Somalis suggest, in contrast, that he may have felt protected by God because he was a holy man rather than a witch (as the Samburu suggest). Another Somali elder suggested that he was just stubborn—he would stay in his home and live there or die there. Perhaps, given that many Samburu who attacked were familiar with him and had perhaps received treatments from him for infertile wives or other problems, he felt that he had nothing to fear from his friends. Nobody, however, really knows with any certainty.

Far more significant than these minor factual discrepancies or uncertainties, however, is how Samburu and Somali narratives use essentially the same facts to convincingly argue that their opponents are "people of demons." If we consider what Somalis and Samburu mean by the epithet attached to the other, it is not easy to deny either's claim. Yet, we are not left in a position where we might say, mirroring Herodotus, that "these are the stories told variously by the Somalis and Samburu, and concerning these things we cannot say they happened one way or another." As anthropologists, we need to come to terms with them, not in order to pick who should wear the proverbial black hats and who the white, but to understand how these understandings and misunderstandings on each side lead to subject positions that are to a great degree justifiable in objective terms while simultaneously spurring indefensible violence—a contradiction that in essence constitutes a single social landscape inhabited by both sides. As seen through a multivocal ethnography of violence—violence perhaps writing in bolder script processes that are characteristic of human life more generally—we understand both sides of the story to be not necessarily more or less mendacious than the other, but rather subtly different but no less accurate versions of a truth that both memorializes past violence and frames the present and future in both war and peace.

Neither group, of course, is as Fatuma and Lekutaas have characterized the other: literally "demonic." They are people like any other, victims as well as perpetrators, yet it is hard to deny the inequities each has wrought upon the other. If Samburu truthfully describe their suffering at the hands of well-armed and aggressive enemies, Somalis assert that Samburu habitually steal their cattle and hold grudges against people who have nothing to do with attacks against them. They have no civilization and no true religion, so their primitive mindset causes them to spear in cold blood an old man sitting peacefully under a tree—a holy man, a teacher, peacefully reading his Koran beneath a tree. They are savages of the bush, of little consequence but capable of causing great harm in their petty cruelties. And those most responsible for perpetrating those cruelties suffered the wrath of their sins, the loss of their lives or their minds as the wages for shedding an innocent's blood.

"Blood, blood, blood." A bearded hero sits elsewhere babbling, shifting abruptly among several languages, only one or two of which he actually knows, tossing twigs at those around him with childlike glee. As most Samburu agree, this man saved their people, but at the cost of his own mind. Were it not for him, where would the Samburu be? Were it not for him, how would they have been saved from those people of demons, who slit men's throats as if they were goats, who burn children and women alive in their houses? Were he not a lion of a man who could thrust his spear through the chest of the sorcerer, where would the Samburu be? But he stood up while the ashes of the house were still smoldering in Lpusi and killed the Sheik even at the cost of his own sanity, temporarily blinded and permanently the prisoner of a damaged mind. And when the Somalis returned, when his son's generation was strong, others arose. When the Somalis came again to ravage their livestock and slit men's throats and burn the houses of women to the ground, other heroes arose to launch black-market Russian rockets into the mosques where the people prayed, and once again the Samburu lands were safe, and the world was whole.

· · ·

In a different anthropology, the chapter probably should have ended right there. There is no resolution, nor perhaps should there be. At our best, anthropologists translate something meaningful about a world that we have grasped deeply, but subjectively and imperfectly, to an audience who will rarely fully grasp even that translation. There are no complete answers; there are incorrect versions and even offensive ones, but we, like our subjects, always see and portray worlds through gazes that are incomplete, if also in some senses true, though in stark contradiction to other "true" versions. Where, then, do we take this?

This chapter has several aims. Ethnographically, it engages with issues of interethnic violence that, even seen through the lens of a fairly specific and historically particular case study, are resonant with broad and continuing issues in northern Kenya and indeed globally. It moreover has theoretical aims concerning the cultural construction of violence and the role that memory plays in defining relationships between groups both in times of peace and in eruptions of new violence, dimensions of which I explore in other ways and through other material throughout this book. Yet most centrally, this chapter is both about and presented through the multivocality that is intrinsic to this context of violence, to similar contexts of ethnic violence around the globe, and indeed to virtually every context human beings inhabit. I am not simply trying to present an array of voices to demonstrate that different people are always going to disagree, nor to present a multitude of disagreeing voices that I as the anthropologist can resolve with monolithic conclusions about "what really happened" and "what it means." Rather, I am aiming to explore what ethnography looks like when we embrace multivocality as an intrinsic aspect of our subject matter, an intrinsic aspect of the worlds our informants inhabit and live through, and thus necessarily an aspect of how we interpret the data. This is different from rehearsing a postmodern cliché of multiple truths; rather it explores how our subjects act in accordance with a knowledge that these multiple truths shape their worlds (even if they do not acknowledge all of them as "truths").

Thus, in the "preconclusion," the ethnographer riffs off of his Samburu friend's riff off of a Somali friend's diatribe against people who her grandfather may or may not have been implicated in slaughtering, and whose subsequent murder, therefore, may or may not have been to some degree justified. It is not a multivocality of the monolithic Samburu voice versus the monolithic Somali voice that may be mediated by the monolithic ethnographic voice that declares as best as possible what happened and constructs its true meaning for the benefit of a scholarly audience. Rather, these are Samburu and Somali versions that agree and disagree on varying points with other Samburu and Somali versions and which themselves contain contradictions that actors may or may not recognize or express.

The ethnographer's voice, then, in striving to capture these varying and contradictory voices is rightfully similarly fractured. We can hardly believe that the ethnographer really means it, for instance, when he suggests that the "world was made whole" by the act of firing black-market rockets into a mosque full of innocents. The act must necessarily strike us as repugnant. At the same time, we may respect and understand the predicament of the Samburu, who view this brutal act as beneficial in obtaining the peace they sought, and perhaps justifiable in the face of the aggression to which they had been subjected, aggression from neighbors, from sometime friends / sometime enemies whose own aggression may be justified by Samburu aggression.

Anthropologists are not, of course, oblivious to the tensions, contradictions, and discordances I emphasize here. We are trained to understand that the truths of our informants are inherently partial, but we are not always methodologically or analytically equipped to do justice to that in the accounts we produce. We understand that the lives of human beings are a messy business, more so when, as in cases of violence, so much is at stake. What this chapter has aimed to do is to push us and suggest directions where, rather than simplifying this messiness for the sake of analytical or theoretical clarity, we as anthropologists embrace the ambiguities and contradictions within ethnographies that mirror, and thus more truly capture, the uncertainties in the world that our subjects (and ourselves) inhabit.

5

BAD FRIENDS
AND GOOD ENEMIES

Let us consider Sartre's most famous line from his most famous play. In the play, three people are condemned to hell, but not the fiery hell of the Christian imagination; this is the Hotel Hell, complete with a valet. Trapped for a sleepless eternity in a stark room, their suffering is wrought by the words of their companions, refractions of themselves through these companions, whom they cannot escape, cannot escape forever, for as the title of the play tells us, there is no exit, and "hell is other people" (Sartre 1958).

Let us move now from an imagined hell of French existentialism to northern Kenya, as the Samburu elder Lekutaas contrasts the relationship of his people with their longtime neighbors, the Pokot—a relationship of ritually sanctioned peace that formed long ago after a now barely remembered war—and the Turkana, with whom they have frequent conflict:

> [Samburu and Pokot] made an oath between them. They exchanged spears. The ground was dug and the head of the spear was put into the earth and buried. And then each shot an arrow into their own cow, so that blood was drawn from each, and the Pokot drank from the Samburu cow and the Samburu drank from the Pokot cow. [Since then] anyone who killed a person from Pokot, he goes mad. . . . And that is

how it is also for a Pokot man who killed a Samburu. Anyone who kills someone from the other tribe must go mad, they must go mad. . . . But they have never been friends. The Samburu never need them. The Turkana are better, we fight with them but there are a lot of Turkana among the Samburu. . . . There is no one from Samburu who goes to the Pokot, and even there is no Pokot who stays with us. . . . But Turkana are free, there are very many of them among the Samburu. Three quarters!

There is an odd triad, then, formed at the confluence of Samburu with Pokot and Turkana. The Pokot and Samburu were long bound together to forever do no harm to the other, but this in a context where doing harm to your neighbors, now and then anyway, is to a great extent the normal course of events. Irrespective of long periods of peace, your neighbors (or even your friends) have cattle you covet, have pasture you may compete for. Living side by side always brings the likelihood of provocation. Perhaps, because of the oath, they know they can go ahead and steal your goat, or go ahead and keep your lost cow because there is really nothing you can do about it. If you try to do something about it—take the cow back by force, spear the person who has your goat— you are bound to go insane or die. Thus the Pokot and Samburu—like Sartre's characters in *No Exit,* perhaps like some married couples, or colleagues in lifelong service together at a university—could treat each other in unpleasant ways, treat each other in ways that they could not treat others. If one takes seriously the half-joking truism "A well-armed society is a polite society," the Pokot and Samburu may be seen as two groups who—by their own accounts—have put their weapons aside, and all manners and most affection along with them.

As Lentiyoo, a Samburu Lkishilli elder, characterizes the relationship between the Samburu and the Pokot: "No, no, they have no friendship. It is just an oath . . . so that we are no longer enemies, we no longer fight." The Turkana are essentially the opposite. The Samburu have long fought with the Turkana, chronically and often bitterly. If there is one group that could aptly be termed archenemies with the Samburu, it is the Turkana. And yet they are also friends—as Samburu express it, true friends—with whom genuine affection exists. As another Samburu elder says, "Wars with the Turkana, even if they go and fight, they will just fight, but they liked each other. When they make friendship, they make friendship that will last."

In this chapter I explore this ironic conundrum, considering the ways peace and war are mediums for refracting the identities of self and other. I will do so largely from a Samburu perspective—owing to my longer history among them, and consequently my richer cultural understanding of them—though playing this off Pokot and Turkana reflections on the same dynamic. Although the content of Samburu stereotypes of Pokot and Turkana is accepted to a significant degree among all the groups, the interpretations can sometimes be quite different. For instance, Samburu portray themselves as relatively wealthy compared with Pokot or Tur-kana, and commensurately Samburu are generally characterized as having a more aristocratic bearing. While Samburu tend to positively value what they see as a kind of nobility, their neighbors typically regard it in nega-tive terms, as being highfalutin, effete, or leading to foolish hubris.

Samburu characterize the Pokot as poor people, variously described as "people with big stomachs" (i.e., bloated from disease) or "people with eyelashes" or "tears dripping from their eyes," as though suffering from chronic eye infection. The Turkana are regarded as also poor, but tough and hardworking, although brutish—ready to do anything to survive. Turkana are well known for taking whatever work they can get, and many Turkana work as herders for the Samburu. As a Samburu elder characterizes the Turkana, "A Turkana who has nothing, who feeds on ostriches, can come and attack you. He has nothing. He has only one hen, but he comes and takes your cows." One clear cultural marker of perceived Samburu superiority is that both Pokot and Turkana will eat almost anything. This pertains in particular to wild game, and the Sam-buru joke that in areas where the Turkana and Pokot live, the only creatures you find alive are snakes and bees. The Turkana take a certain pride in their willingness to eat anything—it is a sign of their strength and resilience, as opposed to the effete, perhaps over-mannered Samburu. The Pokot—who also eat a wide variety of wild animals—also take issue with the Turkana diet, particularly their practice of eating donkeys.

Samburu, then, view each of these neighbors as flawed—not surpris-ingly, given that ethnocentrism is likely one of our few cultural univer-sals. The Turkana are stereotyped as something between a wild animal and an overgrown child, lacking basic qualities that should have been developed in a fully enculturated adult, but raw rather than immoral. While the Turkana might be seen as an untamed force, the Pokot are stereotyped as pitiful little things. Considering these in tandem, I suggest that from a Samburu point of view, these are two sides of the same coin: being "bad friends" in the case of Pokot and "good enemies" in the case of the Turkana are drawn from what might be regarded as fundamental aspects of human relationships, as well as the specific ways Samburu map these onto their own cultural categories. I aim to examine both relationships and the ways they form a triad in Samburu understandings and are colored by the memories and consequences of violence. In doing so, I engage with the central question of the book: how do neighbors—often friends and partners in economic cooperation—become killers of one another, and then move back to conditions of peace. Consequently, I consider how conditions of peace sow the seeds for conditions of war, and how the conditions of war similarly sculpt the landscape of peace. In this context, I explore how being "friends" or "enemies" is often not as simple as in commonplace portrayals. There are many different types of each relationship, in northern Kenya as elsewhere. Thus, by exploring in detail the contours of these dynamics in a specific context, the chapter aims to shed light on how these may lead to peace and violence in broader contexts across the globe.

FORMS OF FRIENDSHIP IN SAMBURU

Examining the nature of the Samburu relationship with the Pokot on one hand and with the Turkana on the other requires an understanding of the ways in which "friendship" is constituted in Samburu.[1] Samburu characterize their relationship with both groups, at least sometimes, as a form of friendship. Consequently, how Samburu view these groups and the relationships with them are refracted through the lens of the types of friendship Samburu have with other Samburu. As with any instance of translation, there can be difficulties in the extent to which a concept translates from one cultural context into another. Multiple types of Samburu relationships could be readily glossed as friendship but have very different characteristics in regard to how they are formed, what type of affect is presumed to exist, and proper forms of behavior. An exegesis of all of these is beyond the present scope, but it is important to highlight a key opposition between friendships predicated on affection and those predicated on respect. These map reasonably closely to classic anthropological characterizations of the distinction between joking and avoidance relationships (Radcliffe-Brown 1940). The core Samburu term for "friend" or "friendship" in general is *sotua,* which can refer to either relationship, though its core meaning focuses on those in which affection is paramount. Relationships predicated on affection may involve transgressions of proper forms of conduct—affection can even develop through less than proper forms of conduct—while those built around respect are predicated exclusively on proper forms of conduct.

Various types of relationships that have at least some component of friendship could be characterized as "respect-based." Most obvious is an institution termed *lang'atta,* which is a formal friendship formed between kinship groups in settling a dispute. For instance, if a member of one family or kinship group has killed a member of another group, for a period of time there is a full break in social relations between the groups, but when it is eventually mended (with the passing of time, negotiations, and compensation payments), lang'atta will exist between them. While this is viewed as a close relationship, there is no requirement to have affection for the "friend," only to treat the person like a proper friend. A similar distinction between respect and affection may be seen in kinship relations. The term *apiyo* may be used to address someone whose family or clan is the same as one's mother's natal clan, while *lautani* is used to refer to one's wife's family. These terms are somewhat flexible; a clan your mother came from (apiyo) is also a clan that has given your family a wife, and Spencer (1965) notes that apiyo is sometimes a friendly, affectionate relationship and sometimes based on respect (typically decided by the dispositions of the group that has given the wife). In my observation, however, while lautani is generally used respectfully, *apiyo* is used reciprocally, affectionately, and rather promiscuously—it sometimes appears that almost anyone can figure out a way that they are someone else's apiyo. Ostensibly, Samburu relations with the Turkana are analogous to the first type of friendship or kinship relation—affection without respect—while the Pokot represent the second, respect without affection.

The key concept through which to understand this dynamic is *nkanyit,* translated roughly as "respect," which is the most fundamental Samburu value (Spencer 1965; Holtzman 2009). Nkanyit is in some ways a peculiar concept in that it is predicated principally on outward appearances. While Samburu acknowledge that it to some degree reflects an inner state, Samburu hold firmly that what is in someone's head is ultimately unknowable, such that people can only be judged by their actions. Moreover, nkanyit may create obligations—even conflicting ones—that cannot always be met. It is a truism in Samburu that you should show respect to elders by giving them small amounts of money, food, or tobacco, but clearly it would be impossible to show this respect to every elder without completely bankrupting oneself. Consequently, nkanyit is based on maintaining appearances and not visibly showing disrespect. As a result, nkanyit, the highest good in the world, may ultimately be maintained through deceit (Holtzman 2009). It is not as important to actually be good, but rather to appear good—or at least not be caught being bad. Thus, for instance, refusing to give your father tobacco may be a breach of nkanyit, because you have openly refused something, albeit something small, to someone you should respect completely. In contrast, secretly starving your elderly father to death is not a breach of nkanyit (even if it may be bad in other ways) because it does not involve openly refusing him anything or defying his stated will. Similarly, one need not be truly generous with guests, but only to appear to be generous, as exemplified in the Samburu aphorism to "cheat the eye" when feeding guests—that is, one may conserve scarce resources without breaching respect by arranging the food served to guests in a way that makes it appear to be more than it actually is.

Nkanyit is cultivated by the Samburu over time. Children do not naturally have it, and while it is modeled and to some extent promoted in them, it is expected that they by and large lack it. It is also gender based. While it is expected and valued in women, it is neither as fundamental to their self-definition nor believed to be as fully developed. In men, developing nkanyit is a long process. Indeed, the institution of murranhood—in which young men spend roughly the years fifteen to thirty as unmarried bachelor warriors—is filled with prohibitions that in part serve to develop the qualities that an elder should have. Although murran are considered to be "hot" in temperament, there are extensive restrictions on their behavior, especially in regard to food. They may not eat food that has been seen by women, and they may eat only in the company of other murran. These restrictions serve a variety of ends. They teach proper social forms of respect, self-discipline, and putting one's social obligations above one's material needs. The projected outcome is that as they move into elderhood, they will be polite (if not always kind), relatively soft-spoken (though firm), and even-tempered.

Not everyone (either in reality or in perception) actually achieves this ideal standard of behavior, and just as there are stereotyped ways of being a virtuous person, there are also prototypical ways of breaching nkanyit. Yet all ways of transgressing nkanyit are not equal. Some forms are simply all bad, for instance being mean-spirited or nasty. One can also violate nkanyit by being a stingy person (*laroi*) or greedy (*lobu*), and although these sound fairly similar in English, Samburu generally view these two very differently. A stingy person (laroi; pl. laron) is cold, refusing to share anything with anyone, to the extent of being essentially antisocial. In contrast, lobu people may be reputed to breach norms of sharing but simply because they excessively desire things for themselves; unlike stingy people, they may be extremely social. A lobu person may circulate among the homesteads looking for something to eat. They may, then, cross proper social boundaries but be talkative, friendly, and lively companions. Consequently, elders who are regarded as lobu—despite not carrying themselves with nkanyit—can be well liked. One might say that the lobu person "lives large," with a friendly and manly bearing. Lobu people can be gregarious, and—though not exactly virtuous, given that they may not truly exhibit nkanyit—they may be considered basically good people, while a laroi is a small, cold thing of no consequence.

As this relates to friendship, people may have a lot of affection for a lobu person, and such a person may, in fact, have many friends (perhaps more than a typical person, even if their flaws are well known). While it may seem paradoxical that people can be well liked while displaying deficiencies in the highest social value, nkanyit, the respect that defines nkanyit is in some ways the opposite of affection, or perhaps creates a social world in which emotion (whether positive or negative) does not play a role. Nkanyit ostensibly involves suppressing emotion, behaving in a manner that is not modified by either positive or negative feelings. The lobu person has emotions, and while it can be expressed as greed, this greed can break through the coldness of nkanyit, such that a lobu person can be good-hearted, friendly, and well liked as an ironic consequence of a sometimes-flawed sense of respect.

The character flaw archetypes that Samburu attribute to their peers model the ways they understand their neighbors. To the extent that nkanyit takes a long time to cultivate, it is not surprising that Samburu would hold that their neighbors lack it, albeit in varying ways and to varying degrees. Somalis perhaps come closest to what Samburu regard as proper adult behavior, being brave and full of pride and self-regard, though they are seen as hot-tempered and overly quick to anger. Kikuyu, as discussed in chapter 3, while respected for their intelligence, are cowardly, greedy, and dishonest. These flaws, while defined in respect to Samburu values, do not fit a clear Samburu character type. Turkana and Pokot, in contrast, do fit such types. Turkana are like prototypical lobu people, gluttonous (as would be expected of people who are like children) and lacking in manners, but in a way that is gregarious, "living large." On the other hand, the Pokot are prototypical *laron,* covetous and stingy. The Samburu stereotype of them is that they are poor (or at least appear to be poor),[2] cowardly, and petty thieves.

These are, of course, gross ethnocentric stereotypes. Individuals of all these ethnic groups behave in a wide range of ways and may characterize culturally ideal behavior quite differently. It is notable, however, that Samburu descriptions of typical or idealized behaviors and attitudes are largely consonant with Turkana and Pokot descriptions of their own behaviors and attitudes. While I would hedge this slightly because my research among Turkana and Pokot is nowhere near as extensive as among the Samburu, such that my level of nuance and certainty is considerably lower, I suggest that Turkana idealized behavior tends toward what Samburu see as characteristic of lobu people: outwardly emotional and ready to do anything or engage with anyone to gain sustenance. Pokot behavior tends toward how Samburu characterize laron, valuing cleverness and stealth in ways that Samburu regard as unmanly cowardice. Thus, the differences are not so much disagreements about behavior or ideal behavior (though doubtless some of these exist) but differing moral valuations of these behaviors. That is, while among the Samburu what a lobu person does is bad, among the Turkana it is positively valued, and the same may be said to a lesser degree of laron behavior among the Pokot.

THE BASIS OF FRIENDSHIP WITH THE POKOT

At present one certainly cannot call the Samburu and Pokot "friends." As discussed in greater detail in chapter 2, they have engaged in low-level conflict for several years, resulting in numerous deaths (mostly combatants, though not exclusively) and the theft of thousands of livestock from each side.[3] Life in border areas is characterized by insecurity, with the threat and sometimes the reality of attack by neighboring communities well armed with modern automatic weapons. Each side has initiated a number of major attacks, involving several hundred raiders, and innumerable smaller skirmishes and thefts. In peace, however—prior to this recent war—the Pokot and Samburu presented a strange conundrum. They were, for at least a century, ritually bound as friends, tied together by an oath that forbade violence. Yet at the same time they appear to by and large not have liked each other. They did not intermarry to any significant degree, as each did with other neighboring groups—even before the conflict occurred. Samburu, moreover, had many negative attitudes regarding the Pokot, particularly that they were poor in wealth and spirit, and wild and terrible thieves. Similarly negative stereotypes of the Samburu appear to have existed among the Pokot.

Despite this broad characterization, there certainly was friendship between specific individuals and sometimes broader cooperation between the groups, for instance in joint herding, or as allies in warfare against other groups. For instance, a massive joint raid against the Turkana at Lolkokorr in the late 1990s ostensibly turned the tables in a war that the Samburu had been getting the worst of, and stopped significant Turkana raiding of the Samburu. The Samburu would likely not have been successful in this effort without the assistance of the better armed and more experienced Pokot. When interethnic clashes occurred with Kikuyu in Laikipia in 1998 (see chapter 3), the Pokot and Samburu stood together in routing their opponents. And yet it is not clear, by and large, that the two groups ever actually liked each other. Because hostilities had already begun between the groups at the time I began intensive research on the relationship between them, there is certainly some bias in some accounts I have recorded. However, these are nonetheless consonant with stereotypes that I have been long aware of (from the Samburu side in particular) and long-standing oddities about the relationship between the groups.

I will explore these issues in a moment. But first, let me detail precisely how the relationship between the two groups came about, and what it entailed. The relationship between these two groups is ostensibly an interethnic version of what Samburu term *lang'ata*. As discussed above, among Samburu, lang'ata forms between families who have experienced ill will in the past, for instance if they fought and a member of one family perhaps killed someone from the other. Eventually peace may be brought about between them with an oath that forms a close, yet circumspect, bond. It is a kind of friendship, but one born of the resolution of a past conflict rather than long-standing goodwill. That is, what exists in lang'ata is nkanyit—mutual respect and fear—rather than necessarily affection.

The relationship between the Pokot and Samburu was similarly born in the aftermath of a long-ago war. The cause, time frame, and events of this war are blurry. Pokot suggest that it occurred in the late nineteenth or early twentieth century, while Samburu place the oath beyond living memory. The Samburu timeline seems more plausible, because their long-term migratory movements took them far from the Pokot—from the Lake Baringo area of Kenya, where they would have made the oath, to the area of southern Ethiopia—for several generations between when they claim the oath was made and when frequent contact was reinitiated. Many knowledgeable Samburu informants can give a detailed oral history going back to at least the 1880s, so it is unlikely that there would be a knowledge gap concerning something this important that occurred after that date. However, some Samburu suggest that the oath was renewed around the time when the Merisho age set were murran (in the early 1900s), so it is certainly possible that the Pokot are referencing this renewal rather than the original oath. One Samburu informant—whose father was born around 1900 and had a strong grasp on oral history— placed the oath around the time of the Lkipeku age set, which was initiated in the 1830s.

Exactly why the oath was made is debated. It is generally held that it followed a terrible war in which many people were killed. It is not agreed how this war was particularly terrible—war is, of course, by its very nature terrible—or why it, among countless other wars with other groups, resulted in an oath. While Pokot are wont to assert that both sides were decimated, Samburu more often claim that the Pokot begged for peace after a punishing defeat. As one Samburu elder asserted, "Then the Pokot just came to plead, it was just the Pokot who came to plead with us. So then there was no way that a person who came pleading could be turned down. Because it was said that you cannot spear someone in the palm of their hand. When a person stretches out his hand to you [begging mercy] . . . that person cannot be killed." The exact reason for this oath cannot be determined. Irrespective of whether it was a mutual decision based on horrific deaths on both sides (as Pokot informants claim) or the result of a Pokot entreaty for mercy, Samburu vary in their accounts of the extent to which the oath actually constituted "friendship." Some assert that it wasn't friendship at all—just an agreement to not kill each other. Pokot were disliked, some claim, not even regarded as true humans. As Lekutaas puts it, "It is like they [Pokot] are not categorized as people, the Samburu looked down upon them because they are some sort of people without eyelashes, with tears dripping from their eyes so Samburu have never wanted them at all."

He continues by asserting that the oath with the Pokot was simply a gesture of charity toward a defeated people, which created no kind of friendship with them: "Oh, Pokot! In history there is nowhere that Pokot came together with Samburu. . . . They are people who are despised by Samburu. They despise them! We don't want them [Jon: But you took an oath.] They came crying! Useless people! They came crying to Samburu, like very poor people." Lenguris, a Mekuri elder, gives a different explanation, claiming that there had been friendship between the Pokot and Samburu, even long ago: "They were living together then. And so then, as they live together, they like each other, people who stay together, they come to like each other. And so they never wanted to provoke each other." Many Samburu assert that there was never any kind of friendship with the Pokot. Lentiyoo, an Lkishilli elder, differentiates between an agreement to not fight and actual affection or goodwill. "No, no, they have no friendship. It is just lang'ata [i.e., a ritual relationship]. It shows that where these people have made lang'ata they fought and very many people were killed. And then they made lang'ata. As a result of that lang'ata, which makes it so that we are no longer enemies, we no longer fight. But we don't like each other. But there is no love between us."

The creation of this oath was, however, unique, an occurrence that no informant from either the Pokot or the Samburu has been able to adequately explain to me. Both groups have fought numerous wars with essentially all their neighbors. The Samburu and Turkana, for instance, fight frequently and later return to peace, as is the case with other groups. And yet they simply enter into a temporary truce. The Turkana and

Pokot fight frequently but seem to maintain a hatred that leads them to fight again. This is, then, an unusual relationship.

The oath puts strong, supernaturally based strictures upon members of both groups, namely that killing a member of the other group will lead to insanity. As Lekutaas describes it, "Anyone who killed a person from Pokot, he goes mad. Did you hear about this old man by the name of Lenaingisae, Lenaingisae who was singing at Maralal? [He killed a Pokot] and he went crazy and he tied strange things all over his body and just sang and sang, going crazy. And that is how it is also for a Pokot man who killed a Samburu. Anyone who kills someone from the other tribe must go mad, they must go mad." I had, in fact, met this man in Maralal many times but had not realized the cause of his madness. Lenguris, of the Mekuri age set, further explained that both Lenaingisae and a Pokot man who suffered a similar fate had killed accidentally—not knowing that the cattle thieves they were pursuing were from the ethnic group they were bound by oath to not harm. As Lenguris explains,

> Lenaingisae, when he killed a Suk [Pokot] man, it was that Suk man who just came to steal cattle, and the warrior just ran to pursue the cattle taken by the thieves.[4] . . . And so he became mad. He never made a family. He just became part of the Maralal streets. He was even killed by a vehicle. He just kept crossing in front of vehicles and was killed by one. . . . Then there was a Suk man who killed a Samburu. He killed a man from Letimba family, of the Kimaniki age set. . . . They went to steal Pokot cows, and the Pokot went to ambush along the path, they waited along the path and the Pokot killed that person. And that Pokot man—because I went there myself, I was doing livestock trading and know him myself—he had had a wife and livestock, he was even a rich man. Now there is not a single thing. It is said he went to die in the bush.

Arguably, the oath to not kill makes stealing more prevalent: if you steal from Turkana (or even from your own ethnic group), you are risking death. If a Samburu steals from a Pokot, or a Pokot from a Samburu, the thief (until recently) could not be harmed. If that person was harmed, it was only by accident, and the consequences to the person who did harm could be dire—ostensibly a living death. Consequently, there are long-standing discourses about the brazen thievery of both sides. As one Samburu elder describes the Pokot, "They take stealing as if it is beautiful thing"—they enjoy it just for its own sake, and thus cannot refrain from it. Most notably, there is a stock story that the Samburu use to illustrate the principal problem with the Pokot, why they are so hard to live with. This account, rendered here by Lekutaas, has been told to me numerous times by many Samburu (even before the war, though with greater frequency after), replete with gestures. "Once a Pokot woman goes out and finds goat kids, she puts one in there [*gesturing as if to pull open a cloak and put her hand inside*], inside her cloth, once she comes across something she takes it with her, she can find no reason to not take something with her. If she comes across a goat kid, she takes it with her, just anything she comes across, a cup, anything, whatever. A Pokot woman cannot go past anything she has seen. And even the men are like that."

Notably, Pokot give virtually the same account of the Samburu, down to the same pantomime. As one Pokot elder explained, "The problem with Samburu is that they are terrible thieves. I think it is just in their blood. Even an old woman, if she comes to your home and asks for a cup of water, you will find that she just slips it in here [*gesturing, as above*]. It isn't just animals. Even very small things. Like a cooking pot. They even steal children." The last reference was to an incident that Samburu asserted was a misunderstanding. A small Pokot child, they claimed, had wandered off and was found by Samburu, who took care of him until a long time afterward, when his parents found him and he was returned. As this was related to me only after the war had started, it is difficult to know exactly how it was viewed at the time it occurred.

Clearly these perceptions are colored by the fact that some of these interviews were conducted during a period of violence between the groups. However, Samburu statements, although likely accentuated by the conflict, were not dissimilar to stereotypes they held of the Pokot during times of peace. Samburu who lived in ethnically mixed zones, particularly Laikipia, often talked about the Pokot tendency to steal, whether as a visitor to your home or collecting a lost goat. One telling incident occurred in 2001—when there was no ill will between the Samburu and Pokot. A Pokot boy, Tinga, had come to live at the homestead of Lekeren, who was my host in Samburu. One day Lekeren's house was locked while he was away, and we needed to retrieve something from inside. Tinga arrived on the scene and managed to find a way in. Our Samburu neighbors attributed his ability to get in to the fact that he was a Pokot, and hence an *mkora*—a Swahili word that technically means robber, but which is in everyday speech extended to any shady character.

One of the most peculiar dimensions to the Samburu-Pokot "friendship" is the general avoidance of intermarriage. Samburu intermarry with many groups, including those with whom there is frequent conflict. The most important example is the Turkana, with whom there is widespread intermarriage despite periods of often-brutal conflict. Intermarriage with groups such as the Dassanetch (when Samburu lived farther north in the late nineteenth century), the Rendille, related Maasai groups, and the Meru has long been common, and marriages with other groups, such as the Boran and Somalis, have also occurred, though the latter are generally more recent.[5] Yet intermarriage did not occur with the Pokot, despite their apparently very close relationship.

Informants give varying accounts of this, some emphasizing the closeness, some emphasizing the enmity, and some oddly both. The Kimaniki elder Lekutaas, for instance, emphasizes the extent to which Samburu dislike the Pokot, seeing this as the primary reason that they do not marry. Others who take a rosier view of long-standing Samburu-Pokot relations focus on the closeness of the bond. Intermarriage, which commonly occurs between friends, does not occur between people who are too close. For instance, although young Samburu have premarital relationships within their clans, in marriage they are clan exogamous. In the view of some, marrying a Pokot would be part and parcel of the dangers inherent in breaching this official friendship. That is, rather than being unmarriageable because there is something wrong with them, Pokot are *too* close to marry. As one Samburu elder asserted, and his neighbor expanded on, in response to the question of why they don't marry:

Maybe because of that oath. Because it is possible that it could reach a point where people get to fear each other because it is like your sister, because of that oath. Because you cannot even afford to differ with these people because of that. And you also can't afford to make a mistake. [*A neighbor continues:*] So, for instance, doesn't the Loimusi [clan] have clans where they fear the girls? So that is what these Pokot girls are like. It is like these people you fear [i.e., avoid, respect], with whom you have lang'ata. And so with people you fear/respect, then you cannot marry the girls from those people. And so it is that way because of that oath. Because of that oath.

Lentiyoo, an Lkirroro elder, oddly takes both views of why Samburu cannot marry Pokot. They are simultaneously too close and also too awful to marry:

> They are very bad enemies, totally bad. And even you know, also because of that relationship with them, they cannot be good for us if we married them. [The wife] could not bring prosperity. She cannot prosper, because they are like our brothers. Because of that blood, because of something called blood. It is usually bad, an oath made from blood is bad. And because that friendship was created out of that oath of blood, and then he goes to marry a girl from that tribe, they cannot be fit with him. And so what I see is the worst thing is that we couldn't match so much because we have that relationship with them. And then they cannot match. And the second thing is that they are very bad enemies, very bad enemies. Yes, they are bad enemies.

This "friendship" is, then, oddly ambivalent. While they are characterized as the closest of friends, closer than friends, they are also drawn as "very bad enemies" who are, as a whole, strongly disliked.

THE BASIS OF "ENEMYSHIP" WITH THE TURKANA

The Turkana's relationship to the Samburu is almost diametrically opposed to that of the Pokot. The oath between the Samburu and Pokot is such that they are required to be "friends" but in a way that essentially obviates true friendship. They cannot harm each other but also do not particularly like each other. I suggest that their dislike for each other is to some extent a consequence of their forced peace. In contrast, the Samburu and the Turkana may be considered archenemies. In the course of the twentieth century, there were at least three periods of extreme violence: the early precolonial period (when the Samburu were nearly wiped out), the 1970s era known as Ngoroko, and the 1990s, when Samburu finally acquired guns and fought the Turkana to a stalemate. Lower-level or sporadic violence is chronic. Only during British colonialism, when violence was controlled by a strong government presence, was conflict not widespread, though even then it was not unheard-of. Indeed, the Turkana might be viewed as the prototypical enemy of the Samburu, the one with whom conflict is always possible, the one most likely to steal your livestock and to whom you would be most likely to look if you wanted to steal animals. Potential for conflict with the Turkana is a constant of Samburu life, and for Turkana living near the Samburu, it is part of Turkana life (though McCabe [2004] notes that more distant Turkana view the Samburu more as potential prey than predators). Yet, as I will describe in more detail below, the relationship between the two groups is also very close, often characterized by genuine affection.

The Turkana are the Samburu's single most consistent enemy. Since well before the colonial period, the specter of warfare has always loomed, and there have been several periods of major conflict between the Turkana and Samburu since significant European contact began in the early twentieth century. The first recorded instance of major conflict between the groups occurred right at the time of European contact and continued at least in incipient form until an actual European presence was established in the area. Captain Stigand, traveling north to Sudan, documents brokering a peace deal when he passed through the Baragoi area in 1908 (Stigand 1910). He is said to have established the official ethnic boundary between the two sides, which follows the main road passing through what is now Baragoi town, the western side of the road being Turkana and the eastern side Samburu. This peace, if it had any substance at all, did not last, and by the late 1910s there was brutal warfare over control of the rich grazing area of the Lbarta plains east of Baragoi—an area believed to have been the sphere of influence of the Purko Maasai before they were moved south by the British in the Second Maasai Move of 1913. In this conflict, the Turkana apparently were by far getting the better of the Samburu, and the Samburu still recall entire settlements being annihilated as the Turkana moved east. The Samburu were saved by most accounts through the intervention of the colonial government. This intervention was not principally for the benefit of the Samburu; rather, the Samburu proved to be useful proxies in government efforts to pacify the Turkana. Thus, the colonial government, with the aid of the

Samburu, pushed back the Turkana and subjected them to colonial authority. These events certainly framed colonial perceptions of both groups, the virile and brutal Turkana as opposed to the effete and mercurial Samburu. Moreover, the colonial authorities then largely perceived the Samburu as indebted to the British for their very presence in Samburu, claiming that without their intervention there would be no Samburu remaining north of the Uaso Ngiro River. This did not, however, result in long-term antagonism between the Turkana and the colonial government or a pronounced love for it by Samburu (at least on an individual level). As the British established a permanent presence in Samburu, it was Turkana who filled out the native staff, while Samburu showed disdain for all forms of wage work.

The colonial period was a time of relative peace. While there were some periods of tension and mild violence, the presence of the British kept large-scale conflict under control. Post-independence, however, there have been several periods of hostility between the two groups. The first was the Ngoroko attacks in the late 1970s and early 1980s, when well-armed Turkana raiders engaged in large-scale raids against Samburu and other neighboring groups, resulting in significant loss of livestock and human life. It is well documented that the Ngoroko were, in fact, more than just traditional stock thieves; rather, it was a paramilitary organization combining Turkana ex-military personnel and youth of fighting age (Oba 1992), and in 1978 it was linked to national politics as an alleged hit squad for political assassination (Daily Nation 2001). The Samburu were hit quite hard by the Ngoroko until the early 1980s, when the Kenyan army crushed the Ngoroko following raids on the herds of the commander of the armed forces, who was a Samburu. The mid-1990s also saw significant conflict on a pattern similar to that of the Ngoroko period, with heavily armed Turkana launching major raids deep into Samburu territory. Normalcy returned only after the Samburu began to acquire guns in significant numbers, enabling them to both effectively raid Turkana and kill large numbers of raiders. Raids and counterraids began again in 2008 after a period of relatively good relations, though they did not result (as initially feared) in another stint of widespread violence.

Yet, despite warfare, sometimes brutal and occurring on a regular basis, Samburu connections to the Turkana are arguably closer than with any other ethnic group.[6] There are high rates of intermarriage between them, as well as frequent adoptions of children. By and large these adoptions appear to be disproportionately in the direction of Turkana joining the Samburu, but there are also large numbers of Turkana with Samburu roots, some of whom sought refuge with the Turkana during famines or other catastrophes. Indeed, while Turkana have very different origin stories for themselves, which are well researched and certainly more accurate for the ethnic group as a whole (e.g., Lamphear 1992), the Samburu often construct the Turkana as ostensibly lost Samburu. One Mekuri elder, for instance, dismissed comparisons between the Pokot— who he believed were simply malicious—and the Turkana, whom he described benevolently as "just lost children of Samburu." Another elder gives a more detailed account, tracing Turkana origins to the disastrous time in the late nineteenth century known as *Mutai* (literally "the finishing [of people and livestock]"), when a combination of livestock and human epidemics created famine and disarray among the Samburu, such that young people took to the bush to fend for themselves before being initiated into adulthood (see also Straight 2006). As this elder explains:

> When Mutai killed people, when Mutai killed the people and big boys like these ones who are now being circumcised went into the bush, they went and became strong. And the boys and the girls went, they just went and they went for good. And as they had gone for good from that place, they went and they stayed until they became grown people. And so it was through that that the Turkana came to be. And so now, with wars with the Turkana, even if they go and fight, they will just fight but they liked each other. When they make friendship they make friendship that will last . . . we are even related in our origins.

Turkana women marrying into Samburu is extremely common, and it is also quite common for Turkana boys or men to be adopted by Samburu families. A high proportion of Samburu families have Turkana origins, some in the father's line and others from women who married in. Lekutaas states, "Turkana are free, there are very many of them among the Samburu. Three quarters!" suggesting that most Samburu families are related to the Turkana. Sometimes women marry Samburu, and upon marriage (and the accompanying initiation ceremonies) become

Samburu, while males may become Samburu after a period of living with a family. Often these are poor individuals who are quasi-employed as herders by wealthier Samburu. If they stay for a long period, the family often decides to formally make them part of the family. Principally this involves initiation into a Samburu age set. The person for whom they have been herding adopts the Turkana as a son and sponsors his circumcision. Following completion of initiation rituals, he is no longer considered Turkana, but is a member of his Samburu family. Of course, his Turkana birth will not likely be forgotten. Thus, during times of conflict between Samburu and Turkana, an individual with Turkana roots—especially men who were born and perhaps spent part of their lives as a Turkana—will create suspicion and perhaps tension. Other Turkana families living among the Samburu may simply assimilate, though their Turkana roots are still recognized. These assimilated Turkana have an official designation as *Ltigira,* literally "they stay quiet" (because of their inability to speak Samburu properly).

Samburu and Turkana can often be close friends. In border zones in particular, it is not uncommon for Turkana and Samburu to live in close proximity, and it is common for Samburu to hire Turkana herders. Much more than Samburu, Turkana seek work of various forms outside of herding their own livestock. Most of the first government workers in Samburu District during the colonial period were Turkana. Samburu showed disdain for all forms of work apart from pastoralism, while some Turkana eagerly sought out such work. One rather whimsical example comes from the colonial period, when Samburu murran were forced onto road gangs as collective punishment for livestock theft and murder. While Samburu hated this unpaid work, colonial officials claimed that the Turkana would actually try to sneak onto the road gangs in hope of future gainful employment (CPK 1934). Turkana communities can be found outside of their home areas throughout much of northern Kenya—in Isiolo and Laikipia, for instance—largely as a consequence of the search for casual work.

Because of this Turkana tendency to leave their home areas, significant numbers of Turkana live with the Samburu. This puts them in an ambiguous position during times of conflict or potential conflict. On one hand, Samburu suspect them of being spies who will go back to their own people and communicate information about the location of Samburu

FIGURE 9.   A Turkana family.

herds and how well they are defended. On the other hand, such Turkana friends can also serve the opposite function, warning their Samburu friends of an impending raid. As Lentiyoo, an Lkishilli elder, explains:

The Turkana, there are very many of them living among the Samburu. For there are those that people made herdsmen. And the person would just stay, for a short while, not very long, and then you hear someone being told, "I want to go and see my family." And now he goes to Lbarta (Baragoi region), and of course he gives out information, our secrets. Then also he is good on both sides, because he may go and hear that there is a Turkana invasion that is coming, he comes to this side and tells Samburu that Turkana raiders are coming. And also he can go from here and then take the secrets of these people and go to tell the Turkana that the cows are here, and that the place is a certain way. And so he lives on both sides.

It is difficult to know which in reality happens more, but it is important that Samburu recognize each as a common practice. Moreover, in border zones Samburu and Turkana may be on good terms, particularly on an individual basis. Thus, these friendships can serve to give warning to the opposing side about impending attacks. As the Samburu elder Lekonchella relates, "Look [in Baragoi], Samburu live on one side of town and Turkana on the other. So we as friends can just go to each other and we drink together, and we talk together, you can even tell me that there is a group of Turkana that is coming to attack us. . . . We can just joke together, then even talk secrets. With the Turkana there is no raid where we don't know when they are coming."

Turkana are enemies, but enemies with whom they are on good terms. They are, in a sense, official adversaries, but by virtue of this have a long-standing relationship, which is by and large characterized by conflict but can also create a level of understanding and even friendship. As we will see, this situation is very different from that of the Pokot.

WAR WITH JACKALS

Lentiyoo, a Samburu elder, describes the Pokot style of fighting:

The Pokot, the kind of fight he can fight, is to fight under cover. If he shoots at you he will shoot when you haven't seen him. When a Pokot sees that you have seen him he would no longer dare shoot you. He fights like a cat or jackal. He cannot fight like a man. And so it is cowardice. They don't stand up. Their standing up is running away. . . . With Samburu, now, they can run to them while fighting, until they just reach where they are, and Somalis are also like that, they run to each other when they fight. But there is no Pokot who dares to run to another person. No, no, he lies down like a cat unless he is being chased, and then it is only his gun that he turns backwards towards you, [*shooting*] dadadada, while he runs away, so that he gets a means to take himself away. . . . And then they are terrified and they start shitting, so that when you follow them you can't even pass their trail because of the shit.

Lentiyoo observes and emphasizes a key—and agreed, though differently valued—distinction in Samburu and Pokot warfare, an emphasis on stealth. His claim that Pokot operate to a large degree through stealth is widely held among Samburu, who attribute it to unmanly cowardice. Notably, this stereotype of Pokot stealth is largely agreed upon by Pokot, though the suggestion that this is a form of cowardice is not. Indeed, it is lauded by Pokot, who (while also emphasizing bravery in their war songs) beseech their warriors to be like tadpoles, deep in the water and difficult to catch, or like slippery stones (*mnyunyuk*) that are hard to hold. Stealth is a form of intelligence; its absence is not bravery but idiocy.

These differing attitudes thus have less to do with stereotypes per se than with how stealth is valuated. Nothing illustrates this better than the differences between Samburu and Pokot settlements, differences that would be readily apparent even to a casual, untrained observer. Samburu settlements are typically in an open plain. Particularly in the lowlands, they may be set on the side of or atop a hill. They are completely enclosed by a fence cut from acacia thorns, with a gate for the house of each wife, which is usually opened and closed simply by moving a cut thorn bush out of the way. The soil is typically dry and packed from human and animal traffic, taking on a very different appearance from the surrounding area. The result is that—even though the houses are small, simple constructions of sticks, mud, and cattle dung—a Samburu settlement can typically be seen from many miles away. Even abandoned settlements can usually be picked out at a great distance many years after the occupants have left. Footpaths are well worn and obvious, so that except in the most remote lowland areas, where settlements may be miles apart, it is rarely difficult to locate settlements (although it may not be the settlement you are looking for).

A Pokot settlement could not be more different. More than once I have approached Pokot settlements and not even realized that I had arrived until I was inside. Sites for Pokot settlements are typically selected within bushy areas.[7] While the areas inside the settlements differ in how much live vegetation remains, paths leading to the settlements twist and turn through a tangle of trees and scrub. While staying in Pokot settlements, I have gone not more than fifty yards from the settlement only to spend well over an hour circling around trying to figure out how to get back. With Samburu settlements, by contrast, I might walk a mile or more even in an unfamiliar area and have no trouble finding my way back.

Samburu and Pokot both acknowledge the hidden nature of Pokot settlements. Samburu, however, speak mockingly of how Pokot settlements are ostensibly "of the bush." This is used to show that Pokot are truly like animals, but more importantly as proof of their cowardice. They hide, unlike real men, who show themselves and are not afraid. Pokot, however, take pride in their settlements. They like the fact they are able to conceal their homesteads and their herds in such a way that it would be a daunting task for a raider to find them, especially at night. They explain that they don't particularly like to keep dogs (though some do), because their barking reveals the location of the settlement at night, which only an idiot—or a Samburu—would willingly do.

This emphasis on allowing yourself to be seen or not seen is central to differences in styles of cattle raiding, both in the manner of combat and the way livestock is captured. By and large, Pokot have come to favor stealthy raids using small groups of not more than twenty or so men. Although Pokot did launch large raids after the initial outbreak of violence in 2006, these did not always prove successful. Approximately fifty Pokot were killed, for instance, in a raid against Nturoto Arus in Samburu, and while some cattle were successfully taken, the majority were returned. Consequently, Pokot by and large shifted to smaller raids, ideally avoiding combat. Some Pokot maintain that these are, in fact, far more effective. As one man indicated to me, "Even with the big raids there is usually nothing that you get." Thus, Pokot prefer more opportunistic theft of livestock, often raiding a poorly guarded herd where little or no fighting is necessary. Late afternoon is a favored time for such raids, because owners may not even realize that the animals are gone until it is close to dark, and thus have difficulty pursuing them, while government forces are unlikely to come to their assistance until morning, giving raiders a twelve- to fifteen-hour head start to get away. Samburu do sometimes speak in awe of how the Pokot are "professionals" (i.e., polished thieves), making Samburu livestock disappear without the owner even being aware of it at times. Yet at the same time this is seen as a cowardly way to raid, making them like hyenas or other scavengers.

Samburu also engage in small-scale raids. However, more than Pokot, they tend to favor large raids involving upward of five hundred to a thousand combatants. The first such raid, in Laikipia in August 2006, was relatively effective. Although nine Samburu were killed, they succeeded in getting a considerable number of livestock. Future attempts have proved far less successful. In one raid some livestock were successfully taken, but perhaps a hundred Samburu were killed by government forces aided by Pokot (see chapter 6), and in a second raid no livestock were taken and a dozen Samburu were killed. In these latter instances, the main problem Samburu encountered was that their plans were well known. Samburu acknowledge that this was the case but do not believe they should change their plans, even if they are known to have been revealed. They believe that even if their plans are known, it will be impossible for their enemies to withstand their onslaught, and thus attribute their refusal to change their plans to their strength and bravery. Pokot attribute this Samburu tendency mainly to stupidity. If Pokot believe plans have been compromised, they modify them, and they have seen Samburu killed because they will not. Pokot also attribute an element of bravery to this, but they cannot quite understand it. Many Pokot claim, for instance, that apparently "Samburu are not afraid to die," though this is sometimes recounted in a baffled tone—as if there is something abnormal about their behavior, as if they might be suicidal rather than possessing admirable courage.

Samburu, at least publicly, assert that you should not be afraid to die in battle. As one Samburu friend declared, "To be born is luck, but to die is a must." Thus, he proclaimed, you should be brave in battle because you will die one way or another. This public face is not always reflected in private action. There is, in fact, a less visible counterdiscourse that cowardice is akin to cleverness. Well-known tales of the ingenious actions of famous cowards constitute a genre of Samburu humor at the same time as they imply admiration for these not-brave men. That the face of bravery is not always authentic is reflected in that fact that the man who noted to me that "to die is a must" had, in fact, turned away before the launch of one of the most unsuccessful Samburu raids. His family members told me that they had never been concerned about his safety when he was at the encampment where Samburu massed before the raid. They mused that they knew he would return home before the raid actually happened because he is, in fact, quite cowardly.

Thus, Pokot assertions that Samburu can be insanely brave are partially supported by Samburu themselves, although they do not characterize it as such. Pokot make other assertions about Samburu that Samburu would not agree with, despite not being entirely discordant with their own stereotypes of their differences from the Pokot. Pokot assert that in combat Samburu are overly emotional, which can lead to great bravery, extreme cowardice, or simply bad decisions. One man, for instance, mentioned the Samburu tendency to use what both Samburu and Pokot refer to by the English term *force,* which means switching their guns to full automatic to provide cover to their fellows. This was a ridiculous waste of ammunition, my Pokot friend explained, and was not a consequence merely of the Samburu having less experience than the Pokot in using guns in combat. Rather, it was a consequence of Samburu getting overly emotional in battle. As he put it, "Pokot hearts are here," pointing to his stomach, "and Samburu hearts are here," pointing to his throat. Such emotion can lead to insane bravery but also unexplained cowardice. For instance, this same man claimed, Samburu commonly throw away their guns when they are scared so that they can run away faster, even when they are not in extreme danger. While Samburu would not agree with either the claim of insane bravery or that of poor combat decisions, it is not inconsistent with Samburu cultural expectations that murran (who have not yet acquired the calm demeanor of elderhood) are like wild beasts in battle. The contrast is also consistent with the Samburu's characterization of the Pokot as "professionals" who coldly, calmly, and slickly go about their business in theft and warfare.[8]

The emphasis on manly valor versus cowardly stealth is extended beyond stereotypical styles of combat to differences in their weapons. As Lentiyoo stated above, the Samburu emphasize that the Pokot always fight while running or else lying down. In the Samburu view in particular, this has consequences for the guns they prefer. Pokot tend to use the much more lightweight AK-47, while Samburu typically have older-style rifles or European-made G3s, which are heavier and have a longer range than a Kalashnikov. There are reasons why each group more readily acquires the favored type of gun. Many Samburu guns are issued to them

FIGURE 10.   Lekeren milks a cow in a war zone bordering Pokot.

as Homeguards (police reservists) and thus reflect the type that is more common in the Kenyan military. Military weapons are also more desirable because ammunition for them can be far cheaper (Mkutu 2008), as it can often be purchased illegally from soldiers or policemen. Pokot weapons are almost exclusively illegal and tend to come from Uganda, where AK-47s are more common.

Although differences in the supply chain are likely the key factor driving the types of guns that predominate among each group, Samburu value their own guns as connoting moral superiority, in contrast to their opponents' AK-47s. Indeed, Samburu do not view differences even in the supply chain simply in practical terms, but use them to create multi-layered globalized discourses concerning themselves and the Pokot. This is neatly summarized by a Samburu elder, Leshornai: "That one of Islam, we aren't afraid of those. Ours do serious work, these ones of America have strength." Here Samburu curiously play on global discourses, mapping onto their own conflicts absorbed tropes of righteous strength—for instance from radio broadcasts portraying the strength and moral certitude of the United States in "the War on Terror." Their guns are not actually American, while their opponents' guns are not really, as they describe AK-47s, either Arab or even directly Russian. Their characterization of their guns as American, British, or "of the government" does not strictly reflect their provenance, but is used by Samburu to emphasize their strength and their manliness (and their closer relationship to whiteness), as opposed to the Pokot. Samburu guns are heavier and have a stronger recoil. Samburu claim that the Pokot like the lighter guns because "they fight while they are running," which would not be possible with a G3. Thus, they maintain that the use of AK-47s, as opposed to G3s, is in part a cultural choice, based on Pokot combat style but also reflecting their cowardice, their defects as men. Samburu guns are appropriate for combat by men who stand and fight like men, whereas Pokot guns are for people who fight while running, which may often mean running away.

Samburu like to emphasize the greater power of their guns, and I have heard numerous accounts of Samburu bragging of firing at Pokot who were bewildered at being shot at from places far outside the range of their own guns. The guns Samburu tend to use do, in fact, have a much greater effective range—about five hundred meters for the G3, while the older rifles are accurate within a slightly longer range and have a maximum range up to a kilometer.[9] In contrast, the AK-47 was developed following observations by the Russian military during World War II that most lethal combat occurred within three hundred meters, such that it was specifically designed for use by relatively untrained combatants fighting at close range (Kahanar 2007). While Samburu not only believe and are proud of what they see as the superiority of their guns, they also emphasize that the Pokot like AK-47s better because they are conducive to their style of fighting. For their part, Pokot give mixed reviews of their own weapons. Occasionally, Pokot will maintain that their guns are, in fact, inferior, a consequence of alleged government aid to Samburu. Thus, one Pokot man complained in 2006 that Samburu were being given powerful guns by the government while Pokot were forced to make do with "these ambush weapons." By and large, however, Pokot speak favorably of the usefulness of AK-47s to the style of fighting they prefer. They also regard Samburu as not particularly competent in combat, rendering their preference of weapons somewhat dubious, a choice founded in ineptitude.

WAR (AND PEACE) WITH REAL MEN

If war with the Pokot is a kind of "war with jackals," with people who are supposed to be your friends but instead steal your livestock, people whose version of standing to fight is shooting while running away—with guns pointed backward and shitting in fear as they run—Samburu view war with the Turkana in very different terms. Turkana are real men. When they make peace, they make meaningful peace, and when they make war, they make war completely.

This is not to say that Samburu view the Turkana as equals. Indeed, there are many ways in which they view the Turkana in deprecatory terms. Because they do not practice circumcision, they are often characterized as overgrown children, and Samburu use the epithet *layiok* (boys) to refer to them, an explicitly derogatory reference to the absence of circumcision rituals for initiation into manhood, and more generally suggestive that they are poorly enculturated, overgrown youths. Also notable in this respect is that their food habits are seen as gluttonous in that they eat virtually everything, in contrast to the refined Samburu diet and self-control that is central to nkanyit. Along with eating all forms of wild game, Turkana even eat donkeys and drink donkey milk.

These stereotypes do not fully contradict self-appraisals by the Turkana, who see flexibility in respect to food especially as a function of their toughness, as doing whatever it takes to survive. Turkana suggest that there are even cannibals among them. They term these "night runners": people who wait for sick people to die so they can eat them. Turkana migrate to Samburu and other places in search of work, such that they are regarded by Samburu as poor people and beggars.[10] This does not, however, mean that they are not dangerous adversaries. In the words of a Samburu elder, "A Turkana who has nothing, who feeds on ostriches, can come and attack you. He has nothing. He has only one hen but he comes and takes your cows."

Unlike Pokot attacks, which are described as stealthy—more akin to stealing than manly cattle raids—Turkana attacks are open, overwhelming, and brutal. A murran from the Lemarash family describes the scope and the consequences of Turkana raids in the 1990s that forced Samburu to retaliate:

We were attacked, when Saar was attacked. They attacked a very big area and we did not have weapons to fight with, but pain just forced us to go. People were crying. People were crying for lives and for their animals. Because people had gotten finished and there were no animals, no cows and no sheep or goats. But what drove us a lot was the problem we were seeing. There was no food for people to eat. It was that problem that took us most of all. . . . There is no double death. Because even starvation can kill us. It is better for us to go so that those who will die, then they will die, and those who will survive, they will survive, because a person cannot die if his days are not over. And even if you can die in battle, you can also die at home.

Samburu recognize—based on extensive experience—that the Turkana are fearsome in warfare. To some extent the almost precultural caricature of the Turkana accentuates Samburu characterizations of what they see as essentially animalistic brutality. As Lekutaas describes it, "It is Turkana culture to kill everything. A woman. Samburu and even the Maasai before cannot kill a woman. No, no, you cannot kill a woman. They'd kill even a dog. The Turkana are like this, even, like if we are running away now with this woman, we are running away, and as we are being chased I will escape myself but they will kill the woman because they usually think that it is the woman who produced the seeds." Similar sentiments are echoed by the Lkishilli Samburu elder Lekonchella:

Samburu just raid to seek for animals but Turkana do a lot of other nasty things. Because sometimes instead of killing women they just rape all of them. . . . The Turkana, they kill anything they get. But the Samburu do not kill women or children or the old or anyone who does not resist. And the Turkana kill even dogs. Turkana leave nothing. Even a breast-feeding child can be killed with her mother. Samburu don't interfere with a woman and children, they are just interested in live-stock. It's only the brave enemy that they try to kill. But when Turkana see people in a home, they enter the home and kill everybody. Pokot are the same. Somalis don't kill women a lot. The raid of the Turkana is very bad. They even break into boxes, they kill dogs.

Samburu, thus, emphasize Turkana brutality in killing everyone, dec-imating a settlement and leaving nothing behind. Turkana informants respond to these accusations in quite interesting ways. They deny killing dogs, but admit killing women and children. They assert, however, that everyone—Turkana, Pokot, and Samburu—kill women and children because the bitterness of war leads people to do most anything. Turkana suggest that they are merely straightforward about this—forthrightness being a Turkana characteristic that is emphasized also by Samburu (along with ethnographers who have worked with them [e.g., Itaru Ohta, personal communication]). This is also consistent with the fact that groups are frequently accused of killing children in the region, particularly the enemy of the moment. For instance, Pokot informants insisted that only Samburu kill children, while Turkana do not—and had little to say when I informed them that Turkana had told me that they do.

Not surprisingly, Samburu typically portray the Turkana as the aggressors in their conflicts. This is not wholly without substantiation. McCabe (2004), for instance, notes that the more distant Turkana with whom he has worked view the Samburu as a group to prey upon rather than to fear. At a more local level, the small-scale raids of Samburu certainly serve as provocation, even if the response is disproportionate. And in some cases—for example, fighting that began while I was in the field in 2008—conflict was instigated primarily by Samburu. In that instance, Samburu had given the Turkana permission to graze animals well within Samburu territory. When Samburu decided that the period for this permission had passed, the Turkana refused to leave, so Samburu attacked them at a watering point, taking large numbers of livestock and killing several individuals. The large-scale raids and broader fighting that followed were a direct consequence of that initial attack.

By and large, however, broad-scale warfare and major attacks are launched first by the Turkana. Yet, despite this experience with brutal aggression, the Samburu view the Turkana as quite reasonable people with whom they can communicate. Of course, one of the ways Samburu believe they "reason" with Turkana is by killing them. That is, by feeling pain, the Turkana understand that fighting is no longer worthwhile. As a Samburu of the Mooli age set discusses one such battle:

> There were Turkana who attacked that side of Ndoto. Sixty Turkana were killed that day. And what caused the death of those was thirst. Our warriors went at night to keep watch at a well in Kawop, because the

Turkana could only drink water there, nowhere else. So, we let the Turkana take the animals. Then the warriors went and kept watch at that well. When the Turkana tried to run to that well, they found that our warriors were keeping watch. And there was terrible heat, they were being burned by the fire of the bullets from 3 A.M. until those Turkana were killed at six o'clock sharp. They were being chased and killed in that plain until they became weak and hopeless. When it reached 3 P.M. they were let to drink at that oasis. Imagine if over one thousand people are allowed to drink from one well. One warrior could just come and start targeting at the oasis, shooting the Turkana one by one. When they lie down to drink the water they get shot. When one is killed and his blood is still streaming into the oasis his friend pulls him out and starts drinking that bloody water. Then thirty of them were killed there, not counting those who were killed elsewhere. When another is shot, his comrade pulls him out and enters the well to drink the water. And they were being shot by one person. Then that pain sent away the Turkana for good.

.   .   .

The wars between Samburu and Turkana, then, are brutal and merciless. The Turkana, in particular—in their estimation and that of the Samburu—wage a total war, fighting vigorously and bravely, sparing nothing and no one. Yet, when there is peace, the Turkana are straightforward about keeping peace. As the Samburu elder Lentiyoo described it, "With Turkana, once it comes that people agreed to be friends, they can stay well together. And they can stay, for instance, even if the children [i.e., murran] go and provoke each other, the Turkana elders may still be ready to come and, for instance, meet. And something is discussed so that if it is difficult to solve, then they just fight. And then even though it happens that they had a fight, they can go back to peace discussions, so it is possible for them to come together again."

Samburu live with the antipathy and potential for violence with Turkana, but also regard the Turkana as potentially reasonable. Fighting is inevitable but sometimes avoidable. Unprovoked attacks occur, of course, but there is also the desire to avoid escalating violence. The Turkana are regarded as people with whom Samburu can sit down as elders to attempt to resolve differences. If they cannot resolve these differences, violence becomes diplomacy by other means.

Another elder, Lekupano, describes a specific incident in which "big boys"—young men around twenty who were not yet initiated into manhood—stole calves from Turkana living a few hours away. They got the calves back to their home area, but the Turkana managed to follow the tracks:

[The boys who stole the calves agreed that each] was free to give out one calf to his friends. Then the Turkana followed their calves until they came to know the people who took them, then they told them to return the calves. . . . The Turkana took the cattle of those boys that were in Marti, and said that the boys will not get those cows unless they bring the calves back. [We got the boys to collect the calves but] as the boys prepared to return them, one of the calves was killed by a hyena. So the number of calves for the Turkana was not filled. The boys took the still living calves back, but the Turkana said they did not want their calves back without their dead calf, and that calf was already dead, having been eaten by a hyena. So the calf was paid for by giving out cows. Then when that case got over, people said that a Turkana had been killed. It was said that it was the Lmooli [murran] who killed but others said it was the boys. . . . That case continued until Samburu agreed to pay compensation for the death of that Turkana.

Cases like this indicate—irrespective of the conflicts that frequently arise—that the Turkana and Samburu regard each other as capable of talking and negotiating with one another. A violent incident or theft *may* escalate to something bigger, but mechanisms exist between the two groups for resolving problems in a peaceful manner.

This is, of course, contingent on having a relationship with those particular neighboring Turkana. Turkana do not attack as a collective ethnicity (and are not always viewed by Samburu as doing so). Thus, Samburu may form friendships, or at least a truce with those living nearby, though this may not be respected by Samburu from other areas. That is, having a good relationship with particular Samburu does not protect Turkana from raids—perhaps carried out for purposes of revenge—by Samburu from other areas. Lelenguya, a Samburu elder from the Lkishilli age set, describes the efforts of other Samburu to prevent him when, as a murran, he set out with his peers to recover stolen cattle and, losing the tracks, decided to instead make a revenge raid on other Turkana. Other Samburu tried to stop the raid, characterizing the proposed targets as "our Turkana"—that is, those Turkana who were their neighbors, whom they (perhaps patronizingly) regarded as their own, and who were not responsible for the raid that Lelenguya and company sought to avenge. Lelenguya recalls, "The Lorokushu people [i.e., the Samburu neighboring those Turkana] then said, 'Let us stop these people, because these people would now go and attack these Turkana of ours who live next to us here. And later on in the day we will be attacked ourselves. And so they should not be attacked, yes these Turkana of ours should not be attacked because if these ones are attacked today then we will also today be attacked by these Turkana.'" In the end Lelenguya's group was not persuaded, casting sticks and Sodom Apples at those who were trying to stop them, and they went and successfully raided the cows of the nearby Turkana. As predicted, however, those Turkana did return to avenge the raid on their neighbors.

Turkana present to Samburu several of what would seem like quite disparate facets. On one hand, they launch horrible, brutal raids, with large numbers of warriors who pillage and wreak havoc beyond simply capturing cattle, killing everything in their way, raping and destroying property in the process. Yet at the same time they are reasonable people who can be dealt with, poor people who can even be looked upon in a patronizing manner, as not simply Turkana but as "our Turkana"— people working for you as herders, or simply living as your neighbors.

THE POSSIBILITY OF FRIENDSHIP

To Samburu, both the Pokot and the Turkana are in their own ways bad. The irony here is that the Pokot were—until very recently—officially "good," but in practice held in low regard, while the Turkana were officially enemies but generally viewed in positive, if ambiguous ways. The Pokot were official friends of the Samburu, the two bound together by a time-honored oath, while the Turkana were consummate enemies with a long history of brutal warfare. Thus, living side by side as friends created a kind of enmity, while living side by side as enemies created something more akin to friendship. As Lentiyoo compares the two groups:

I think the Turkana are somewhat better, even though we have no lang'ata with them. That is because with the Turkana, when it happens you have formed a friendship with some people you sit with, then they can stay in peace. But the Pokot, even though that lang'ata (oath-bound relationship) is there, if the women come and pass here, and come across the goat kids that you just passed by over there, the woman would put the kid inside her cloth and then she'll go with it. And a man of the Pokot, when he gets your cow if it goes astray and goes to his settlement, he takes it away so that you can't get it. But the Turkana, they don't have such filth. No, no, when the Turkana women come, for instance, they will just come properly to your settlement. And, as well, if your cow goes astray, that cow would just then stay there [with the Turkana] until the owner is called to come and take it. And so it is something like that so that the Samburu and Pokot can't be on good terms, they can never be in good terms because the Pokot are a class of people with very bad manners.

The Pokot are, thus, not truly seen as friends. It is even asserted that they may be incapable of friendship, even among themselves. Many cite the fact that among the first Samburu killed by the Pokot as the war broke out was someone who had been friends with Pokot, having herded cattle with them during a recent drought. One Samburu elder attributed this not to enmity between themselves and the Pokot, but as simply the fundamental absence in Pokot of a capacity for actual friendship. "They have no friendship," this elder asserts, and then cites as proof the killing of the Samburu, Lolmodooni, whose killing—from a Samburu perspective—was the spark for the war. "They don't have friendship, like the family of Lolmodooni, he was their friend and he was the one who was killed." Or, as another man put it, "Pokot are people who cannot be friends with anyone completely."

This does not, however, merely apply to their relationships with Samburu, Samburu assert. They claim that this is characteristic of Pokot relationships even with one another. In support of this claim, Samburu cite their observations from when they went with the Pokot to raid the

Turkana at Lokorrkorr, in a massive jointly organized raid that brought warfare between the Samburu and the Turkana to a temporary halt. In the course of the raid, Samburu assert that the Pokot left their own wounded behind, being unwilling to assist the injured and leaving the Samburu to do so. These assertions, made by Lekutaas, are supported by Samburu generally: "They can just kill a person of their own, as if they didn't see them as a Pokot anymore. For instance, can they carry anyone who has an injury? They can't help someone once he has a serious injury, wounded like that, they can't help him. Instead they kill him and take away his gun. Recently when they were going together with Samburu, to go attack the Turkana, most of them who were injured, they usually left them so that it was the Samburu who brought them. Yes, they can't carry a person of their own who is wounded." To a great extent, then, the oath between the Samburu and the Pokot is not viewed as the ultimate form of friendship between the groups, blood brotherhood to cement an already strong bond. Rather, the Samburu view it as the only way to maintain peace with a group that was impossible to deal with. As one man explained, "Pokot have no sense of respect. And when they have discussions, the usual discussions of men, they are not going to remember it later. Once they leave, they just act like boys. There was nothing that was discussed by men and was agreed upon once and for all."

The extent to which this reflects actual differences in the behavior of Pokot and Turkana is highly debatable. Although Samburu frequently maintain that Pokot are incapable of real friendship, close and genuine friendships were formed between Samburu and Pokot, particularly in Laikipia before the onset of violence—for instance between my Samburu host, Lekeren, and Simba, as well as with the father of Tinga (the boy Lekeren semi-adopted). Samburu assertions that Pokot leave their wounded on the battlefield—or even kill them and take their guns—is contradicted by Pokot assertions that they cleverly hide their wounded aside in the bush until the fighting has stopped, rather than foolishly trying to carry them off in the direction of the battle, as they assert Samburu try to do. Nor do Samburu have a positive attitude to the Turkana during times of conflict, as they harass as potential spies Samburu who were adopted from the Turkana or whose close ancestors were Turkana.

Although their perceptions may to some extent reflect reality, Samburu decidedly perceive the Turkana and the Pokot to be quite different, both in times of war and peace. I have argued that these perceptions are to a great extent derived from the moral basis for relationships they have among themselves, with concepts of virtue and friendship (or their absence) then projected onto other ethnic groups. Pokot are seen as the consummate laroi, violating nkanyit through behavior that is cold, selfish, and secretive. Turkana also ostensibly lack nkanyit, but they do so (in the Samburu view) as lobu people, living life with abandon. They are enemies who rapaciously consume anything in their path—whether elephants, snakes, or Samburu cattle—but part and parcel of this is their outgoing nature. They are seen as gregarious and likeable people with whom you can be true friends in time of peace and who are forthright when ending war.

.　　.　　.

In October 2008 a local NGO sponsored by European ranchers held the Highland Games, an athletic competition designed to bring together warring groups in northern Kenya, particularly the Samburu and the Pokot. While the intention was good, I was skeptical that bringing together groups of youth to run some foot races would have any notable effect on relieving the then extremely tense context of violence. It struck me as inherently low-impact in the context of war, but moreover, the people likely to attend such events—more educated or church-going youth—were unlikely to be the ones engaged in shooting one another. Indeed, although I would have preferred to have been wrong on this point, the violence continued—and indeed, the second annual games were nearly canceled after a major raid killed twenty-two people, followed by counterraids and further violence.

It is not my intent to criticize a laudable attempt to stop violence. However, it is in some senses informative in respect to the discussion of this chapter. The games were based on the often-repeated truism that if people simply got to know each other, if they somehow humanized each other, they would find peace. However, it is often not the case that people fight because they do not know each other; sometimes they fight because they do. In this sense, the book's defining question of how neighbors—oftentimes friends or economic partners, but in any case people who are familiar and on good terms—become killers of one another may be seen in a different light. I have suggested that we need to understand how people make the cognitive shift that allows them to resituate a group or an individual from the category of intimate to the category of enemy, where lethal violence is an acceptable, perhaps even valorized act. On the surface, killing a friend seems far more difficult to understand than killing a stranger—even if we have all heard that most victims are murdered by someone they know—and yet it is possible that intimacy may itself be a component underlying lethal violence, rather than something that prevents it. Indeed, I am reminded of the oft-repeated words of my Pokot friend Simba, who at the height of the war with the Samburu claimed that it was easy for those who were unfamiliar, who had never interacted, to leave aside the bitterness of war. Those people had no issue with one another, unlike "the ones who had been friends before," who found it difficult to put aside their new hatred.

In exploring how people alternate between being friends and killers of one another, I have sought to both provide rich, specific detail that moves us beyond easy categories of "timeless enemies" or "uneasy coexistence" to understand the specific ways relationships may be constituted in this part of the globe, but also to suggest what may be generalizable to contexts of violence and peace more generally. In a sense, I aimed to show in this chapter that not all friends are the same, just as not all enemies are the same. Of course, the world is not simply constituted of "neighbors who are like the Turkana" and "neighbors who are like the Pokot," yet these may minimally serve as models to help us understand the relationships of communities in conflict elsewhere in the globe.

This chapter has been framed to a great extent by a subjective, Samburu point of view. This view might be summarized thus: they fight with Turkana, but despite this warfare, Turkana are "better" than, or preferable to, Pokot, with whom they (until recently) did not fight. This view is useful from a broader comparative perspective in that we might understand the situation with the Turkana to be one of "peace constituted through violence"—they get along well partially because of the constant threat of lethal conflict—whereas the situation with the Pokot is one that eventuated in "violence constructed through peace." That is, in the Pokot case, the form of peace that existed created behaviors that ultimately culminated in violence. Yet from a broader perspective, we may also ask if we should take the Samburu view that the Turkana situation is "better" as our own subjective point of view. Our concern is less that groups around the world love their neighbors than that they refrain from killing them. Ironically, these goals may in some ways be in contradiction. While anthropologically there is something intriguing about the notion that peace does not lead to love, it is perhaps more significant in real-world terms that love does not necessarily lead to peace.

6

VIEWS ON A MASSACRE

Government and the Making of Order and Disorder

> It's like we don't have government. It's then we saw that
> the government only defends those ones, the Pokot. We
> don't have government. They took us like we were
> people of another country . . . It's like we aren't citizens.
> It's like we are rebels. We were just hit, you see, like
> people of another country . . . They had no desire to
> arrest us. They had no desire to arrest us, although they
> were the government. They had the desire to kill. So,
> they hit us with bombs. It's like their own strength
> consumed them that they felt that they should finish us,
> that they would finish us.

Such is one Samburu man's experience of the government response to
an early morning Samburu cattle raid on neighboring Pokot in early 2007
in which eighty to one hundred Samburu died. Samburu undertook the
raid in the border zone between the two groups in Laikipia as retaliation
for a series of smaller, persistent attacks by Pokot. Despite foreknowledge
of the raid by many on both sides—including people affiliated with the
government—the Samburu initially succeeded in capturing cattle and
began to drive them away. After that, however, things went badly. They
were pursued by an indeterminate mixture of Pokot and government
forces, and though many Samburu escaped, some with Pokot cattle, large
numbers were killed—according to many Samburu, by government
bombs dropped on them by helicopters.

In the violent incidents so far explored in this book, as well as the narratives used to explain them, the government of Kenya has been featured
as little more than an occasional player. The intention has not been to
create the illusion—perhaps as in some early twentieth-century anthropological account of internally cohesive and self-contained systems—that
these northern Kenyan groups exist in a realm geographically beyond or
temporally before the effects of government. The government of Kenya

is not absent from these violent conflicts, and it is certainly the most potent military force in northern Kenya. It does, however, frequently sit on the sidelines or, when entering the fray, does so for varying reasons and in ways that may appear counterintuitive or counterproductive to interests of peace.

The government is, moreover, central to understanding violence as a cultural system made up of a frequently shifting triad of perpetrators, victims, and observers (Riches 1986; Stewart and Strathern 2002). Viewed as a cultural system, violent acts not only *do* something but also *say* something. They may say something to the perpetrators' co-ethnics (e.g., about their resolve) and to the victims (e.g., about how far they might go, about future actions). Adversaries each have much to say to observers—for instance, about the legitimacy of their actions, or who is the "perpetrator" and who is the "victim," since an attack may be justified as retaliation for a greater wrong, as preemptive self-defense, or as a police action (e.g., to recover stolen cattle). The most important observer is, of course, the Kenyan government, which possesses tens of thousands of troops and police and heavy weaponry far outclassing that of its citizens. Consequently, an important aspect of local narratives is to establish legitimacy that may bring this most potent observer onto one side or another.

Yet the role of the government is far more complex. The government may at various points take different positions in the triad of perpetrator-victim-observer. Most obviously, it is an observer empowered to decide how to police responsibly in the context of violence, but at times it shifts to being an actor that those on all sides come to construe as a perpetrator. Sometimes the ways it is seen as a perpetrator are straightforward, sometimes they come deep from the conspiracy mill, and sometimes they are impossible to evaluate to the extent that accurate interpretation depends on disputed or unknown facts. And indeed, it may even on rare occasions shift to the role of victim.

Our readings of the discourses of violence detailed in this book must, then, to a significant degree be refracted through the complex roles the Kenyan government plays as actor, audience, and symbol in these conflicts. The government is in principle accepted by local actors as the agent of order among disorder, even though it is in practice seen as not always approaching this ideal. Thus, the stories that people on all sides tell to describe and explain what has happened—sometimes true, sometimes misunderstandings, sometimes lies, or sometimes a brew of all of these—are stories told to someone. Sometimes they tell these stories to themselves, sometimes to me, and sometimes to their enemies. Yet in many ways the most important body that they hope will hear their versions of war is the government, for their opinions have implications in the form of military force. Words, then, may be used to sculpt legitimacy, to raise the alarm for action, or to deflect blame upon someone else. Words may affect whether your cattle are seized or returned, whether the conflict is neglected or policed, or whether it is you or if it is your adversaries who bear the brunt of a government intervention. Thus, how actors understand the government, how it behaves, and how it is spoken to and about are fundamental to making sense of these conflicts.

WHERE'S THE GOVERNMENT? WHAT GOVERNMENT?

As the war between the Samburu and the Pokot dragged on into 2009, I asked Charles—a Pokot who grew up with many Samburu—if perhaps the government could put an end to the conflict. Flabbergasted, he responded, "Truly, Jon, because there is nothing the government can't do. There is none. There is no citizen who could be more powerful than the government. The government has the ability even up to using an airplane to seek a gun inside a house. So you see, it is just apparent that they have agreed to this [war]. Why is it in Nairobi if criminals have guns they are searched for until they are found? Why is it that here they don't search for them, and guns are guns? Criminals are criminals."

His response is telling on many levels. The most obvious claim is that the government is, at a minimum, indifferent to the conflict. He asserts that they have the ability to stop the conflict but have not. Beyond indifference, there is a suggestion of complicity—and indeed, as I explore further case studies over the course of this chapter, complicity can rapidly melt into conspiracy and claims of deliberately self-serving action and inaction. However, he also reveals a fundamental respect for the principle of government on the part of local actors. They hold the ideal of government in high regard, which makes the actual government all the more wanting. In Charles's account, the government possesses great power—

limitless power, almost superpowers, such as the ability to see into houses—power greater than any citizen they are charged to protect, or to prosecute should that person break the laws of the state. And yet, despite these great powers, it fails to fulfill even basic responsibilities.

His contrast of northern Kenya with Nairobi is also provocative. On one level he suggests that lawlessness in northern Kenya is most significantly the result of government neglect. Yet this assertion is to some extent naïve or misleading. Nairobi is hardly an example of safety grounded in sound governance. It is a place that Kenyans playfully nickname "Nairobbery," where it is said that—based on large income disparities and high rates of crime—one third of the people hire the second third of the people to protect themselves from the other third of the people. Nairobi, rife with crime and private security services to prevent it, is hardly an exemplar of a place where criminals live in fear of an all-powerful government.

In considering the role of government policing in Kenya generally and in northern Kenya specifically, it is instructive to turn briefly to Nairobi and look closely at one of the best-known criminal incidents in Kenyan history: the 2013 attack on Westgate Mall in the affluent outskirts of Nairobi. In addition to looking for parallels between the response to this attack and government responses in northern Kenya, we may consider what the response to an incident that commanded intense international attention suggests about responses in out of the way places, far from the public eye.

THE KENYAN GOVERNMENT AND MILITARY IN THE SPOTLIGHT: WESTGATE MALL

On September 21, 2013, an unknown number of gunmen entered Nairobi's Westgate Mall, a high-end shopping center even by Western standards and a favorite place to congregate both for wealthy Kenyans and expatriates. Initial reports indicated that there were as many as fifteen gunmen armed with heavy weaponry such as rocket-propelled grenades.[1] The gunmen moved through the mall, at first shooting on sight, then more methodically quizzing potential victims to determine whether they were Muslim—for instance, asking them to recite parts of the Koran or name the Prophet's mother—then releasing Muslims from the mall and shooting them if they were not.

The steps taken to deal with the attackers were disjointed. In the initial stages, the task of rescuing civilians fell mainly to ad hoc groups of off-duty policemen and security personnel (some of whom were in the building at the time of the attack), while the Kenyan police cordoned off the building. Roughly three and a half hours after the attack began, the elite Recce Company of the General Service Unit of the Kenyan police (an Israeli-trained unit most often responsible for the security of high-level officials) entered the mall and began a firefight with the gunmen. By some accounts, they also attempted to make targeted rescues of high-status individuals trapped in the building. While the Recce Company had allegedly pinned down the gunmen, the Kenyan Army Ranger Regiment then also entered the building. With no coordination or communication between the two units, shooting ensued between them, leaving at least one Kenyan officer killed and three wounded by friendly fire. Both units withdrew due to casualties and allegedly because of a lack of night-vision goggles.

Over the next two days, a variety of attempts were made to retake the mall from the gunmen, who were allegedly holding hostages. Finally, on September 23, a large explosion caused the roof to collapse. Everyone remaining inside was presumed dead, though it is unclear who was still inside. Government sources claimed that the gunmen were still in the mall and were killed by the explosion, but that no civilians remained alive at that point. However, many points remain fuzzy. For instance, there was no evidence that the gunmen were still in the building when it was blown up. What caused the collapse of the mall is also unclear. By many accounts it was caused by rocket-propelled grenades fired into the mall by Kenyan security forces, such that most of the physical destruction was caused the rescuers rather than the terrorists. While there initially were said to be as many as fifteen terrorists with heavy weaponry, security cameras indicated that there were four, lightly armed with AK-47s. Controversy later emerged when footage from security cameras showed Kenyan soldiers looting the mall, stealing cell phones and other items.

The mall attack and the government response, although beyond the focus of this book, are nonetheless instructive for considering the nature of the "third actor" in the conflicts described. A short and only slightly unsympathetic summary of the events would suggest that the government was slow to respond; when it did respond, it was disorganized; the government was responsible for much of the destruction; and then members of the rescue team looted the mall. Accurate information is scarce: Was it four gunmen or fifteen? Were civilians killed in the explosion? Were the gunmen killed? Were government forces responsible for the explosion? Indeed, having observed the workings of security forces in northern Kenya, as horrific as were the events at the mall, I found them in many respects unsurprising. Though I had followed their actions closely only in the very different context of remote northern Kenya, I understood that government forces could be disorganized, corrupt, and destructive, so it was not shocking to see the same elements play out on a larger stage. Yet this larger stage is also instructive for considering the dynamics in northern Kenya. For if so many things could go wrong in the spotlight of an international stage and with the direct assistance of international bodies, it is not difficult to imagine how these dynamics must play out far from the gaze of most anyone but the citizens of northern Kenya.

BOMBS OF THE GOVERNMENT, DISCOURSES OF THE GOVERNMENT

In the massacre in which eighty to one hundred Samburu were killed, according to their accounts by bombs dropped on them by the government as if they were "people from another country," precisely what occurred is impossible to disentangle. Everyone agrees there was a raid and many Samburu died, but who killed them and how is far more ambiguous. Analyses of the events and accounts, though differing, tell us much about the real, imagined, and asserted roles attributed to the state as an actor in local violence. Notably in these discourses, the idealized state is highly regarded. Its failings are seen not in terms of a rejection of governmentality as a principle, but rather as a failure to live up to the ideals of government.

This particular raid occurred in the context of a back-and-forth between Samburu and Pokot in their low-level conflict. About ten months prior, Samburu had launched a massive raid in retaliation for persistent losses of cattle, with mixed results. They successfully captured a large number of livestock, losing fewer than ten lives. Yet along with this success came a tangible Samburu loss. The typical pattern Samburu follow in warfare is to withdraw their residential settlements from nearby areas just prior to launching a raid in order to keep their livestock, children, and women safe from counterattacks. As a consequence, the Samburu ceded large areas of territory to the Pokot through their retreat prior to the raid and—irked both by this loss of land and by the Pokot's continuing theft of cattle—planned further major attacks. Their second major raid, in May 2007, met with more disastrous results. Samburu plans were well known—the Samburu have a reputation (even among themselves) for not being good with secrets and for refusing to alter plans even when detected. The Samburu raided around dawn and successfully captured a large number of livestock. However, they found some of their escape routes cut off, and a large party of Samburu was surrounded. In the ensuing fighting, an estimated eighty to one hundred Samburu were killed.

How these Samburu died is unclear and complex. Samburu, for their part, tend to give a fairly simple answer: it was the government. Widely circulating stories following the raid indicated that the large number of Samburu killed was the result of a brutal military response, including helicopters that dropped bombs on the raiders. Samburu closer to the event later indicated to me that there was no helicopter, but tanks and mortars were used on those attempting to leave with Pokot cattle. One man who successfully returned from the raid with stolen goats responded to the question of who killed his companions in these terms: "It is the government who killed them. It is the government. Do the Pokot have bombs? Do the Pokot have big bombs that they kill people with? It is the government who has killed."

There is, then, he asserts, no doubt that the government killed his peers. He agreed that some people were killed by Pokot—though he claimed that those Pokot had been ferried ahead in government vehicles to cut off the Samburu escape—but predominantly they were killed by government forces, in a manner that he sees as being at odds with the way a government should maintain law and order for its citizens. He continues:

Bombs are meant for people from other countries. The right thing is to arrest people and put them in jail. The footprints can be followed to some point and they can confiscate the cows and have the stolen ones brought back and arrest the people. You remember that's what they used to do was just come and seize the cows, because the government is powerful, and the cows will be given back by force, and it's a must that people will also produce the guns. . . . I don't understand why the government used the bombs on its citizens. If they needed to kill, why don't they use guns? They killed people who were just running away, but they followed them in order to kill. They were just running away. Some people were driving cows but others were just running away. The ones who were killed were not even going with cows. They were just killed with bombs as they were running away.

By all accounts a large number of young Samburu men died in this raid, although accounts of how they died differ significantly. Samburu universally attribute it to an inappropriately brutal government response: they were bombed "like people from another country." Yet Pokot informants paint a very different picture. When I related the Samburu description of these events, my Pokot friends laughed: "Those are just their words, lies of the Samburu. We Pokot killed them. The cattle owners themselves killed them. Whenever we defeat [the Samburu] they say it is the government." Many Pokot would not admit that government forces were even present, emphasizing that the owners of the cattle killed the Samburu. As one man told me, "They were killed by Pokot. [Jon: Really? Because Samburu say they were killed by the government.] Not the government. You know they feel embarrassed. They feel embarrassed. They feel embarrassed to say they were killed by Pokot." Pokot agree, if pressed, that government vehicles assisted them with transport in pursuit of the cattle but deemphasize any role the government played in the fighting. Moreover, they assert that government assistance was appropriate given that the Samburu were cattle thieves. No Pokot agreed that the government had used bombs, and some expressed surprise at the claim. One man noted that if they had used bombs, blown-up cows would have been left behind, which he asserted (albeit with no hard evidence) there were not. Some claimed that the government might have used tear gas canisters to stop the movement of cattle, but nothing else.

Pokot, thus, take credit for the work that Samburu attribute to the government, typically portraying Samburu as rampant liars, but also as people who are too ashamed to admit they were bested by their adversaries, the

Pokot. Indeed, Pokot deny that they are shown any favoritism by the government, sometimes suggesting quite the opposite. When they have fared badly in their conflict with the Samburu, they often attribute it to favoritism that the government purportedly displays toward the Samburu.

Parsing facts from these disparate accounts is difficult if not impossible. By Samburu accounts, the government cordoned off the battlefield for several weeks after the incident, meaning that no one could come to see exactly what had occurred—which Samburu attribute to a desire to cover up their atrocities, though it also means that Samburu (or anyone) can construct any account they wish without any ability to confirm or falsify it. Samburu—particularly the combatants in a not very successful mission—obviously have an interest in placing blame on the government rather than offering respect to the martial abilities of their foes. Conversely, Pokot have an interest in taking credit, in asserting their dominance even in what they often claim are adverse circumstances. And indeed, in other contexts Pokot, like Samburu, blame the government for their own failings, complaining in particular about what they see as a government propensity to supply the Samburu with guns. While the Pokot are themselves well armed, they predominantly have AK-47s, which some derisively dismiss as "ambush weapons," since they are lightweight firearms with about half the effective range of the European-made G3s that are more common among Samburu. As one Pokot man asserted:

> The thing is, the way things are now, the Pokot have no one to defend us. To tell the truth, we have no big leaders who will come to our aid, no government to come to our aid. Maybe just God alone. . . . The thing we really feel now, the thing we believe completely, is that if we could get weapons we could assist ourselves completely. The Turkana attack us in the lowlands, and the government says the Pokot are bad people. The Samburu attack us up here, and the government says the Pokot are bad people. And so they come to collect our animals and bring our animals to Samburu. And it is guns that deliver those cows. It isn't pens. So now we have seen how it is, and we pray because there isn't another way, except to get assistance in the way of guns.

In the view of many Pokot, it is only through government assistance that the Samburu are able to resist them. And indeed, some assert that this assistance emboldens the Samburu to an extent that peace becomes impossible:

> We won't get peace because the government helps those people [Samburu]. Because they've grown used to it, to gathering the cows of the Pokot and driving them away. And when the Pokot come to get them, they are blocked by the government. But, if the government were to leave those people, and to leave the Samburu without their assistance. . . . You know, you've seen ranches, and also Nairobi. Those places are full of Turkana. They are full of Turkana who have been made homeless. It's us Pokot who've made them homeless. But these people [Samburu], these people—they think they are something because the government is helping them. If they were to be smart they would seek peace. But if they say no to peace, that's it. Pokot—we will awaken and if we fight with Samburu, Samburu will be driven very far away. They won't live in these parts.

Thus, Samburu and Pokot both hold a similar view of the Kenyan government. Both hold the government responsible as a scapegoat for their failings. Samburu point to such things as the large number of their warriors killed in this particular raid, or the greater success Pokot seem to enjoy in making off with Samburu cattle, which—unlike Pokot cattle, they claim—are rarely if ever returned. Pokot, for their part, attribute government aid (mainly in the form of guns) to the fact that Samburu fought them to a standstill after some early Pokot successes, and claim that the government returns cattle to the Samburu but not vice versa. These assertions typically have a certain nefarious, hidden quality to them. The mechanism behind this is typically shrouded in rumor or mystery, such that one imagines that where, as Evans-Pritchard (1937) famously asserted, the Azande use witchcraft to explain unfortunate events, Samburu and Pokot use the trope of government to explain misfortune.

This is not to say that the explanations of the two groups are identical. Where Pokot tend to focus on what the Kenyan press likes to vaguely term "prominent figures in the government," Samburu tend to blame the national government as a single nebulous body. Pokot tend to focus on specific Samburu leaders, who often have greater stature on the national scene than their own leaders do, and who strive to ensure their standing within the community by aiding their co-ethnics in waging war. Samburu sometimes focus on individual Pokot leaders, though there are fewer of them. Thus, Samburu tend to reprise long-standing tropes about their marginality from the Kenyan state, particularly from a Kenyan state led by the Kikuyu, such as Kenya's first president, Jomo Kenyatta, or more recently, Mwai Kibaki. Unlike the Pokot, they sided with the opposition in the recent referendum on the new constitution and in the 2007 election. Some Samburu also assert that the Kikuyu or the Kikuyu-dominated government want Laikipia for themselves. In this version Kikuyu are simply using the Pokot as tools to drive off the Samburu, on the assumption that less-educated Pokot will be easier to oust from the region than a better-connected and more "enlightened" group, as Samburu see themselves.

But there is another trope regarding the government that Pokot and Samburu share much more closely. When asked about the possibility of the government bringing peace, the almost universal response from both groups was to ask, with a laugh, "What government?" or simply to state, "There is no government." Despite being blamed when something goes wrong, the government is seen as generally uninterested in the conflict and certainly not inclined to take the necessary actions to bring peace. As Charles asserted, "Truly, Jon, because there is nothing the government can't do. There is none. . . . So you see, it is just apparent that they have agreed to this [war]."

Government indifference to fighting is, in fact, a widespread theme not only among Pokot and Samburu, but also among other northern Kenyan pastoralist groups. Turkana, for instance, have also complained to me that despite the presence of a nearby military camp, soldiers do nothing to fight cattle raiders or return stolen cattle. Rather than risk their lives to retrieve someone else's property, they prefer to remain safely in their camps until the dust has cleared, emerging only to take credit for whatever livestock civilians successfully recover by themselves. The perceived government indifference to fighting and cattle theft contributes to the outrage of both Samburu and Pokot when the government actually does take action. As one Samburu man argued, "Why is the government attacking us and it's not attacking the Pokot? It shows that we belong only to God. . . . Our cows that were raided the other day at Kanampio, were those returned? Yet their cows were returned when the government used bombs to kill people. Is there any cow of ours that the government has ever returned?" On other occasions, Pokot make precisely the same case—that the government allows the Samburu to raid them freely but takes action to return cows they have taken from the Samburu. As one man noted above, "The Samburu attack us up here, and the government says the Pokot are bad people. And so they come to collect our animals and bring our animals to Samburu."

Clearly there is a measure of government inaction in this conflict. If one looks beyond cattle raiding, this is all the more obvious. One might excuse the government for its inaction on cattle raids, on the grounds that stolen cattle can be difficult to retrieve. This is especially true of cattle taken by the Pokot, who by all accounts have adopted tactics that make retrieving cattle far more difficult. Yet land is more difficult to explain. Among both the Samburu and the Pokot, many individuals have bought title deeds to land that they cannot use because it now falls within territory controlled by the other ethnic group, who freely utilize it. No government efforts have been made to return the legal owners to these farms, either Samburu or Pokot—not to mention Kikuyu, some of whom abandoned their farms because of insecurity from both the Samburu and the Pokot.

Why does the government fail to act in these conflicts? Or, perhaps more central to this book, how do Samburu and Pokot explain this inaction? There are two main explanations, applied by both groups to varying degrees. One is that the government simply doesn't care, that they are concerned with the doings of larger ethnic groups and the mainstream Kenyan political economy, hence conflicts between relatively small, remote ethnic groups are not of major concern to them. Others take a more conspiratorial view—that the government actually wants smaller groups to fight among themselves so that they will drive each other from land coveted by larger tribes closer to the power structure of the nation, particularly the Kikuyu. This view is held particularly by Samburu, who are apt to assert that the Pokot are something between mercenaries and dupes to the Kikuyu, who want to gain control of Laikipia, but some Pokot also adhere to the idea that the government, dominated by large ethnic groups, wants fighting as a means to later gain the land for itself.

"BIG PEOPLE" IN THE NGOROKO PERIOD
AND IN RECENT TURKANA RAIDING

If widespread discourses among various northern Kenyan groups explain violent events through government indifference, bias, and overexuberance, other discourses paint the government in darker terms—as sometimes shadowy perpetrators. One example can be found in Samburu recollections of a visit by then president of Kenya Daniel arap Moi to the Samburu District headquarters, Maralal, in the 1980s. He is said to have advised the Samburu with words that they quote to this effect: "It is good to keep only a few cattle and sell the others. If you have too many cattle, people will see them and become interested in them." What Moi was purported to have been conveying in this possibly apocryphal piece of "friendly advice" was that in modern Kenya groups like the Samburu are vulnerable—vulnerable to predation from elements who see something of value and weave plans to separate it from its rightful, but weaker, owners.[2] In this context a prominent Samburu discourse has emerged that explains much cattle raiding directed against them through reference to their marginality and vulnerability in modern Kenya.

I turn now to a focus on conflicts mainly between Samburu and Turkana, for whom the discourse of government conspiracy is particularly prominent. Indeed, government involvement is an often-cited Samburu trope in explaining raiding by neighboring Turkana, first during the infamous period of Ngoroko raiding in the 1970s and early 1980s, and again during a massive upturn in raiding in the mid- to late 1990s through the present. These discourses center mainly on rumors that explain much of the large-scale raiding as a largely commercial enterprise undertaken by local, regional, national, and even global "Big People." Thus, the economic losses and physical sufferings they endure through raiding are frequently narrated through reference to what they construe as their position within postcolonial Kenya, politically and economically marginalized and vulnerable to predation by "Big People" within a kleptocratic state.

These discourses play out differently among various northern Kenyan groups. Here I focus on Samburu discourses, simply because I know them most intimately (given the length of my work with the Samburu). The idea that cattle raiding had moved beyond locally organized stock theft between Samburu and their neighbors first arose during the

Ngoroko attacks in the late 1970s and early 1980s, when well-armed Turkana raiders engaged in large-scale raids against the Samburu and other neighboring groups, resulting in significant loss of livestock and human life. As discussed in chapter 5, it is well documented that the Ngoroko was composed of more than just typical local Turkana; rather, it was a paramilitary group that included both Turkana ex-military personnel and youth of fighting age (Oba 1992). Intriguingly, many Samburu linked the violence of the Ngoroko period to the national scene via the Anti-Livestock Theft Unit of the Kenya police stationed to quell the threat, rather than the attributing it to Ngoroko themselves. Many Samburu still assert that members of the Anti-Livestock Theft Unit were participating in (rather than preventing) the raids, owing to Kikuyu dominance of the independent government and their significant presence in the Kenya police—a rumor that harkens to those of vampiric firemen and policemen that Luise White (2000) evocatively describes in colonial Kenya and elsewhere.

Thus, rumors of police participation in cattle theft were construed centrally within Samburu perceptions of their position within postcolonial Kenya: vulnerable to predation in the new context of a government dominated by an ethnic group they not only perceived (rightly or wrongly; see chapter 3) as harboring considerable post–Mau Mau antipathy toward them, but which had earned a general reputation of using their new political power to enrich their co-ethnics. Today, some Samburu dismiss police participation in Ngoroko as mere rumors—lies—while others debate whether it stemmed from Kikuyu antipathy toward the Samburu or simply served as an economic activity, part and parcel of a perceived strategy to replace rich whites in colonial Kenya with rich Kikuyu in postcolonial Kenya. That is, the theft of their cattle was perhaps simply part of a trend throughout the country: if in other areas Kikuyu got differential access to land or other benefits to make them rich, in Samburu what was of value was cattle.

The Ngoroko raiding ended in the early 1980s, when the army crushed the group following raids on the herds of the then-commander of the armed forces, who was a Samburu. In recent years, however, new rumors have emerged that at least some cattle raiding is market oriented, organized at some level by the rich and powerful, some of whom are specifically identified, while others are more vaguely seen as "Big People."

The main thrust of these rumors is that raiding—particularly by the Turkana—is commercially oriented, and a range of evidence is cited in this regard. As one young man asserted, contrasting Turkana raiding (which Samburu conclude is often commercial) with Somali raiding (which they see as merely intended to add animals to Somali herds): "Maybe there is somewhere that [the Turkana] take them. Nobody knows. Because now if we go and take revenge, when you raid them you will never find your animals. You will never even get the ones with your family's earmark.[3] But those Somalis from down there, when you go to recover your animals you will just get your own cows. But the [Turkana], you will never find them. There was a time that the government pursued the raiders, but they only brought back animals that don't belong to us, just as compensation."

Informants cite a range of evidence that Turkana raiding is commercial. For instance, the tracks of their stolen cattle are said to simply disappear in the bush, the implication being that the animals were loaded onto trucks and taken to markets in Nairobi or elsewhere to be sold, as various sources claim is a common occurrence elsewhere in the northern Rift Valley (Eaton 2010). The contrast between the Turkana and other ethnic groups is especially notable, since when raids were conducted by groups such as the Somali and Boran, for instance, informants asserted that their actual cattle were returned, while with the Turkana it was at best only an *equivalent number* of cattle, but never the *actual stolen animals*.

Samburu widely assert that what accounts for these differences is that the Turkana had presumably already sold the missing animals—the raid being only a means to "fill an order."[4] As one elder explained, "You can't raid unless someone has placed an order [for the cattle]. . . . People aren't fools. There must be an order. How can someone raid without an order?"

The accuracy of this assessment is debatable, given the infamous difficulty of tracking animals in the wide expanses of Turkana (e.g., Lamphear 1992). Yet the vastness of spaces can hardly account for differences in Samburu discourses concerning raiding, since they assert that the specific cattle taken by Somali raiders are recovered—despite the equal vastness of Somali areas. However, informants frequently tied these raids to "Big People" inside and outside the district—principally politicians or unknown businesspeople, but sometimes condensed under a nonspecific notion that it is "the government." It is important to note in this regard that while Samburu occupy about two thirds of the district and make up a similar portion of the population, the remaining third is Turkana, administered by the same district commissioner and with a vote in both national and local elections. One elder, for instance, denied the notion that it was "the government" as a general institution that encouraged or assisted the raiding, but suggested that particular politicians might be involved.

> [People thought] the government was assisting the Turkana because during the fighting you would encounter people in army uniforms. And some people said, in fact, it is the government that is attacking us. . . . But I think it is just because they [many Turkana] don't know how to use guns, so those of them in the armed forces teach others. . . . And you also have politicians who are looking for votes; for instance, councilors can help them look for guns or food during fighting. It is true that the government favors the Turkana, but secretly. You will never see it openly.

Rumors take a variety of forms, with varying levels of plausibility. Some, such as this suggestion concerning councilors (and similar ones implicating more prominent politicians) contain relatively straightforward motivations and mechanisms: garnishing favor among their constituents by supplying them with weaponry. Insofar as those making such claims are often close to the parties involved, they appear plausible, though there is no way to confirm their accuracy. Other rumors contain assertions that go far beyond the local context, however. One rumor suggested, for instance, that Samburu cattle were being used to feed the Sudanese People's Liberation Army (SPLA), one of the main rebel groups in southern Sudan. In this scenario, the SPLA had placed a large order for cattle through intermediaries in Nairobi and were willing to pay many times the market price for the animals. Turkana raiders were said to steal Samburu cattle and turn them over to middlemen, who brought them on trucks to Nairobi, where they were butchered and the meat sent to the SPLA in southern Sudan. Samburu are adamant that Sudanese accompanied the Turkana on one raid. Oddly, though, the alleged proof suggests no connection to the SPLA. According to one Samburu man, "When people finished the battle they discovered that there are Sudanese there who were killed. The dead person was white, and he had things in his ears." Since the SPLA was composed of Nilotic peoples, such as the Nuer and Dinka, whose skin is typically much darker than the average Samburu, it is difficult to imagine what sort of Sudanese person this was purported to be.

Rumors can become extremely complex, even circuitously counterintuitive. Perhaps this is best exemplified by rumors concerning the death of the Samburu District commissioner, who was killed when his helicopter was shot down while pursuing Turkana raiders who had struck deep into Samburu territory in 1996. The fact that he was killed by Turkana while pursuing Samburu cattle would seem to construct him as an ally of the Samburu. Many Samburu, however, construed it in exactly opposite terms: his death, many asserted, proved his favoritism toward the Turkana. While it is impossible to know where his sentiments may have lain—or if he was simply an unbiased public official—it had previously been rumored that he favored the Turkana, and his death in the helicopter served as the final piece of evidence. Informants suggested that he was known to be too cozy with the Turkana community. They noted that the Turkana had demonstrated their friendship by giving him many goats for his Christmas celebration, and believed it likely that he, like other "Big People," was getting kickbacks from the raids, which were extremely intense at that time. That his helicopter was downed by small-arms fire, killing all aboard, was seen, rather ironically, to have conclusively proven this theory. The argument was that he was only shot down because he was flying too low, something he would do only if he felt he had nothing to fear from his friends the Turkana. Another informant claimed to have heard that the individual who had shot down the helicopter had been rather surprised to discover that something as small as an AK-47 could destroy something as big as a helicopter. The death was, in that account, quite accidental.

It is easy to find such rumors farfetched. And indeed, when multiple rumors use the same evidence to prove opposite things, it isn't possible that all are true. If one presumes that at least a good deal contained in these rumors is false, the question becomes how and why these falsehoods emerge. Partial answers lie in some of the commonplace explanations through which anthropologists deal with rumor: rumors fill in gaps when

information is imperfect; rumors reflect the anxieties of societies undergo-
ing change (White 2000)—in this case, concerns of Samburu and other
marginalized northern groups regarding their problematic fit within the
political economy of "modern Kenya." At the same time, it is important
to highlight the links between two key facets of these rumors: first, that
contemporary raiding is a radical shift from long-standing patterns, and
second, that these changes are attributed to the actions of specific groups
or individuals. Thus, the drastic shifts in raiding associated with the
Ngoroko period were viewed not simply as a shift in the balance of power
when the Turkana (or some Turkana) got greater access to guns. Rather,
there was a fundamental shift in the nature of raiding when, in the context
of postcolonial Kenya, the Samburu became vulnerable to predation from
"the government"/the Kikuyu—viewed in this context by many Samburu as one and the same—with aggression based both in greed and animosity. In contrast, rumors concerning recent raiding highlight issues that
are predominantly based in class and politics. On one hand, these involve
the perception of an emerging modern elite (which can include the Samburu) preying on those who have ostensibly been "left behind." On the
other hand, it involves politics, pure and simple—fomenting conflict or
aiding one side to gain votes—though it is difficult to disentangle politics
from personal enrichment. And here the rumors are not linked to some
ethereal, abstract modernity; rather it is a modernity driven by particular
kinds of people—"Big People" using their economic and political power
for exploitative ends, a prototypical actor who has wide recognition
within the political economy of contemporary Kenya. While at times
these "Big People" are a vague, nefarious category, at other times they are
specific individuals who could be named but may be considered too powerful and dangerous to do so freely.[5]

Whether these accusations are correct cannot be proven. The point is
that—right or wrong—these rumors are spread by particular groups and
individuals who (for good reasons or bad) find themselves at odds with
these people as individuals, as representatives of rival localities, as political
opponents from other clans, or merely as visible "Big People" who may
provoke envy and fear of exploitation. Thus, irrespective of whether they
are the cause of these events, such figures can be usefully linked to the
types of unfortunate events—devastating cattle raids—that the Samburu
see as having become part of life in postcolonial Kenya.

THE USUAL SUSPECTS: WHEN THE GOVERNMENT
BLAMES THE GOVERNMENT

On November 10, 2012, approximately 160 Kenyan police (a mix of regular police and local police reservists) descended into the forbidding Suguta Valley, commonly nicknamed the "Valley of Death" for its scalding temperatures, rough landscape, and well-armed and lawless cattle raiders. They were in pursuit of Turkana livestock raiders who had taken a significant number of Samburu cattle. While such cattle raids are commonplace, the events that followed are highly notable. Despite being exhausted, short of water, and on unfamiliar terrain, the police, intent on recovering the cattle, successfully tracked the perpetrators. The raiders, however, neither fled nor surrendered the cattle. Rather, they turned their guns on the police, staging a well-planned ambush that left forty-two policemen dead, the largest number of police killed in any incident in Kenyan history.

As we have wound through events and discourses involving the government in northern Kenyan violence, the government has predominantly been seen as a powerful if unreliable and sometimes corrupt force. While the victims of violence—whether Samburu, Pokot, Turkana, or others—have enmity for the perpetrators, there is nonetheless a persistent theme that the government also bears responsibility, whether as inert or indifferent observers or as unacknowledged and unsanctioned perpetrators of violence. The latter may take the form of explicit yet excessive force in which the government is seen as a partisan combatant—for instance, in dropping bombs on fleeing Samburu raiders—or as a shadowy, kleptocratic instigator that is in some senses orchestrating violence.

But what about when the government's position changes to be neither observer nor perpetrator but rather that of victim, as in this massacre of forty-two policemen? Who then takes the blame? In this instance the government—surprisingly or unsurprisingly—blamed the government.

In the days following the massacre, I was startled to find an internet video of my Turkana host, Christopher, in handcuffs on Kenyan television. He was among a small group of locals who had been arrested in conjunction with the incident. Everyone arrested was associated with the government, one being a local councilor and the rest government chiefs. While I was startled to see my friend from a remote spot in northern Kenya arraigned via an internet video, I was not shocked at the development itself. His settlement, where I frequently stayed, adjoins the police encampment from which the ill-fated police mission was launched. This was not the first time that Christopher had been arrested. I slept at his home on all of my visits to his community, a Turkana village not far from ethnic Samburu areas, but for a few months he had been "away," having been arrested in conjunction with an earlier Turkana raid on Samburu.

Without question, Christopher was uninvolved in the raids for which he was arrested. It is impossible to know whether he had foreknowledge of some raids. Sometimes perhaps he did, given that I—a foreign anthropologist—had foreknowledge (if not precise information) about some Samburu raids. However, he in no sense resembled the people that I knew or strongly suspected participated in or otherwise benefited from raiding. Christopher was not wealthy in either livestock or cash. He had a modest number of goats and (despite earning a small salary as chief) lacked the cash to buy a mobile phone—which increasingly everyone in northern Kenya has and uses regularly. I have seen people who seem to have large influxes of wealth that are not easily accounted for, people who have livestock for sale with no clear origin, and Christopher was not this type. Christopher did not live in, and rarely traveled to, the area where the raiders settled with the stolen livestock. He frequently investigated even minor incidents, like the sound of gunshots (which are most often attributable in his area to guys celebrating while leaving a place of drinking). And in any case, he was arrested not for livestock theft but for the murder of the policemen, yet he was nowhere near where the policemen were killed.

Why arrest Christopher, a man who certainly did not take part in the raids and is not plausibly associated with the raiders in any meaningful way? How Christopher can be held officially responsible for raids such as these is complex, tied to the Turkana's political position in Samburu District and the historically constituted position of "chiefs" in Kenya at large.

As discussed extensively in chapter 5, Samburu-Turkana relations are rife with contradictions, as they are both archenemies and close neighbors, adversaries and friends. Partially this is because the Turkana are a large, diverse ethnic group—numbering over nine hundred thousand, according to the 2009 Kenya census, and spanning Samburu District to Uganda and the Sudanese border, with a large number of clans and other subgroups. It is, consequently, frequently ambiguous as to whether all

Turkana are enemies or whether some are friends, while the Turkana who are deemed "friendly" by some Samburu may simply appear to be representative of all Turkana to other Samburu. Recall, for instance, the incident described by the Samburu elder Lelenguya in chapter 5, where a group of Samburu tried to prevent him and his fellows from undertaking a revenge raid against what the local Samburu characterized as "our Turkana"—their friendly neighbors, who they argued were not the Turkana responsible, but who would attack them if Lelenguya's sortie of more distant Samburu followed through on their raid (both of which subsequently occurred).

This largely autochthonous dynamic of differing groups of Turkana being differently positioned vis-à-vis Samburu is, moreover, further complicated by divisions caused by political boundaries within Kenya. Significant numbers of Turkana live within the Kenyan political entity of Samburu District.[6] These Samburu-residing Turkana are in the awkward position of ostensibly belonging to neither group. While by virtue of proximity and political boundaries they tend to share interests, develop social ties, and to varying degrees assimilate with Samburu, Samburu clearly view them as members of a different ethnic group with whom there is frequent antagonism. On the other hand, Turkana living in Samburu district maintain that their co-ethnics in other regions see them as being aligned with the group's enemies since they live close to or even among them. They claim that raiders from other parts of Turkana actually raid them, though not as frequently as they raid the Samburu. Indeed, during periods of severe conflict between Turkana and Samburu—for instance in the mid-1990s—it was common to find Turkana communities establish themselves within Samburu territory as "refugees," rather than flee to what one might assume would be safer haven among their co-ethnic Turkana.

There is, then, a complex dynamic for communities such as Christopher's, which sits on the border between Samburu and Turkana (though well within the administrative boundaries of Samburu District). Naturally, this border area is one of the most common areas for conflict, and even when raids occur elsewhere or if raiders are from elsewhere, they of necessity pass through the border regions. Turkana raids—which are more common, though unprovoked Samburu raids also occur—tend to occur in areas where the two groups live in close proximity and where local Turkana appear to be on reasonably good terms with the Samburu, at least much of the time. Local Turkana will insist that they did not undertake the raids, which they say are conducted by Turkana from more distant areas, perhaps "those from Lodwar" (a major center in Turkana District) or Ngoroko. Local Turkana may claim that they too are victimized by these groups.

Samburu tend to view these claims with suspicion. They recognize that Turkana are not uniform, and that particularly aggressive groups of distant Turkana attack even other Turkana, who as one Samburu informant agreed, "even other Turkana are afraid of." However, rarely do Samburu fully absolve neighboring Turkana of responsibility. Samburu frequently claim that even if the raiders are from far away, they could not negotiate the terrain without locals who serve as their guides. Moreover, they believe that even if the instigators are not from the area, locals take part to garner livestock from the attacks. Samburu claim (though admittedly without substantiation) that in the course of raids for which local Turkana disavow any responsibility, individual Turkana with whom they are familiar from Baragoi town have been killed and their bodies identified. For their part, local Turkana are ambiguous about their roles. They do not admit participation but also do not flatly deny that people from their area could play a role in such raids. They insist, however, that if any individuals assisted the raiders it would be due to coercion. Those "Turkana from Lodwar," as they are characterized, are dangerous people, well armed and brutal. If they asked for assistance and it was not provided, they might attack or kill local Turkana instead of or in addition to Samburu, such that some admit the possibility that locals might sometimes serve as guides.

This returns us to the issue of collective responsibility and irresponsibility discussed first in chapter 2. Where in the classic anthropological conception, a whole naturally takes responsibility for the actions of its members as a means of creating solidarity with the group—an attack on one is an attack on all—whether it is beneficial to take responsibility clearly is contingent on the implications of responsibility within a particular social and political context. Responsibility can become culpability with implications for reprisals by the opposed group or the third leg of the triad of perpetrator-victim-observer: the government. Consequently, it may be beneficial for actors to distance the group from the actions of individual members. That collective responsibility, or denial of collective responsibility, can be situational and one sided, is well illustrated by the assertions of a Pokot man in reference to a cattle raid undertaken by his co-ethnics: "If there are cows that were taken, those were thieves. Those were thieves. Not [like] those people [i.e., Samburu] coming with weapons. This is just stealing. If I go and steal a chicken, isn't it just said that *I* stole a chicken? It isn't *Pokot* who stole the chicken." He thus denies responsibility for the actions of his co-ethnics—characterizing it instead as the act of individual thieves. In contrast, he nonetheless asserts shared culpability for actions taken by Samburu.

This ability for responsible, or possibly responsible, parties to evade culpability ironically explains why someone like my friend Christopher could be arrested for such raids (or in actuality for the massacre of police officers following the raid, as that is what the charges involved). His arrests have seemingly come in the spirit of Captain Renault's famous call in *Casablanca* after Humphrey Bogart's character, Rick, shoots dead a villainous German officer: "Round up the usual suspects." Renault realized that someone needed to be held responsible, for his sake perhaps and also to protect Rick. Similarly, in the case of the massacre, *someone* has to be held accountable. *Something* has happened such that someone needs to be arrested to demonstrate that someone is being held accountable (irrespective of that person's ties to the event).

Thus within the complex dynamics of this context it may not be possible, or even necessary or desirable, to determine what exactly happened and who is responsible. Even if we had perfect knowledge, there might be various at least partially correct answers for who bears responsibility or blame. If no one actually knows who did it, the next best thing is to arrest whomever you can—for instance, Christopher. Indeed, the typical pattern in Kenya, historically and today, is to arrest those regarded as the leaders of a community, irrespective of whether they are connected to violent events, and even if they are government-appointed bureaucrats rather than leaders arising organically out of the community. In regard to the Baragoi massacre, Christopher was one of five local administrative officials arrested—these being, to my knowledge, the only individuals arrested (despite them having actually taken no part in the raiding). In another community, a different friend/informant was arrested and imprisoned for over a year in connection with a raid undertaken by co-ethnics in an area far from his home area, though neither facts nor logic connected him to the attack and the police making the arrest were unaware of who he was or what he looked like, instead employing a trick to make him identify himself at a public meeting. To cite a famous Samburu example from the colonial period, the *loibon* (seer) Leaduma was arrested for allegedly playing a role in instigating the killing of a white settler (despite having no direct role in the killing) (Holtzman and Straight 2005; Fratkin 2015). Thus, we may ask what dynamics lead to figures such as these being arrested for events in which they likely played no role.

Several motivations can be cited here, some based in logic and some in expediency. The official government position is largely that chiefs are expected to be in charge of "their area." Thus, if a crime occurs in their area, they are expected to either arrest the perpetrators or be held responsible. This has the effect of creating a situation in which chiefs have a strong incentive to, as much as possible—in appearance at least, if not always in fact—control "their people" to avoid being punished themselves, thus keeping the chiefs on the side of the government rather than with their constituents.

Perhaps most importantly, however, the reason for arresting Christopher and those like him is that he was available to be arrested. Those who actually took the cattle remained, heavily armed, in the inhospitable Suguta Valley. Efforts to arrest them and recover the cattle had already born a concrete result: forty-two police officers had been killed. The government needed to demonstrate that it was doing its job. If no one were arrested, officials might be blamed for doing nothing. And moreover—though I do not know of this occurring in Christopher's case specifically—others can benefit from placing the blame on someone. In the famous colonial example of the arrest of the Samburu loibon Leaduma, it is clear that rival Samburu clans jockeyed to have the blame placed on one another, using the government to settle unrelated grievances. And a Pokot friend arrested in 2010 and imprisoned for about a year insists that he was implicated for events socially and geographically distant from him because Pokot rivals envied his wealth and influence.

.   .   .

This chapter has examined the role of the government as an often-shadowy "third man" in northern Kenyan conflicts. I have considered the government to a great extent as an actor, but perhaps even more importantly, in the discourses that agents in these conflicts use to explain conflicts, and to whom much of their discourses is aimed. That is, as warring, or sometimes-warring, groups move between the roles of victim and perpetrator of violence, the government serves as an inconsistent audience for these events and the stories that are told about them. It serves most clearly as an observer—a powerful observer that may intervene with overwhelming force, and thus an audience whom actors strive to convince of their victimhood or their righteousness. And while the principle of government is respected by virtually all actors in these northern Kenyan conflicts, in practice officials are most often seen as negligent in their roles or even as malicious actors, using power in biased and sometimes corrupt ways.

In this sense, one may compare the role of government, its role in explanatory narratives, and the incomplete and uncertain understandings of its actions to other quite different contexts. We may think of similarities in the structure of rumors about the government in northern Kenya to the kinds of rumors Luise White (2000) stunningly described in colonial Africa, where firemen were believed to not only start fires but actually be vampires of a sort. Rumors are often a product of anxiety, in contexts of change or adverse circumstances one cannot explain. In this we may think back to one of our most classic anthropological texts, in which Evans-Pritchard richly explicates how among the Azande "witchcraft explains unfortunate events." In northern Kenya I argue that to a significant degree "the government explains unfortunate events." That is, it is a higher power, a body seen as having almost superpowers, yet one that is fickle and escapes a common person's full understanding. In this sense we may consider how the beliefs of Samburu, Pokot, and Turkana about the nature of government share much not only with traditional conceptions of the role of the supernatural but also with our own perceptions of government. Rumors of shadowy government malice—whether true or not—on all sides of the political spectrum in a country like the United States are structurally similar to both Samburu views of the government and Azande views of witchcraft: Did the CIA blow up the Twin Towers? Was the code in electronic voting machines rigged to produce outcomes desired by those who design and operate the machines?

Such rumors resonate not simply because we don't know, but because we know they *could* be true. And moreover, we are not in a position to decide when they are true and when they are nonsense. The forces are sufficiently powerful and sufficiently hidden that we have no way to assess them. Such rumors can reflect a genuine fear, they can be an excuse where the reality is uncomfortable, they can (whether true or false) be used to evoke action, and they can also reflect actual events. We don't know, and the actors do not know. Perhaps no one knows precisely how it came to pass that 9/11 happened, that the attack on Pearl Harbor was a surprise, that a mall was destroyed in Nairobi, or that eighty Samburu died with the government at hand. Whether those Samburu died by the government's bombs, by their bullets, or by those of the Pokot is unknowable. The most important thing we know is that a massacre happened, and we are left to try to make sense of it and to understand the structural forces that shape how and why actors make sense of it as they do.

CONCLUSION

War Stories

> You can tell a true war story by the questions you ask.
> Somebody tells a story, let's say, and afterwards you ask,
> "Is it true?" and if the answer matters, you've got your
> answer.
>
> TIM O'BRIEN (1990), *"How to Tell a True War Story"*

In 1993 the Nobel Peace Prize was awarded to Rigoberta Menchú, a young Guatemalan peasant woman turned activist who grippingly described the horrors experienced by herself and her indigenous Quiché community at the hands of the army during the Guatemalan civil war. Though she was uneducated, her story, *I, Rigoberta Menchú* (1987)—told to and edited by anthropologist Elisabeth Burgos-Debray—drew international attention to the oppression of poor, mostly indigenous Guatemalans by a brutal right-wing regime supported and armed by the United States. Thus, for instance, in one of the most gripping accounts of savagery described in the book, Rigoberta describes looking on as her brother, Petrocino, already horrifically injured from torture, was publicly burned in the village square with twenty-two other villagers who were said to support one of the rebel movements.

> In my brother's case, he was cut in various places. His head was shaved and slashed. He had no nails. He had no soles to his feet. The earlier wounds were suppurating from infection. And the woman *compañera,* of course I recognized her; she was from a village near ours. They had shaved her private parts. The nipple of one of her breasts was missing and her other breast was cut off. She had the marks of bites on different parts of her body. She was bitten all over, that *compañera.* She had no

ears. All of them were missing part of the tongue or had their tongues split apart. I found it impossible to concentrate, seeing that this could be. You could only think that these were human beings and what pain those bodies had felt to arrive at that unrecognizable state. All the people were crying, even the children. I was watching the children. (p. 178)

Menchú continues to describe the scene, with the military commander exhorting the peasants to look and understand what happens to you when subversives bring foreign, exotic ideas aimed at destroying the democratic government of Guatemala and saying that the same would happen to them if they followed this path. He describes the power of the army, the various weapons they have to destroy those who oppose them. And at the end of the speech, the prisoners, naked, swollen, and unable to walk, are dragged to the town square.

> He called the Kaibiles and they poured petrol over each of the tortured. The captain said, "This isn't the last of their punishments, there's another one yet. That is what we have done with all the subversives we catch because they have to die by violence. And if this doesn't teach you a lesson, this is what'll happen to you too. The problem is that the Indians let themselves be led by the communists. Since no-one's told the Indians anything, they go along with the communists." He was trying to convince the people but at the same time he was insulting them by what he said. Anyway, they lined up the tortured and poured petrol on them; and then the soldiers set fire to each one of them. Many of them begged for mercy. They looked half dead when they were lined up there, but when the bodies began to burn they began to plead for mercy. Some of them screamed, many of them leaped but uttered no sound—of course that was because their breathing was cut off. (p. 179)

This is the savagery that Rigoberta Menchú witnessed and brought grippingly to the attention of the international community.

These things, it turns out, did not all happen.

.   .   .

It was once well known in certain circles that the Kaiser's army did not, in fact, lose the war.

You can take this all the way back to the *Niebelungenlied,* the German epic poem focusing on the adventures of Siegfried. Siegfried killed a dragon and, by bathing in its blood, became invulnerable, except for a spot between his shoulder blades where a large leaf had fallen. Knowing he was a great warrior, the princes of Burgundy, Gunther and Hagen, befriended him, and later he helped them defeat the invading Saxons and Danes against overwhelming odds. But from there things started to go bad—women, jealousy, and the like. Gunther was set on marrying Brünhild, queen of Iceland, but he knew that, like all her suitors, he would have to best her in a contest of strength for which he was no match. Siegfried secretly helped Gunther win, and Brünhild was forced to marry him. Later, the powerful Siegfried helped Gunther sleep with his new wife, who otherwise would wrestle and pin Gunther every night in order to prevent it. By and by, rumors started flying that Siegfried had been the one to deflower Brünhild, and angered at the deception, she demanded that her husband take revenge. So during a hunting trip arranged on false pretenses, Gunther's best warrior, Hagen, speared Siegfried in his one vulnerable spot as he drank water from a spring unarmed. Though he could never have been defeated in a fair battle, the hero Siegfried died through the treachery of those who claimed to be his friends, stabbed in the back by those close to him.

It was once well known in certain circles that World War I followed more or less the same course. When Germany surrendered in November 1918, their troops remained in French and Belgian territory, and on the eastern front the Russians had already been defeated. The Kaiser's army was undefeated and, upon the signing of the treaty of Versailles, retreated to Germany in an orderly manner. What led to the defeat—the surrender—was the fact that the German army had been stabbed in the back. They had been stabbed in the back by internal dissent, socialists, profiteers involved in the war effort not out of patriotism but only as a means to enrich themselves. Those perhaps most responsible for this stab in the back were the Jews.

This version of the defeat of Germany in World War I is not true. But the Holocaust is.

．　　　．　　　．

Working with communities who are often at odds with each other has required me to be open concerning the history of my research in

Kenya—that I have entered this project as a longtime researcher in Samburu, that these are people I know well. This was never more important than when I began my work with Pokot in 2006. Not only were tensions much higher than in other communities where I was working—the conflict we were discussing was active and ongoing, rather than in the relatively distant past—but before I met Pokot face to face I had attended a peace meeting between the Samburu and the Pokot in which I had literally been on the Samburu side. It had not been my plan to attend the meeting at all. I had gone to Laikipia to interview Kikuyu about the 1998 clashes, but everyone had gone to this meeting—organized by politicians and government officials to bring together the warring Samburu and Pokot—including most of the people I had intended to talk with that day. So, if part of anthropological fieldwork is to go with the ebb and flow of daily life, I simply did what the people in the community were doing and went to the meeting.

As I approached the place where the meeting was being held, I saw many Samburu I knew, who brought me to sit with them at the meeting, which was arranged in a partial circle, with Pokot ringing one side and Samburu the other. A gap separated them, and at the front was the area where speakers (whether Samburu, Pokot, or neutral parties) would address the collected body. I sat with my Samburu friends facing off against their Pokot enemies and, as I would do in any such ethnographic circumstances, watched my friends, to some extent mimicked them, and followed their instructions for behaving in a culturally appropriate manner. Pokot and Samburu have very different ethos surrounding such meetings. Pokot, for instance, are more apt to display emotion. For the Samburu, by contrast, the highest social value is *nkanyit* (Spencer 1965; Holtzman 2009), a sense of respect, such that they tend to be calm and polite even when saying the nastiest things. At one point, the Pokot were angered over an issue of stolen cows that they claimed needed to be returned before any peace discussions could take place, and they rose collectively and temporarily left the meeting. The abrupt movement en masse suggested imminent violence— I half expected that the Pokot group was leaving to fetch weapons. Perhaps others in my Samburu group felt the same, and some of us started to rise, but the Samburu elders called out, "Sit, sit, let the boys go." And so, like them, I sat beside my Samburu friends. I could not have looked like anything other than a Samburu partisan.

FIGURE II.   Kalashnikov and a milking gourd.

Two days later I unexpectedly found myself sitting beneath a tree with a group of Pokot, elders and herders. I was in Ol Moran with a Samburu acquaintance who was still on good terms with the Pokot, and he directed me to someone who could take me to talk to the Samburu's enemies. I don't know if the Pokot regarded me as being in league with the enemy—I had sat on the Samburu side, but I clearly was a white man, not a Samburu—but I certainly suspected that they might feel that way. Some of them mentioned having seen me at the meeting. So, whether they thought I needed to or not, I definitely felt that I had to explain myself to them. I told them that I was a researcher, and I was studying peace and war.

"I have studied in Kenya for a long time," I said. "And now I am studying this war. I have stayed with Samburu for a long time, and I have heard their views and now I want to hear . . ."

"The truth," one man finished my sentence for me.

.   .   .

The truth. Where does "the truth" figure into all this? This Pokot elder did not, of course, finish my sentence as I intended it. I meant to say that I wanted to hear their views, their perspectives on things. To a certain extent, I do aim to get at what "really happened" through the material I have presented in this book. However, what people say and believe (I don't always know if even those two mesh that closely) is much closer to the heart of this project. Why do they fight? What do they think about these people who are sometimes enemies and sometimes friends? How do understandings and misunderstandings of the Other lead to conflict or create contexts that even in times of peace lay the groundwork for future violence between friends, economic partners, or neighbors? The stories they tell are important irrespective of whether they are "true," whatever that means.

.   .   .

As quoted at the beginning of this chapter, author Tim O'Brien offers a compelling, if counterintuitive, formula for testing whether a war story is true: does it matter if it *really* happened? As a prototypical example, he takes the well-worn story of a guy jumping on a hand grenade to save his buddies. If it never actually happened, we would feel cheated by this "trite bit of puffery, pure Hollywood." He contrasts this with a different version of the same story:

> Four guys go down a trail. A grenade sails out. One guy jumps on it and takes the blast, but it's a killer grenade and everybody dies anyway. Before they die, though, one of the dead guys says, "The fuck you do *that* for?" and the jumper says, "Story of my life, man," and the other guy starts to smile but he's dead.
>
> That's a true story that never happened.

O'Brien's point is that there is an essential truth, which may be captured in an account irrespective of whether it really happened. In fact, something could have *really* happened and still not be "true" to the extent that it stands in counterpoint to this essential truth. The Hollywood puffery version of the story might have happened sometime, but O'Brien says we shouldn't care, shouldn't regard it as "true" because altruism, heroism is not what war is really about.

We all can probably agree with this to a certain extent. We read fiction not simply as pure entertainment, for the appreciation of its beauty or its humor, but also as a means to gain insights into aspects of the human condition that might not be accessible either through direct experience or through a nonfictive account. Anthropologists themselves, while ostensibly in the business of producing true information—we are not supposed to make stuff up, even if we may report on things our informants make up—often assert that you may learn more about a culture or place from a fictional rendering than from one of our own presumably factual books. Even empiricist "methods guru" H. Russell Bernard (2011) points out that you might gain insights into the human condition from *King Lear*—it just isn't, in his view, anthropology.

O'Brien sees an essential truth to the experience of war: "In the end, of course, a true war story is never about war. It's about the special way that dawn spreads out on a river, when you know you must cross the river and march into the mountains and do things you are afraid to do. It's about love and memory. It's about sorrow. It's about sisters who never write back and people who never listen" (p. 91). Of course, someone else might hold that a true war story is about how people are hideously evil. O'Brien's accounts do highlight the senseless violence and tragedy of war, yet there is also a romantic beauty to his storytelling and his writing—a romantic beauty that is not found in, let's say, Menchú's account of the massacre in which her brother was killed. Perhaps it is found in the German legend of the "stab in the back" but only in the Siegfried version from the *Niebelungenlied,* not in the one that led to the Final Solution.

It might be noted in this regard that O'Brien's writing has been well received, and deservedly so, as it is beautiful, intelligent, and in his own sense, very true. However, an almost identical text written by an SS trooper storming the Warsaw ghetto would certainly not be well received in the contemporary United States. To Vietnamese in 1970 those two texts—O'Brien's and that of our apocryphal storm trooper—would probably have been essentially indistinguishable.

Those are both true texts that never happened.

O'Brien offers us two notions of truth: the things that really happened and the things that are at the essence of reality. He tells us that they may be in opposition. But he does not tell us who is entitled to decide which is important or how they should decide.

.   .   .

How to decide? Convention has it (at least in social science) that, as the author, I might tell you how to decide. I could tell you that as far as I know when L killed the Sheik he was like any other murderer killing an old man in cold blood, or I could tell you the opposite. I could tell you my guess is that Simba was trying to hide in a warthog's den while the Samburu stole his cows because he's really a coward and just brags about the people he's killed or wants to. Maybe the Turkana are the only good guys in the whole bunch, because all the groups kill children but only the Turkana own up to it. Maybe since Samburu have been my friends the longest, some sort of loyalty compels me to say they are the good guys. Though on the other hand, they never gave me a cow as a present—just goats to eat. I had to buy their cows, but after just being friends for a little while, a Pokot man gave me a heifer as a gift. Though it turns out it was maybe stolen from Samburu. Story of my life.

So if I've succeeded in this ethnography, I've taken you into the proverbial grove, so maybe I'm expected to lead you out of it. But I don't know that I can or would want to even if I could. Maybe I should, maybe it's a moral obligation of some sorts. If I gave some postmodern he said / she said on the Holocaust or Wounded Knee, I trust someone out there would have the guts to string me up, or that no one would have the poor sense to let this book see the light of day. People have died in this book, a lot of people, and it doesn't do them justice for me to slither off to my university job and get paid decent money to say that I don't really know who is to blame, that maybe it is everyone or no one. Because someone killed those people, so to them, to their loved ones, or maybe to our sense of humanity, who did it and how it happened matters.

Or maybe it does and maybe it doesn't. Would it matter if the officer who ordered my grandfather's entire village killed was named Hans or Fritz, or if he was German or Austrian? Or even Russian or Polish for that matter? Would it matter if they were all killed then and there, as I've heard it told, or if some of them were shipped off to the concentration camps to work before dying?

Sometimes blame isn't really the point. A major issue here is the way the stories people tell about their wars contain understandings and misunderstandings of other groups that sow the seeds for future violence. Samburu conflicts with the Kikuyu are infused with memories of past violence, which shape them and give them meaning irrespective of their relation to actual events. When Somalis and Samburu go to fight one another, they do so with images of the Other shaped by battles a generation before, and indeed speak of them in those terms. Understanding that dynamic is, I have argued, important. If there is a way to peace, or at least more peace, in the world, perhaps it involves coming to grips with how people—people who are neighbors, even friends—can end up believing things that justify doing horrible things to each other. But there are also larger structural issues. Why do they fight at all? All around northern Kenya, people are shocked and bemused to hear that there are so many guns in the United States and yet they are rarely used on other citizens—and when they are, the perpetrators are customarily locked up quickly. Individuals in Kenya suffer in violence, and sometimes individuals also gain. But by and large the overriding conditions of war cause suffering to groups as a whole, to essentially all the groups that are described in this book.

Part of this answer perhaps lies in the juxtaposition of Rigoberta Menchú and the epic of Siegfried, which gave us the trope of the "stab in the back" that justified the Holocaust. Neither tale really describes how things actually happened, but nonetheless we are comfortable drawing conclusions about Truth from Menchú's account but not from the other. Anthropologist David Stoll (1998) spurred vehement criticism for saying that Rigoberta Menchú gave a false account. Stoll's critics don't claim that his conclusions were wrong. Even his most vehement critics more or less agree that her account was at least highly embellished (though they do not necessarily agree about why or how the embellishment occurred). The deeper question is why in the world would he devote such energy to picking on Menchú? Stoll claimed that he wanted to reveal the plight of all poor Guatemalans—those who were not necessarily sympathetic to the Marxist struggle, those who were not indigenous, those who collaborated with the death squads out of self-interest drawn from their own plight. His pursuit of truth (that is, telling us "what really happened") masked a larger Truth—that a U.S.-sponsored government was terrorizing, torturing, and killing civilians to maintain a structure of oppression. Just because Stoll was right that Menchú was wrong in some specific points should not distract us from the deeper truth, an important truth, that Menchú and her followers highlighted.

So let us return to Kenya. I can't tell you the truth, the whole truth, but I can tell you that the truth does matter. It matters because the Holocaust matters, it matters because the genocide in Rwanda matters, and it matters because the stories that made the Pokot erupt in rage are the same sorts of stories that made the United States coldly tear apart Iraq in search of weapons of mass destruction that lots of people already knew did not exist. Telling stories matters, and how people listen to those stories matters. If this book has made us listen to our own war stories, the stories that drive us to war, even a little bit more critically, it has achieved something. And, perhaps ironically, the fact that we don't quite know what is true tells us something important. The truth of Rigoberta Menchú wouldn't matter so much if it was an argument about a goat or an argument between former lovers. It mattered because the structural conditions put people in positions that empowered them to kill and convinced them that it was in their interests to kill.

And so it is in the northern Kenyan context that I have described. People get rich supplying people with guns. People covet other people's property, land, and livestock, and there is no fair way to adjudicate this. Historical inequities remain unresolved. Oftentimes violence could be stopped, but it is not. Oftentimes perpetrators could be punished, but they are not. So whether my friend Simba, my dear friend Simba, is or is not a killer—or perhaps whether he is a vicious one or a righteous one— is really little more than a trivia question as long as the conditions exist that make stealing someone's cows, or picking up an AK-47 and putting a bullet through someone's skull, just a normal part of a world that he and his fellows, his enemies and his friends, live in but did not make.

LIST OF VIDEOS ONLINE

The following videos can be found at http://www.ucpress.edu/go/neighbors:

At a Samburu Cattle Camp

Simba Tours the Ruins

Bleeding a Cow and Debates About Loyalty

Lekeren on Tinga

Conversations With Tinga

Song and Prayer at a Pokot Dance

The Pokot Buffalo Dance

Dialogues on the Sheik

NOTES

INTRODUCTION

1. Research for this paper began with a pilot study of multisited fieldwork in 2006, followed by eight months in 2008 and two months in 2009. It is also informed by long-term research among the Samburu since 1992.

CHAPTER 2

1. Both Samburu and Pokot use the English word *patrol* to describe scouting activity and forward movement ahead of the cattle. Interestingly, much of the vocabulary for contemporary warfare is borrowed from English, such as *cover* and *force,* the latter meaning to switch one's weapon to fully automatic. Though I have not confirmed this, most likely this vocabulary comes by way of individuals who fought in the Kenyan armed forces.

2. Given that it is a volunteer army, there is consent in joining the U.S. military, but once one is a member of such an organization, one is bound by force to adhere to its rules and dictates.

CHAPTER 3

1. Ramon Goodwin served as a policeman in Samburu District during the period discussed here.

2. In this 2005 comment, he was referring to Kenya's third president, Mwai Kibaki.

CHAPTER 4

1. I use the term "ethnic Somalis" as a general term to distinguish Kenyan Somalis from nationals of Somalia. As I will discuss in more detail, there are many divisions within the Somali identity even within Kenya.

2. For more detailed discussion of this question, see Whitaker (2008) and Reisman (1983).

3. The words "border dispute" were actually banned from Kenyan media.

4. This and similar incidents are also recounted in Hjort (1979).

5. The kudu is a large antelope with a spiraled horn.

6. "He" refers to the man to whom the Sheik's death is attributed, as will be discussed in more depth below.

7. Some Samburu corroborate accounts of him healing Samburu.

8. Although he is widely known among the Samburu, the Sheik's family assert a different man was the Sheik's killer, a man who in fact was unsuccessfully tried for murder.

9. For their part Samburu share little credit with the Boran in defeating the Somalis.

10. Samburu involved in the raid uniformly maintain that "L" killed the Sheik. However, another man, Letimalo (who was unable to take part in the raid because of problems he was attending to at home), was put on trial by the government, though later acquitted.

11. *Lmangatti* is Samburu for "enemy," a term with which resident non-Samburu are very familiar.

12. The term used here—"shetani," or demons—has a double meaning in colloquial Kiswahili usage. It can be used simply to connote those who are pagan, who do not follow a major faith, or it can be used to specifically mean sinister elements. Lekutaas moves between these meanings in this passage.

CHAPTER 5

1. Ideally this would involve an exegesis of Turkana and Pokot forms of friendship. However, attaining that type of cultural depth was beyond the scope of this project.

2. It should be noted that Samburu *laron* may be wealthy individuals who appear to be poor—apparently starving to death and wearing old, tattered clothing—because they may be as miserly to themselves as they are to others.

3. The conflict has abated somewhat between the main research period for this book and the finishing of this final text, though one would not characterize the groups as having returned to being on good terms.

4. Suk is the name used by Samburu and other Maa-speaking peoples to refer to the Pokot, and is also found in earlier European literature on the Pokot.

5. A number of Samburu families come directly from Boran, although some informants maintain that they came from children who were adopted by Samburu, rather than intermarriage.

6. The only group arguably closer is the Rendille, with whom there is sufficient cooperation and intermarriage—and essentially no conflict—that a group has formed essentially betwixt and between the two, the Arialle. The only conflict noted by Samburu is that during the *Mutai* of the late nineteenth century, Rendille were alleged to have burned to death starving Samburu who tried to steal milk from Rendille camels.

7. Here I am referring to Pokot settlements I have observed in Laikipia. There is a wide range of regional variation in Pokot lifestyle, such that settlements in other areas may differ somewhat from what I describe here based on my own observations and discussions with informants.

8. Notably, this description of the Pokot as "professionals" contrasts with Samburu descriptions of Pokot behavior when they together raided the Turkana at Lokoror. In that raid Pokot were said to have engaged in odd behavior, such as singing over cattle they had seized while still in the midst of battle. However, somewhat consistent with this portrayal is the claim that Pokot essentially abandoned the battlefield to drive off cattle, leaving Samburu to fight on their own.

9. The difference in effective range is, however, somewhat exaggerated by Samburu, perhaps for rhetorical purposes. Samburu stories of firing at Pokot at ranges that are said to shock and baffle Pokot do not involve hitting anyone, but rather pitching rounds in the general direction of a group of surprised Pokot.

10. They may also, however, be seen favorably as having a tremendous work ethic.

CHAPTER 6

1. A summary of these events can be found in *Kansas Intelligence Fusions Center Report: Lessons Learned*.

2. I say "friendly advice" since it contains potential overtones of extortion. However, since Samburu view Moi (from the relatively small cultural grouping of Kalenjin pastoralists) as having been relatively favorable toward them (particularly in comparison to Kikuyu-dominated governments), Samburu downplay the implied threat in these words.

3. Samburu cut the ears of their cattle to designate ownership and aid in identifying their own animals.

4. The Samburu term used for "order" is *odah,* from English.

5. For the obvious reasons, I will not name them here.

6. Samburu has recently been subdivided and redesignated a county under the 2013 constitution, but this does not bear on the dynamics described here.

BIBLIOGRAPHY

Abbink, Jon. 2000. "Violation and Violence as Cultural Phenomena." In *Meanings of Violence,* edited by Goran Ajmer and Jon Abbink. Oxford: Berg Press.

Amnesty International. 1998. "Kenya: Political Violence Spirals." AFR 32/019/1998.

Anderson, David. 2005. *History of the Hanged: Britain's Dirty War in Kenya and the End of Empire.* London: Orion.

Aretxaga, Begoña. 1997. *Shattering Silence.* Princeton, NJ: Princeton University Press.

Bauman, Richard. 1986. *Story, Performance, Event.* Cambridge: Cambridge University Press.

Bernard, H. Russell. 2011. *Research Methods in Anthropology.* Lanham, MD: Altamira Press.

Borneman, John, and Abdellah Hammoudi, eds. 2009. *Being There: The Fieldwork Encounter and the Making of Truth.* Berkeley: University of California Press.

Brenneis, Donald. 1996. "Telling Troubles: Narrative, Conflict and Experience." In Briggs, *Disorderly Discourse.*

Briggs, Charles, ed. 1996. *Disorderly Discourse.* Oxford: Oxford University Press.

Campbell, Colin. 1994. "Capitalism, Consumption and the Problem of Motives: Some Issues of Understanding Conduct as Illustrated by an Examination of the Treatment of Motive and Meaning in Weber and Veblen." In *Consumption and Identity,* edited by Jonathan Friedman. Reading: Harwood Academic.

Chagnon, Napoleon. 1977. *Yanamamo.* New York: Holt, Rinehart and Winston.

Chenevix-Trench, Charles. 1993. *Men Who Ruled Kenya.* London: I.B. Taurus.

Chomsky, Noam. 1992. *Manufacturing Consent: Noam Chomsky and the Media* (film). Mark Achabar and Peter Wintonick, directors. National Film Board of Canada.

Chomsky, Noam, and Edward Herman. 1988. *Manufacturing Consent: The Political Economy of Mass Media.* New York: Pantheon.

Clifford, James, and George Marcus, eds. 1986. *Writing Culture.* Berkeley: University of California Press.

Colony and Protectorate of Kenya (CPK). 1934. "Samburu District Annual Report." Kenya National Archives, Nairobi.

———. 1952. "Samburu District Annual Report." Kenya National Archives, Nairobi.

Daily Nation (Kenya). 1998a. "Stench of Death as Raids Toll Rise." January 25.

———. 1998b. "Government Assailed as Killings Persist." January 26.

———. 1998c. "Fresh Killings in Njoro Area." January 27.

———. 1998d. "Bishops, Kibaki Heap Blame on Government." January 31.

———. 2001. "What Friends Think of Kanyotu." July 19.

Daniel, Valentine. 1996. *Charred Lullabies.* Princeton, NJ: Princeton University Press.

Eaton, David. 2010. "The Rise of the 'Traider': The Commercialization of Raiding in Karamoja." *Nomadic Peoples* 14, no. 2: 106–22.

Englund, Harri. 2001. *From War to Peace on the Mozambique-Malawi Borderland.* Edinburgh: Edinburgh University Press.

Evans-Pritchard, E.E. 1937. *Witchcraft, Magic, and Oracles among the Azande.* Oxford: Clarendon Press.

———. 1940. *The Nuer.* Oxford: Oxford University Press.

Ferguson, Brian. 1995. *Yanomami Warfare: A Political History.* Santa Fe, NM: SAR Press.

Fratkin, Elliot. 2011. *Laibon: An Anthropologist's Journey.* Lanham, MD: Altamira Press.

———. 2015. "The Samburu Laibon's Sorcery and the Death of Ted Powys in Colonial Kenya." *Journal of East African Studies* 9, no. 1.

Gardner, Robert. 1961. *Dead Birds* (film). Documentary Educational Resources.

Geertz, Clifford. 1973. *The Interpretation of Cultures*. New York: Basic Books.

George, Kenneth. 2004. "Violence, Culture and the Indonesian Public Sphere." In Whitehead, ed., *Violence*.

Gilsenan, Michael. 1996. *Lords of the Lebanese Marches: Violence and Narrative in an Arab Society*. Berkeley: University of California Press.

Gluckman, Max. 1940. *Analysis of a Social Situation in Modern Zululand*. Rhodes-Livingstone Papers no. 28. Manchester: Manchester University Press.

Goffman, Erving. 1959. *The Presentation of Self in Everyday Life*. New York: Anchor Books.

Gourevitch, Philip. 1999. *We Wish to Inform You That Tomorrow We Will Be Killed along with Our Families*. New York: Picador.

Government of the Republic of Kenya. 2003. *Report of the Judicial Commission Appointed to Inquire into Tribal Clashes in Kenya* (Honorary Justice A. M. Aki-wumi).

Grindal, Frank, and Bruce Salamone, eds. 1995. *Bridges to Humanity: Narratives on Anthropology and Friendship*. Long Grove, IL: Waveland.

Gupta, Akhil, and James Ferguson, eds. 1997. *Anthropological Locations*. Berkeley: University of California Press.

Heider, Karl. 1988. "The Rashomon Effect: When Anthropologists Disagree." *American Anthropologist* 90, no. 1: 73–81.

Herodotus. 2003. *The Histories*. Edited by John Marincola. New York: Penguin.

Hinton, Alex. 2004. "The Poetics of Genocidal Practice." In Whitehead, ed., *Violence*.

Hjort, Anders. 1979. *Savanna Town*. Stockholm: Stockholm Studies in Social Anthropology.

Holtzman, Jon D. 2004. "The Local in the Local: Models of Time and Space in Samburu District, Northern Kenya." *Current Anthropology* 41, no. 5: 61–84.

———. 2009. *Uncertain Tastes*. Berkeley: University of California Press.

Holtzman, Jon, and Bilinda Straight. 2005. "The Echoes of the Vultures." Presented at the Society for Ethnohistory annual meeting, Chicago Illinois.

Jarvenpa, Robert. 1998. *Ethnography and Apprenticeship among the Subarctic Dene*. Long Grove, IL: Waveland Press.

Kahanar, Larry. 2007. *AK47: The Weapon That Changed the Face of War*. New York: Wiley.

Kansas Intelligence Fusion Center. 2014. *Kenyan Westgate Mall Attack: Lessons Learned*. https://publicintelligence.net/kifc-westgate-attack/.

Kenyatta, Jomo. 1962. *Facing Mount Kenya*. London: Vintage Books.

Lamphear, John. 1992. *The Scattering Time: Turkana Responses to Colonial Rule.* Oxford: Oxford University Press.

Lesorogol, Carolyn. 2008. *Contesting the Commons.* Ann Arbor: University of Michigan Press.

McCabe, J. Terrence. 2004. *Cattle Brings Us to Our Enemies.* Ann Arbor: University of Michigan Press.

Menchú, Rigoberta. 1987. *I, Rigoberta Menchú.* Edited by Elisabeth Burgos-Debray. New York: Verson Books.

Mills, C. Wright. 1940. "Situated Actions and Vocabularies of Motive." *American Sociological Review* 5, no. 6.

Mkutu, Kennedy. 2008. *Guns and Governance in the Rift Valley: Pastoralist Conflicts and Small Arms.* Bloomington: Indiana University Press.

Nordstrom, Carolyn, and Antonius Robben, eds. 1996. *Fieldwork under Fire.* Berkeley: University of California Press.

Oba, Gufu. 1992. *Ecological Factors in Land Use Conflicts, Land Administration and Food Insecurity in Turkana, Kenya.* Pastoral Development Network Paper 33a. London: Overseas Development Institute.

O'Brien, Tim. 1990. *The Things They Carried.* New York: Houghton Mifflin.

Payne, Leigh. 2008. Unsettling Accounts. Durham, NC: Duke University Press.

Powdermaker, Hortense. 1967. *Stranger and Friend.* New York: Norton.

Rabinow, Paul. 1977. *Reflections on Fieldwork in Morocco.* Berkeley: University of California Press.

Radcliffe-Brown, A.R. 1940. "On Joking Relationships." *Africa* 13, no. 3: 195–210.

Rampton, Sheldon, and John Stauber. 2003. *Weapons of Mass Deception.* New York: Tarcher.

Rapport, Nigel. 2000. "Criminal by Instinct." In *Meanings of Violence,* edited by Goran Aijmer and Jon Abbink. Oxford: Berg Press.

Reisman, Michael. 1983. "Somali Self-Determination in the Horn." In *Nationalism and Self-Determination on the Horn of Africa,* edited by I.M. Lewis. Los Angeles: Evergreen.

Riches, David. 1986. *The Anthropology of Violence.* Oxford: Basil Blackwell.

Roth, Wendy, and Jal Mehta. 2002. "The *Rashomon* Effect: Combining Positivist and Interpretivist Approaches in the Analysis of Contested Events." *Sociological Methods and Research* 31, no. 2: 131–73.

Rutherford, Paul. 2004. *Weapons of Mass Persuasion: Marketing the War against Iraq.* Toronto: University of Toronto Press.

Sapir, Edward. 1938. "Why Cultural Anthropology Needs the Psychiatrist." *Psychiatry* 1: 7–12.

Sartre, Jean-Paul. 1958 (1944). *No Exit.* Translated by Paul Bowles. New York: Samuel French.

Schneider, Harold K. 1967. "Pokot Folktales, Humor and Values." *Journal of the Folklore Institute* 4, nos. 2–3: 265–318.

Sorel, Georges. 1999. *Reflections on Violence.* Cambridge: Cambridge University Press.

Spencer, Paul. 1965. *The Samburu.* London: Routledge and Kegan Paul.

Steedly, Mary. 1999. "The State of Culture Theory in Southeast Asia." *Annual Review of Anthropology* 28: 431–54.

Stewart, Pamela, and Andrew Strathern. 2002. *Violence: Theory and Ethnography.* New York: Continuum.

Stigand, Chauncey. 1910. *To Abyssinia through an Unknown Land.* London: J.B. Lipincott.

Stoll, David. 1998. *Rigoberta Menchú and the Story of All Poor Guatemalans.* Boulder, CO: Westview Press.

Straight, Bilinda. 2006. *Miracles and Extraordinary Experience in Northern Kenya.* Philadelphia: University of Pennsylvania Press.

Taylor, Christopher. 2004. "Deadly Images." In Whitehead, ed., *Violence.*

Tolstoi, Leo. 1877. *Anna Karenina.* Moscow: Russian Messenger.

Van de Port, Mattijs. 1998. *Gypsies, Wars and Other Instances of the Wild.* Amsterdam: Amsterdam University Press.

Von Hohnel, Ludwig. 1896. *Discovery of Lakes Rudolf and Stefanie: A Narrative of Count Samuel Teleki's Exploring and Hunting Expedition in Eastern Africa.* London: Longman's.

Whitaker, Hannah. 2008. "Pursuing Pastoralists: The Stigma of 'Shifta' during the Shifta War in Kenya, 1963–1968." *Eras* 10.

White, Luise. 2000. *Speaking with Vampires: Rumor and History in Colonial Africa.* Berkeley: University of California Press.

Whitehead, Neil, ed. 2004 *Violence.* Santa Fe, NM: SAR Press.

Wolfowitz, Paul. 2003. Interview. *Vanity Fair* (May).

Yanagizawa-Drott, David. 2014. "Propaganda and Conflict: Evidence from the Rwanda Genocide." *Quarterly Journal of Economics* 129, no. 4: 1–45.

Guatemala, 190–191, 198–199

guns: acquisition of, 15, 140–141, 142; characteristics of different models, 151–2, 172;differential access to across ethnic groups, 16, 89–90, 98, 106, 118, 181; disarmament campaigns 86; ethnic preferences for, 67, 150–151; government provisioning of, 46, 172–173; presence during fieldwork, 32; price of 35, 92, 116; throwing away in combat 150; trade in 35, 66–67, 116, 151

hermaphrodite, 108, 121

Herodotus, 7, 9, 122

hierarchy (and war), 45–48

Holocaust, 192, 196, 198, 199

Homeguards (Police reservists), 15, 151

humanizing (as antidote for violence), 161

humor: about eating habits, 128; and cowardice, 149; dark, 55–6, 92

insanity: due to breaking Samburu-Pokot oath, 16, 42, 137; of the Sheik's killer, 109, 112–113, 122

intermarriage: 4, 115; P. 203n5; absence with Pokot, 134, 139–40; infrequency with Somalis, 115; with Turkana, 16, 143

Iraq: insurgency in, 46; interethnic violence in, 2, 3; U.S. war on 23, 39–41, 45, 199

Isiolo (place): attitudes of residents during Shifta war 100, 105; differences among Somali residents, 100–103; political competition in, 114–15

Islam: as metaphor, 151; Samburu criticism of, 119; views on killing, 112–113

Kenyan army: at Westgate Mall, 168–9; colonial, Samburu service in, 78, 102;

colonial, Somali service in, 101–2; corruption 68; defeating Ngoroko, 142, 177

Kenyatta, Jomo (first Kenyan president): alleged pro-Kikuyu bias, 82–83, 174; as leader in Mau Mau 79; colonial imprisonment in Samburu, 78

Kibaki, Mwai (third Kenyan president), 86, 174, 202n2.

Kikuyu: 4, 35; alleged greed/cleverness with money, 83, 91–92, 93, 133; alleged hatred of Samburu, 17, 82, 86–87, 174; as cowards, 76, 83, 88, 91–2, 133; attitudes towards Samburu, 93–95; clashes with Samburu, 73, 84–90; dominance in independent Kenya, 82–83, 175, 177, 181; Mau Mau, and 17, 78–82; post-tribalist discourses of, 95–96; precolonial and colonial contacts with Samburu, 75–78; relationship with Samburu, 16, 24, 73–74, 96–97, 198

Koran, 107; viewed as talisman by Samburu, 111

Laikipia (place): competition for land in, 43, 84, 174, 175; clashes with Kikuyu in, 43, 73, 84–87, 91–92, 96, 97, 134; colonial expulsion of Maasai from, 90, 94; colonial history of, 76; historical claims to, 87, 90–91, 94, 96; interethnic mixing in, 42; Samburu-Pokot conflict in, 44, 62, 149, 164; Samburu purchase of land in, 92–93; supernatural qualities of, 90

Laikipiak (extinct Maasai group), 14, 76, 90

land: competition for, 84, 85; Kikuyu acquisition of, 87, 95, 177; legal rights to, 94–96; loss of in conflict, 170, 175; Samburu purchase of, 92–93

lang'atta (ritual friendship): among
Samburu, 130, 134–135, 140;
between Pokot and Samburu 136,
159
laroi (coward/stingy person): among
Samburu, 132, 203n2; as applied to
Pokot 133, 161
lautani (kinship term), 130
Lbarta (Baragoi region): border region
of Turkana-Samburu, 145–146;
previous Maasai occupation of, 141;
Turkana-Samburu war over, 141;
Leaduma, 187
lies: as source of insights, 21, 27;
difficulties in assessing, 58
lobu (greedy/greedy person): among
Samburu 132; applied to Turkana,
133, 181
loibon: colonial arrest of, 187; consulta-
tion for warfare 14; perceptions of
the Sheik as, 98–99, 107–108; Somali
distinction with the Sheik, 113
Ltigira, 144. *See* Turkana

Maasai: colonial move for white
settlement, 70, 90, 94; intermarriage
with, 139; previous occupation of
Laikipia, 90; previous occupation of
Lbarta, 142; Relation to Samburu,
12, 14, 91, 94, 96
mangatti (enemy), 77, 119, 202n11
Maralal (Samburu District Headquarters): 43, 81, 137, 176; site of
Kenyatta imprisonment, 78
massacre of police (Baragoi), 182–183,
186–187
Mau Mau: history of, 79–80; Imprisonment of insurgents in Samburu
District, 178–179; Kikuyu lack of
acknowledgement of Samburu role
in, 75, 89–90, 96–97; Samburu
opposition to, 78, 80–82; source of
alleged Kikuyu grudge against

Samburu, 17, 24, 73, 75, 82–3,
86–87, 177
mean-spiritedness (alleged, of Samburu),
20–21, 67–68, 117–119)
memory: erasure of, 75, 91, 95–96;
unevenness, 24, 74, 87, 91, 96–7;
violence, and, 5, 25, 26, 113–115,
123, 129
Menchu, Rigoberta, 26, 190–191,
198–199
mercy, 135–136
Meru: Samburu intermarriage with,
139; trade with, 75
methodology, 8, 10–11, 25, 48–52
modernity, 91–93, 96, 181
Moi, Daniel arap (Kenyan President),
85–86, 176, 204n2
multivocality, 10, 11–2, 23, 113, 120,
122, 123–125,
murder (concept of), 3–4
murran: colonial suppression of, 77–78,
144; demeanor, 150; description of,
12–13, 47 development of nkanyit,
131–132; raids by, 14, 16, 20; role in
warfare, 15, 54–55; songs of, 108,
114; tradition of killing by, 14, 76–77;
mutai, 143, 203n6

Nairobi, 166–169
narrative: analysis of, 8–9, 11–12, 25,
34, 48–52; 60–69, 121–2; conflict,
and 6, 26, 50–51, 165; justificatory,
49–50; versus truth, 26, 190,
195–197;
nature conservancies: 58–60
Ngoroko: attacks on Samburu ,140,
142, 185; conspiracy, and 82,
176–177, 181; *See also* Turkana
Niebelungenlied, 192, 196
nkanyit (respect): absence among Pokot,
161; absence among Turkana, 153,
161; as a basis for relationships, 135;
description of, 130–133, 193

O'Brien, Tim, 26, 190, 195–197
oath (between Samburu and Pokot),
    dissolution of 61; general description
    of 16, 42, 127, 139–140; history of
    42–43, 126–127, 134–136; insanity,
    and 139; 158–160; symbolism of
    blood in 126, 154
Ol Moran clashes (1998), 24, 73,
    84–91, 96

parallel accounts: anthropological
    analysis of, 8–9, 99, 121–125, 197; in
    Herodotus, 7; of alleged desire of
    anthropologist's friend to kill his
    other friend 52–54; of "government"
    massacre of Samburu, 169–172; of
    Samburu-Pokot conflict, 21, 22,
    24–25, 43–44, 64–69; regarding a
    wildlife conservancy, 58–60;
    regarding recent Samburu-Somali
    conflict, 114–q15; regarding
    Samburu-Kikuyu clashes, 85–90;
    regarding 1965 Samburu-Somali
    conflict, 100, 106–113, 121; research
    methods, and 10–11
"partial accounts", 8, 124–125
partition of Africa, 103
pastoralists, 12, 16, 42, 43, 84; interac-
    tions with Kikuyu agriculturalists,
    87–88, 94, 97; Somalis, 101–102;
    stereotypes of, 93–94, 97, 118;
peace (perceived benefits of), 54–56
peace meetings: accusations of duplicity
    at, 44, 65; anthropologist's experi-
    ence at, 193; autochthonous,
    between Samburu and Turkana,
    156–157; discourses at, 56, 71, 72;
    organized by outside groups, 50, 56,
    71, 161
poaching, 104, 116
Pokot: allegations of government
    favoritism towards Samburu
    ,172–175; alleged incapability of

friendship, 159–160; anthropologist's
    first meeting with, 193–195; attitudes
    towards Samburu, 11, 19–21, 44, 64,
    67–68, 134, 138, 149–150, 171–172;
    castration by Samburu, 39–41,
    43–44, 61, 69–72; eating wild
    animals, 128; emphasis on stealth, 62,
    64, 133, 147–148; gun preferences,
    67, 150–152, 172; gun trade, 35,
    66–67; joint Samburu clashes with
    Kikuyu, 84–85; lack of intermarriage
    with Samburu, 139–140; oath with
    Samburu, 16, 25, 42–3, 61, 126–128,
    135–140, 160; portrayal by Samburu
    as cowards, 146–148; reputation as
    thieves, 36, 44, 133, 134, 138–139,
    159; Settlement patterns, 147–148,
    203n7; traditional style of raiding,
    63–64 war with Samburu, 21,
    23–24, 36, 39–72, 133–4, 146, 159,
    164, 169–173; wars with Turkana,
    42–3, 64
police: at Westgate Mall attack,
    168–169; conspiracies regarding,
    82–83, 177; failure to recover
    livestock, 43, 64, 174–175, 178;
    massacre of, 182–183, 186–187;
    reservists (Homeguards), 15,
    150–151; Samburu employment
    as, 78
politicians: Kenyan, 58–60, 114, 142;
    U.S., 39–40, 45; raiding, and
    178–181
postmodernism, 23, 124, 197
Powys murder case, 77–78, 187
propaganda, 24, 40–42, 45–46, 72
Purko (Maasai): previous occupation of
    Laikipia, 90–91; previous occupation
    of Lbarta, 141

ranches (white owned): in colonial
    period, 76, 78–79, 81, 94; in local
    communities, 51, 58, 161

rape, 154

Rashomon; "effect" 8–9; film/story as metaphor in this text 12, 197

religion, 112–113, 119, 122

Rendille: Samburu intermarriage with, 139; Samburu relationship to, 203 n6

rocket propelled grenades: in Westgate Mall attack, 168; Samburu use, 114, 123–124; Somali use of, 118

rumor: analysis of, 177, 180–181, 188–189; Anti-Livestock Theft Unit, about, 82–83, 177; commercialized cattle raiding, about 178–9; government involvement in raiding, about 173, 176–177, 180–181, 188–189; nature conservancy, about 58–60; *See also* conspiracies

Russia (as symbol), 152

Rwandan genocide, 2–3, 24, 39,41, 48, 199

Samburu District (and ethnic boundaries), 58–60, 179, 183–185

Sartre, Jean-Paul (No Exit), 25, 126–127

Sheik Ahmed Yassin ("The Sheik"), 24–25, 30, 98–100, 106–113, 118–123

Shifta: history and definition of, 102–105, 117; war with Samburu, 98, 106, 121

Somalia: flag of, 117; referendum for Kenyan Somalis to join, 102–103; role in Shifta war, 103–104; source of weapons in Kenya, 118

Somalis (Kenyan): attitudes towards Samburu, 116–117, 118–119, 120, 122; attitudes towards Shifta, 102, 104; cattle raiding by 178; conflict with Boran, 114–115, 202n9; distinctions among, 100–103; explanations for wars with Samburu, 16, 100, 102, 105, 109, 118, 120;

history as traders, 115–116; history in Kenya, 101–105, 202n1; Islam, and 112–113, 119; oppression by government, 105–106, 117; peaceful interactions with Samburu, 115; positive Samburu views of, 133, 146, 154; temperament, 117–118, 133; wars with Samburu, 4, 15–16, 24–25, 42, 98–100, 106–115, 118, 120–121

songs, 14, 108, 114, 147

sotua, 130. *See also* friendship

Spencer, Paul, 4, 12, 130–131, 193

spies: anthropologists, and 19, 30; Turkana suspected of being, 144–145, 160

SPLA (Sudanese Peoples Liberation Army), 179–180

stealth (Pokot versus Samburu), 44, 133, 147–148, 150

Stigand, Captain, 141

Straight, Bilinda, 14, 76, 77, 143, 187

Suk (synonym), 137, 203n4; *See also* Pokot.

temperament: of murran, 131; of Somalis 117–118, 133; Samburu-Pokot differences, 193

theft, Samburu minimization of *lwambuan* 14, 16; of cattle versus other items, 88; as discourse to avoid group responsibility 62, 186; oath as cause of 127, 137

trade: in guns, 34–35, 66, 116, 118; with Meru,77; with Somalis, 115–16

triad of victim-perpetrator-observers of violence, 8, 26, 165, 185–186

"tribalism", 94–96

truth: complexities of 9–12, 26–27, 195–199; two definitions of 190, 195–197

Turkana: adoption by Samburu, 143–144; alleged favoritism towards,